KU-739-161

Praise for *Memoirs of an Unfit Mother*

'A cracking, unsentimental read . . . love her or loathe her, Robinson has produced a book that revolutionises the celebrity autobiography' Barbara Ellen, *Observer*

'Devastating, original, self-lacerating, glittering with anger and thwarted maternal love . . . The book, like Robinson herself, is a combustible mixture of ferocity and vulnerability' Allison Pearson, *Daily Telegraph Magazine*

'A brilliant read and a lesson to all would-be showbiz biog writers' Keith Waterhouse, *Observer*

'Anne Robinson is brave, funny and honest, and her autobiography is a terrific read' *Daily Mail*

'. . . one of the most courageous autobiographies ever. The queen of put-downs has written an unputdownable book. Read it and weep' *Glasgow Herald*

'To the stereotype, to dominatrix, bully, verbal sniper, we might usefully add . . . survivor, sufferer, fighter' *Sunday Independent*

'Riveting' *Mirror*

'What emerges from this well-written book is the richness of her relationship with her daughter . . . and a much more truthful account of the toughness of *Mirror* agony aunt Marje Proops than anyone has dared tell before' Roy Greenslade, *Guardian*

'. . . Robinson reveals she is now as tough on herself as she is on others. Not only can she write, but there is not an ounce of self pity' Suzanne Moore, *Mail on Sunday*

Anne Robinson continues to live in London and Gloucestershire and hopes eventually to become a full-time Cirencester housewife.

ANNE ROBINSON

Memoirs of an Unfit Mother

timewarner
paperbacks

A *Time Warner* Paperback

First published in Great Britain in 2001
by Little, Brown and Company

This edition published by Time Warner Paperbacks in 2002
Reprinted 2002, 2004

'Happy Mother's Day' by Emma Wilson
reproduced by kind permission of Express Newspapers.
Extract from *Jeffrey Bernard is Unwell* by Keith Waterhouse,
published by Samuel French, reproduced by
kind permission of the author.

All photographs are from the author's private collection.

A CIP catalogue record for this book
is available from the British Library.

ISBN 0 7515 3624 5

Typeset in Minion by M Rules
Printed and bound in Great Britain
by Clays Ltd, St Ives plc

Time Warner Paperbacks
An imprint of
Time Warner Book Group UK
Brettenham House
Lancaster Place
London WC2E 7EN

www.twbg.co.uk

To the two most important women in my life.

My mother, who taught me that the biggest time saver is money. And if you rack up enough of it, you can spend the time saved shopping.

And Emma. A very special daughter indeed.

Acknowledgements

Shortly after this book was commissioned, I received an approach from the BBC to host a new game show called *The Weakest Link*, then in the early stages of development. The schedule to complete my manuscript thus became busier than I imagined. Much had to be written as I began my monthly commute between London and Los Angeles, to tape the show on both sides of the Atlantic.

As always, my husband was a model of calm and reassurance and a reminder of why I love his sunny Italian temperament. Emma regarded my timetable as 'typical of Mum', and accepted it completely. My brother Peter, the scholar of the family, gave his time unselfishly. His observations of our childhood were intelligent and illuminating, and it was a delight to look back together and reflect. And also to laugh. Girlfriends, who know who they are, relieved my burden by their constant electronic reassurances. ('Mum has made it to email, provided someone else turns on the laptop,' Emma was heard to cry.)

Then there was truly the luck of the gods. Ed Victor, my elegant agent, who has moved networking to an art form, introduced me to Philippa Harrison, newly appointed Chairman of Little, Brown (I doubt she cares for 'Chair' or 'Chairwoman'). After years of terrorising newspaper sub-editors to do no more than 'lift and dust' my copy, I found the experience of having such a distinguished editor liberating and instructive, never restricting. So, a huge debt to Philippa for not only sharing her immense professional wisdom but also her genuine kindness and sisterly concern, her encouragement and wonderful sense of the absurd.

The same goes for Viv Redman, my copy-editor, who made it look as if she had 'lifted and dusted', while often doing a jolly good spring clean.

Finally, although this book is dedicated to my mother and Emma, it is meant for all women who have struggled with motherhood, with a career, with trying to do the right thing.

I reckon if we muddle through and achieve even a two per cent improvement in our lives from one generation to another, we have done superbly and deserve to give ourselves a pat on the back.

Contents

Memoirs
of an
Unfit Mother

Prologue

'Have a facial once a month and get plenty of help in the house,' my mother would advise as I was growing up. It was her favoured recipe for marriage. Her contempt for domesticity and her appetite for business dealing and making money and spending money went undisguised.

So where was she when I stood in the witness box defending my lack of housewifery? She was in the back of the court. Ready to take the oath and proclaim her fitness to replace me and become a full-time mother, grandmother and homemaker to her granddaughter.

It was her well-meant and utterly misguided attempt to make ours the winning side. Losing, coming second, was not in her nature.

But where had she been before today? Running a business. Certainly not at home. And never for a second setting an example that might convince me that that is where I should be.

And where had I been as a mother? Frequently in a newspaper office. Often in a pub. Sometimes in a blackout.

It is the dawn of the seventies. Outside, women are marching and proclaiming their right to equality as laid down in Germaine Greer's newly published *The Female Eunuch*.

I have not heeded their cries. I, after all, have a career. I work in a man's world. I have a mother who has had a gloriously successful career. We both *have* equality of ambition. Both have achieved equality of income.

But now I am standing in a courtroom accused of caring more about my career than my family responsibilities.

And what about Charlie, the father of my daughter, Emma? A man who will go on to be editor of *The Times*. He who has shown no less ambition than his wife. He is making no promise – not even being asked to make a promise – to stay at home and look after his child. But he is about to get custody, care and control of her.

March 1973. Court Four of the Family Division of the Law Courts. Men surround me. A solicitor and his clerk, plus two barristers and their clerks on my side. The same again on the other side.

'Get the best,' my mother had ordered. But 'the best' had gone to defend a man who the police believed had murdered his wife. 'The best', before he threw in the towel for a case with headlines and kudos, had asked me how bad my drinking was.

'Do you', he had enquired politely, as we sat in his chambers accompanied by my expensive legal team, 'drink in the morning?'

Of course I drink in the bloody morning. Presuming I know it is the morning.

As it happens, he has his own weaknesses. He is clever and much in demand but there is every reason to believe he too drinks in the morning. He is known for his nervous breakdowns and depressions that require him to absent himself from work.

Later he will become a judge. When he dies his reputation is intact. His obituary in *The Times* is glowing. It does not say if he drank in the morning.

But so what? In court we are without 'the best'. Instead I have a replacement QC, who is less in demand in the Family Division. And as we break for lunch and await the judge's verdict on the final day of that court case, the replacement QC and

I head for the canteen. 'If I say it myself, I did rather well. A lesson in advocacy for any young pupil listening,' he declares, as he puts down on the rudimentary canteen table the chicken salad he has collected from the self-service bar. He tucks his thumbs behind the lapels of his robe. Then introduces me to a youngster in a poorly fitting suit who is hovering in the background: his son who has just popped into the courts.

That morning the judge had announced that his daughter and her boyfriend are in the public gallery and he hopes no one minds.

I mind. My case is meant to be 'in camera'. Half the lawyers there have been hired by me at a sum I no longer dare add up. Yet friend and family of the judge, short of any form of entertainment on a freezing cold Friday in the first week of April, can enjoy my misery for free.

The QC and proud father, sitting with me in the Law Courts' canteen, goes on to boast of his son's achievements. I am a mother about to lose custody of a tiny daughter. Do I care what his son is called or how well he is doing in his maritime exams?

Hardly.

And who else is in Court Four?

There is the judge, summing up and declaring who should have custody, care and control of Emma, aged two and a half. I am advised he is a heavy gin drinker and full of painkillers. His use of both is apparently common gossip. He does not *sit* in judgement as it happens. He paces along the platform at the side of his desk because the leg that needs the painkillers stiffens if he does not exercise it.

Then there is the QC who is representing my husband. He has previously been a Tory MP. Twenty years later he will be arrested for smuggling whisky across from France in his cabin cruiser. He dies in disgrace. His obituary in *The Times* says so.

His junior in the case, a tall distinguished man, asks me to his chambers a decade later and suggests we share a bottle of champagne. By then he is himself a famous QC. (Still later he becomes a High Court judge, knighted and admired. In 1999 he decides whether a young girl who is dying should be treated or, as her parents wish, be left alone.) In 2000 it is he who declares that Siamese twins should be separated so one lives and one dies.

One meeting is taking place because I had phoned for background about a headline-grabbing divorce case. I could have sought advice from others. But I am still raw enough to want to show off the new me. I am curious to see how he reacts all these years later. Charmingly, is the answer. Such a beguiling idea, the bottle of champagne. Such a cosy, friendly gesture. He repeats my newspaper title – Assistant Editor of the *Daily Mirror* – several times. 'For a girl is it not the highest in Fleet Street?' he asks. 'Yes,' I say. 'Wow,' he says. 'Clever, clever you. Well done!'

An odd response from a man who, in Court Four of the Law Courts (Family Division), rises to his feet that week in 1973 to ask if it is true that I once said to my husband that I would rather cover the Vietnam War than Hoover the sitting room.

He poses the question not because he wishes to give the judge a taste of my wit, rather to supply the court with yet another glaring example of my unfitness to look after my baby. To illustrate my regrettable and shameful attitude to the role that I am fighting to be allowed to continue.

A decade on, the champagne is redundant. It stands unopened on his desk. He fishes around, embarrassed because he has no mineral water to hand. His clerk has left for the night.

By now I have had ten lonely years without my daughter. I have learnt first-hand the reality and grimness of 'every other weekend access'.

I have also learnt that the drinking and the career that helped me lose my daughter have never made up for the pain and shame of that loss.

So my drinking days are over. As I leave, the junior barrister, now a QC and later a High Court judge, tells me that he remembers parts of my case as among the funniest he can recall. Imagine. What a laugh!

Across the courtroom is Charlie's solicitor. A truly charmless man. Three months before this court drama my husband took our little daughter away to join the solicitor and his wife at their Esher home on Christmas night. So late on Christmas Day, I was left alone in a farmhouse on the moors of Derbyshire where Charlie and I were living in disharmony. There are certain lows you never forget.

Two decades later Charlie's solicitor writes me a letter. Out of the blue. In it he tells me how much he admires me. He says he has followed my career in the newspaper world. And my broadcasting career. He claims never to miss seeing me on television. He is a faithful listener to my Saturday morning Radio 2 show.

A few years later, remembering his deadly approach and his reputation as a divorce solicitor and his apparent respect for my skills, I think who better to seek advice from about protecting my assets from the next husband?

He is charm itself. He suggests we meet. He suggests dinner and books a table at a restaurant in Knightsbridge. How beguiling. Over dinner he tells me he keeps a mistress. I beat an early retreat. He says before I go there is one other thing he wants to tell me. My case was one of the funniest he can recall . . .

And what of *my* solicitor? *He* says his wife does not understand him. In the weeks before our appearance in Court Four he wines and dines me and kisses me and tells me how he fancies me. And, pathetic me, I think I have found a true friend.

Just before the case begins we learn our smooching was observed and is to be produced as evidence by the other side. Apparently this is a bit of an 'in' joke because when my solicitor is not hiring the barristers on my side, he hires the ones on Charlie's side. But since the case is 'in camera', reputations are safe and a fun bit of legal football will hurt none of them.

When I lose custody, care and control of my daughter on 6 April 1973, I never hear from my solicitor again save for his bill and, finally, a letter which says if I do not pay the bill in full within the month he will start proceedings to repossess my home.

Two decades later *Vogue* describes him as one of the six most sought-after divorce lawyers in London.

And years later what happened to me? And what happened to that little two-year-old with the unfit mother and the dazzlingly glamorous and beautiful and allegedly suitable grandmother? And the apparently responsible and ambitious father?

Our tale will reveal the bitterness and the heartbreak of our marriage. And the part my drinking played in its destruction. There was to be no happy ending for us as a couple. But Charlie's role in Emma's life, when I was far from capable, was vital.

Eventually I learnt to stand upright again. To reclaim my role as a mother. To take a second stab at my career. And live happily and contentedly.

And the two-year-old?

Child experts would have had reason to shake their heads in gloomy anticipation of the problems her troublesome childhood were likely to produce. But she is proof that hope and spirit can triumph over the most unpromising of beginnings. Generously, she delights in her unconventional upbringing and her eccentric, crazy parents. She refuses to criticise or blame either her father or her mother.

Our story proves there is no such thing as escaping maternal influence. But that it is possible to face up to the worst and heal.

1

The Founder of our Plenty

Fifteen years after a mother has left the earth there is a grown-up daughter standing in a shop, saying petulantly to a saleswoman, 'I know it looks nice – but I don't wear purple.' Why doesn't she wear purple? Because as a little girl, and then as a bigger little girl, a voice was saying, 'Don't wear purple, it's for old people.' The same voice that said, 'Once you go into brown you never wear anything else,' and 'Short-sleeved jackets are common', and 'Pull your shoulders back and don't frown.'

And when the little girl had stopped frowning, rejected the purple outfit and the jacket with short sleeves, but was still undecided between the green dress and the blue dress, the final command: 'Have both.'

This is my mother's voice. The stylish, excessive, gold-medal shopper.

There was also my mother the unyielding, unforgiving task-master. So a cleaning lady or a gardener or an offspring foolishly imagining an element of corner-cutting would go unnoticed ended up terrorised and forever regretted the economy.

Then again, there was my mother the empowerer. 'You are', she would declare with an endearing certainty, 'second to none. You can go out into the world and do *anything*!'

The empowering voice, throughout my life, is the one that

girlfriends have envied. 'If only', they have so often cried, '*my* mother had talked to me like that.'

But it wasn't all rosy.

We lived permanently in extremes. A confusing seesaw existence in which best intentions were constantly thwarted by unintentional abuse.

Yet, to her credit, I never experienced a mother who was also a jealous competitor. In her book, disloyalty to a daughter was worse than the murder of a stranger. She believed jealousy was the vice of mothers who wished to stay young and attractive for their husbands and who ruthlessly eradicated any competitors. Especially daughters.

To my mother, the notion of being suspicious or fearful of one's own flesh and blood was unimaginable. She, in contrast, had only a touching and unrealistic faith in the genius of her children. In her order of priorities my brother came first. It was hardly to his benefit. I came second. Her husband, my father, came not first but last. Probably of the three of us under her control being second was the least traumatic position. But it was still a mixed blessing.

Nevertheless, on her tombstone it would have been fair to write: 'She would have died for her children. She did what she thought was her best.'

Alas, a mother's best is rarely enough. A mother's best can result in shocking damage and the second half of a child's life spent recovering from the first.

A mother's place is in the wrong.

To begin with, of course, we didn't know our mother was a star. We accepted as normal her energy, her quick wit, her beauty, her dazzling fearlessness, her scary exacting standards and her startling ability to make money. The last talent matched only by her gift for self-maintenance. Emptying Bond Street was a regular hobby. Then again, her generosity within the family was as huge as her stinginess in business.

Auntie Mame crossed with Howard Hughes out of *Vogue* and Mother Teresa. Eccentricity, secrecy, style, kindness. An exotic cocktail except on a very bad day when, without warning, added to the mix were those unforgettable Stalinesque tendencies. Self-doubt, if it existed, was not on show. With every part she played there was an uncrushable belief in her right to do exactly what she wanted.

And whatever the role of the moment it ran alongside an undisguised contempt for housewifery. The order to have a facial once a month and get plenty of help in the house was just one of her maxims. Being 'up at six and out at five' was another. Ostensibly a bit of Irish nonsense, we were in no doubt what it meant.

In her book, to be second, to be caught out, to be diddled by another who was sharper and quicker and up earlier in the morning was shameful. As was 'being taken for a ride'.

This was the philosophy of the street trader. It whistled round our lives and our home in St Michael's Road, Blundellsands in Crosby. An imposing thirties house bought with three thousand used one-pound notes towards the end of the war. My mother was a third, maybe fourth, generation trader. My great-grandmother and my grandmother before her had been in St John's Market selling chickens.

The family was part of the mass exodus from Ireland. Peasants who came to Liverpool during the famine of the mid-eighteen hundreds. None of the women in the family appeared to have married a man of means. Or one who could turn much of a penny. The women, however, were rather good at it, perhaps out of necessity. And St John's Market, a forbidding early-nine-teenth-century building darkened by years of grime in the centre of Liverpool, offered the dash for freedom. It allowed traders to rent a stall by the day. Or even to stand outside the building selling their wares. The women would journey from other parts of Liverpool. Sometimes they had only worn-out second-hand clothes to sell. The better-off could afford to trade in fruit or fish or chickens they bought early each morning in the wholesale market across the road. By the time my mother came along, the family stall in St John's was a permanent one. Her fresh blood then sent it spinning into an astoundingly lucrative business. First, in the early forties, unashamedly on the black market, dealing in rabbits. After that as a wholesale supplier for ships, hotels and railways in the north of England.

By all accounts, my grandmother, less of a business head, shared her daughter's relish for spending. Her market coats were not the traditional white, but navy blue silk especially tailored for her. A week's profit could sensibly be blown on a new hat from Bon Marché. The bailiffs might be circling the door of her rented home but she would still be demanding her new son-in-law drive her to Southport to inspect a row of houses she fancied buying.

Quite how a family of Irish peasants developed such grandness and appetite for all things luxurious plus, admirably, an appetite to make the money that provided for high living, heaven knows.

My mother's pitch was in the market's second aisle. A. Wilson was comparatively small, but in a prize position on one of the busiest corners. Behind the display of chickens was an office with high stools and a long desk, probably unchanged from the previous century, except for the telephone (ROYal 3841). Outside, the goods were laid out, dressed with price tickets. The giblets (1/6d a plate) were separate. Fresh sawdust was sprinkled on the floor. Sweeping up the sawdust and scrubbing down the blocks were parts of the ritual of shutting down at 6 p.m. after the big iron gates had closed the market to shoppers.

To my generation, the Second World War and the early post-war years were likely to have involved austerity, going without, sacrifice and suffering. In our home, of course, it typically meant exactly the opposite. There were two cars in the drive, which had In and Out gates. There was a housekeeper. A gardener. Occasionally a cook, when from time to time an attempt would be made to ape more precisely the conventional middle-class lifestyles that surrounded us. But these experiments rarely lasted. My mother's patience with anyone who did not automatically move with the speed of sound hovered around zero. For the first decade of our lives my brother and I could have been forgiven for imagining our names were Hurry Up.

Our war, which may not have been your war, was a puzzle for a child growing up in its smouldering shadow. At school they taught you about the loss of lives, the bravery, the going without. At every turn in Liverpool bomb damage was evident. Churches without spires. Holes in the ground. Rows of houses half standing, so you could see the wallpaper from the bedroom. Men without legs, hobbling on crutches or with one sleeve of their jacket empty. At home, however, the grown-ups appeared to have enjoyed the very best of times. This was particularly true of my mother, who naturally judged good and bad on the simple basis of how well the business was going. And business wasn't just good during the war years, it was spectacular.

The black market raged. If a movie writer wanted to illustrate how it operated he would invariably create an image of a man in a heavy beige overcoat and a Trilby hat with a cigarette in his mouth who talked in whispers and produced nylons out of the back of an old lorry. What he would not have described was a slim, strikingly beautiful blonde woman with a husky voice, a new Rover car, dressed in a well-cut suit and a Mitzi hat. Her shoes and handbag by Mr Rayne. Her rings from Boodle and Dunthorne. There ended the difference. My mother's dealings were no less dramatic, her risk-taking every bit as great as the other profiteers.

By being up earlier in the morning than anyone else, she managed to commandeer the entire allocation of rabbits for Liverpool. These came in boxes of ten. Two pounds were added to the price of each box. The man who delivered them got five shillings. My mother kept the rest. All cash. Thousands of cases a week passed through her hands.

The butchers of Liverpool and Lancashire were thrilled. They never asked questions. Nor did my father, who benefited hugely. His officer's uniform (he was commissioned almost immediately because of his education) was hand-stitched by Liverpool's finest tailor, John Snell. So magnificent was business that occasionally one picked up a hint that the most compelling reason for the arrival of my brother in 1942 and me in 1944 was because it ruled out any question of the young Mrs Robinson being enlisted to drive an ambulance.

The avoidance of making a proper effort for the country in wartime, the dealings on the black market and the skulduggery it involved, was normal business practice to her. This neither clashed with nor made a nonsense of Anne Wilson, the good Catholic, who for years since leaving school had risen early to catch the first Mass of the day.

There is a story of George Orwell journeying to the northeast to chronicle the effects of poverty and deprivation during the worst years of the Depression. He found a mother and her four babies barely existing between the walls of a tiny, damp basement room, struggling to survive without water or heat. 'How long have you lived in these conditions?' he asked. 'Ever since they told us about them,' the mother replied.

That punchline mirrored our early backdrop. No one told us we were different. Only as we started to visit other homes did it slowly dawn on us just how bizarre was our family's way of doing things.

Out there, for example, in the post-war years of going without, there were ration books, an absence of luxuries. Often necessities were no easier to come by – or so we learnt later. At the time, my brother and I toddled around in cosy ignorance. One day in our local village I went to buy some sweets. The woman asked politely for my coupons. 'We don't use them,' I replied equally politely. 'In our house,' as my auntie once remarked with Irish pride, 'despite Hitler, there was fruit on the sideboard and nobody ill in the house.'

Legend has it that my father came back from a visit to relatives and told my maternal grandfather that at his cousins' they were sharing two eggs a week between the whole family. 'The fellow is talking through his backside again,' said my grandfather, who had known only juicy steaks, eggs galore, even bananas, during all the time the Germans had been razing Liverpool to the ground.

Directly opposite my mother's stall in St John's was another poultry stall, Harris's. As I type the name I almost bow with respect. Mrs Harris was the opposition. As is still the case with markets, the same goods were on other counters only yards away. Do stallholders today live in any greater harmony than they did in St John's? I don't know. But certainly to A. Wilson the Harrises were the enemy. To begin with there was old Mrs Harris. Then later there were her daughters Eileen and Fanny. Before I was born, Mrs Harris senior had apparently done everything to put my mother out of business. Quite what 'everything' meant was never clear. My mother's customary habit of painting broad strokes on the canvas made it difficult to know. In any case, by the time I came along the Harris family had been kicked into touch. But whatever they did or did not do, we owed them a lot.

Old Mrs Harris had sharpened my mother's brain when it came to fighting dirty or defending her corner. The middle-aged Harris daughters, in their brown felt hats and white market coats, one pinched-faced and thin, the other barrel-like, looked benign enough to me. Perhaps they lacked their mother's appetite for commercial espionage. No matter, it was their mother whose memory we marked.

Every year, from the age of four until my mid-teens, we decamped to the South of France for anything up to six weeks. There on the terrace of our hotel we took part in a first-night ritual. My mother would order us to raise our glasses to Mrs Harris. 'Without her, we wouldn't be here,' she would announce solemnly. Sadly, the Harris family only went to Colwyn Bay for their holidays.

The lesson: learn from your enemies. They are your greatest teachers. It ran parallel with the idea that there were no victims, only volunteers. That to look adversity in the face was the only respectable option. To shy away from a fight was unthinkable.

The details of how, when she lay dying, old Mrs Harris had called for Miss Wilson was one of my mother's favourite stories. Apparently the old girl's conscience would not allow her to breathe her last until she had made peace with her young adversary and congratulated her on her cleverness.

I imagined having a market stall was normal. Unaware that few other mothers, nay, no other mother, in comfortable, middle-class Blundellsands, stood in the kitchen at six o'clock in the evening and cooked with their hat still on. Or asked her children to feel her hands. In winter, still icy after a seven-mile car journey from the market.

Did other families leap with joy at the arrival of a brand-new Morris Minor? A second car that only weeks later was on its way to the Isle of Man because someone had offered over the odds for it.

Did other mothers constantly say: 'Give me a telephone and I'll buy the opposition at one end of the street and sell it at the other'?

Or: 'Don't ever clean a kitchen floor. You go out and make the money to pay others to do housework'?

Who else's mother would declare with unconcealed contempt of almost any Blundellsands wife who stayed at home, 'She's very empty'?

Most people were terrified of my mother. We certainly were.

When years later feminism arrived, heralded by bra-burning, demonstrations and the wholesale condemnation of men, as well as the angry demand for women everywhere to release themselves from the tyranny of domestic duties and domestic violence, it was hard for me to grasp. Sure there was massive inequality in poorer homes, particularly for young mothers on the breadline. In the workplace, yes, the hours and rates for women were atrocious compared to men. But what was so tricky about life for middle-class, educated women? Nothing, I considered, that couldn't be solved by being up at six and out at five. By having a facial once a month and getting plenty of help in the house. By using one's head to save one's legs. By having a job, for God's sake.

My approach to the woes of sisterhood was hardly surprising, coming from a home where men, far from posing a threat, were regarded by the head of the house as variously stupid, incompetent, slow and only very occasionally equal. The odd clever, rich one would have my mother cooing and flirting in the best traditions of Barbara Cartland, but there weren't enough of them for a daughter to form any idea that this sort of male was commonplace.

Unique in working-class Bootle, my mother was sent away to a boarding school, Seafield Convent (Cherie Blair's old school), only a few miles along the coast at Crosby. Alas, when she was fifteen the bailiffs stopped circling her parents and pounced. She was taken away. The legacy is still perhaps in the convent's vaults: 'A. Wilson, fees unpaid.' From then it was she who righted the family business. My grandfather, a ship's engineer, was presumably on the high seas when the furniture was being emptied from the rented home. He appeared not to have involved himself in the family's precarious finances. Perhaps it was his absence that resulted in my mother becoming the parent. The hard-working, conscientious girl who had barely any time for enjoyment and courtship. Money, money, money. It had to be made. How else do you dress like a lady, own a car, become a cut above the rest?

She was twenty-seven by the time she met and married my father, a handsome, dashing local schoolteacher. His mother, a widow, had a small sweet shop opposite St James, the school in

Marsh Lane, Bootle, where my father went first as a student teacher and later as master in charge of science, geography and, unofficially, jokes, japes and entertainment.

A grammar-school boy and university graduate, Bernard Robinson was more than a step up from the dockers in flat caps who cycled to work and who expected no favours from life. A professional man. An exceptional 'catch'. Hadn't Anne Wilson done well? they said around Bootle.

Certainly the wedding was like nothing else the community had witnessed. There was morning dress, the bridesmaids in the finest satin, the bride, exquisitely beautiful in hand-stitched satin. 'The honeymoon is being spent on the Riviera,' said the *Bootle Times*. Impressive, presuming Bootle had the foggiest idea about the Riviera. Or what it represented.

Southport, twenty miles away, was only just dawning as an adventure. Mostly, as it happened, by courtesy of my uncle Paddy Flanagan, only brother to my maternal grandmother (one of four sisters), who had introduced the first coaches to the area. Those who made it further afield to Blackpool for a few days' holiday at a boarding house took their own salt and pepper and expected to be locked out from after breakfast until teatime. Many more would settle for a day trip to New Brighton. A foreign jaunt was a week's camping on the Isle of Man.

That Anne Wilson, the market-stall girl, had upped her station was a forgivable assumption. Bootle wasn't aware that it was the bride who had paid for the wedding and the honeymoon. Why should it be? My mother then and for the rest of her life disliked anyone knowing her business. Nevertheless, being misjudged by her new husband's colleagues was to seal a lifelong scorn for his profession.

Her resentment of teachers – with some justification – had begun at school. She had learnt very little and as a result and to her everlasting regret her spelling was poor, her general education sparse. It made her feel inferior. A deficiency she tried to right by reading newspapers, going to the theatre and generally 'keeping up'. Commendable but hardly necessary since her lack of basic schooling was largely regarded as immaterial and irrelevant to anyone who saw her operate in business. Or add a line of figures faster than a calculator.

No matter, teachers joined, nay headed, the canon of things she distrusted and avoided, along with November, Easter, Winston Churchill, meanness, small portions, crude jokes, nuns (excepting those from the Convent of Adoration), politicians, particularly Bessie Braddock, a famous female Labour MP (but not Michael Foot and Lord Boothby, whom she admired), paying income tax and housewives, especially those whose lives revolved around sewing and making dainty cakes.

With equal passion, she adored fortune tellers, tarot cards, the Irish, the law, barristers, judges, Jews, newspapers, quality bed linen, fresh flowers, well-cut clothes, beautiful hats, a 'good deal', boxing, the theatre and anyone with a sense of humour. In her rare spare time after leaving school she would slip off to the city's law courts and revel in hearing Maxwell Fyfe (later 1st Earl of Kilmuir) and Lord Birkenhead and Lord Birkett. Why and who introduced her to this form of entertainment is another mystery.

If Bootle was knocked sideways by the wedding of the year on August Bank Holiday 1937, the first night of the honeymoon was no less adventurous. By today's standards, it would have made a page lead in a Sunday tabloid.

My mother told the tale with great pride. They were at the Savoy Hotel in London (where else? as she would say). That night 'your father had to ask the hotel to call the doctor. He came and examined me. "Mr Robinson," he said to your father, "you are an exceedingly lucky man – your wife is a virgin."'

Sometimes a piece of oft-repeated family folklore becomes unremarkable simply by its familiarity. Only when I passed on this anecdote in my own middle age and saw the looks of astonishment on the faces of others did I realise just how bizarre the first night of the honeymoon must have been for all concerned. My mother, my father, the Savoy Hotel doctor.

Did my mother have sex that night? Did she enjoy it? Had my father ever had sex before? Did sex remain something to do with doctors and duty? Who knows? I don't ever remember being curious about the details. Although, if I had been, I would not have asked much more. Sex we never spoke of, beyond my mother's firm belief that girls who were 'loose' were never respected.

But even without any further and better particulars, the bare bones of the situation meant that a twenty-seven-year-old who could pay for an exotic wedding and a film-star-quality honeymoon had no idea where babies came from. It set the tone for her future life: rigid convention colliding on a daily basis with a breathtaking lack of orthodoxy.

Was my father a lucky man? My mother never gave the impression that lovemaking was anything other than something to be endured. And, inevitably, nine months from the honeymoon, in the spring of 1938, their first baby, Rita, was born.

Rita's life lasted just fourteen months. When we were growing up we learnt that the doctor had diagnosed her as suffering from diphtheria, which was raging at the time. But in fact, said my mother, she was wrongly treated. Her problem was teething and it was the treatment that killed her. Was this a fudged truth? Or did the diphtheria represent a hint of neglect on behalf of my parents that made their version of events easier to live with? We will never know. In all likelihood, even the central players shied from discussing the truth.

It was a typical family secret. In those days there were no counsellors and shrinks, twelve-step programmes or daytime television shows offering viewers the chance to share their grisly confidences.

In our home, the most obvious result of the loss of the much-adored Rita was the treatment of my brother. When he was born four years later, he was nursed and cosseted. 'Peter arrived during the Blitz and bombing so he was bound to be highly strung,' my mother would explain. This was expected to excuse anything her only son did or said.

(More than half a century later, after giving this version of events on a radio programme, Peter learnt that there was no bombing in August 1942. But there was plenty in January of that year. 'So I was conceived during the Blitz,' he wrote to me recently. 'You, Anne, were born when the bombing had stopped and the country was optimistic about its future.')

My father was another precious son. A working-class prince, an only child whose father was a checker on the docks and a drunk. At some point he was thrown out of the house by his wife Annie (née O'Rourke), who was already running her own sweet shop. Thus Bernard Robinson as a baby found himself surrounded by women. He never mentioned his father, who was later crushed by a crane and died alone from pneumonia.

Presumably, like the women in my mother's family, Annie O'Rourke had taken to trade to put food on the table. All of this was a barely noticed route to emancipation for working-class women. And hardly remarked on by the feminists of later years.

In my mother's formative years, a woman's place was very much at the back of the bus. She was nine when women over the age of thirty were finally granted the vote. In 1937, the year she was married, the divorce laws were extended to give women the right to petition on grounds of their husband's cruelty, desertion or madness. In the thirties, women's dependence on men extended to a restaurant manager being entitled to refuse a woman a table if she entered on her own.

Meanwhile, there was bohemian London. This allowed the upper classes and the artists and writers and actors of the day to ignore all convention. So Vita Sackville-West could conduct a grand and public affair with Violet Trefusis, while living the life of wife to a diplomat and later Tory MP, and travel Europe with her female lover without risk of attracting public scorn. Not that lesbianism or women's rights (or wrongs) ever cropped up in our house. The talk was much more likely to be of the Duke of Windsor and Mrs Simpson. My mother regarded Mrs Simpson, on the whole, as a good thing because her suits fitted and she was elegant.

Born in 1909 and 1911 respectively, my mother and father were still children during the First World War; the Depression was looming as they moved from their teens to their twenties. For them poverty, disease, hunger, children without shoes, mothers without medical treatment, families without homes, ran alongside the dawn of Hollywood, of motion pictures, of dances and music and jazz and the Charleston. Forty years later they were still humming 'Bye, Bye, Blackbird' and 'When the Red, Red, Robin Comes Bob, Bob, Bobbin' Along'. Al Jolson was their musical hero. My father was a talented musician who played the saxophone, the piano and the ukulele. My mother with no hesitation shared his hobbies. Her love of glamour and the theatre complemented his enthusiasm. Fred Astaire and Ginger Rogers, being elegant, carefree and gravity defying, were film stars they copied on a Saturday night at the Lyceum, Reece's Café and the Grafton Rooms.

For the young Catholic men and women from Bootle, if Reece's Café and the Grafton were social cornerstones, the parish church was another. The parish priest, as far as his community was concerned, had the judgement of Solomon.

When the Second World War came my father, at twenty-eight, was immediately called up. My mother accompanied him to sign on at the temporary office in Williamson Square in the centre of Liverpool. She claimed she 'dropped' the clerk ten shillings and had him assure her that my father would not have to leave Britain to fight abroad.

This was absurd. The clerk must have enjoyed his luck and taken the ten shillings anyway. It's true my father never did leave England, eventually becoming a captain in the Royal Artillery, but that was because of his skill in training men. Not that he ever interrupted or disputed my mother's tale or suggested to her that others might find it disgracefully unpatriotic.

He was, as far as she was concerned, an ongoing trial and disappointment. As she remarked despairingly whenever he had goofed, which was often, 'In all the years he has been with me, he's learnt nothing.' She would humiliate him without a second thought. He rarely answered back. Their relationship was an uneven balance of criticism, admiration and a strange sense of commitment.

Only after they had both gone did I begin to understand how the relationship worked. His priorities were different from hers. He wished to be amusing and to be liked. This naturally had no place in her mission statement, which was to be on the lookout for a bargain, a good deal, never to be taken for a ride and to hell with whether people liked you.

So, from the start, the idea that he might profit from watching her way of doing things was doomed. But to take her orders was what he was used to. Women had brought him up. He was trained to service their needs. If at times he resented her power, he didn't often show it. But he would sometimes defy her silently.

People loved his easy charm. His humour. His lack of judgement. Without effort he would have folk believing that bumping into them was quite the nicest thing that had happened to him that day. Probably – as is often the case with the easygoing – his cheerfulness masked a great deal of indifference.

My mother's manner, meanwhile, was one of uninhibited directness. She would shout, she would rail at her staff, her competitors and the salesmen on the market. Confusingly for the recipient, however, a ferocious battle over a halfpenny a pound in the price of a consignment would end with her asking sweetly and with genuine interest whether this son or that daughter had heard from the university of their choice. How a wife's pregnancy was faring and to be sure to remember to tell the wife – whose name she would always know – that Miss Wilson wished to be remembered. The hapless male would end up not knowing if he was coming or going.

She loathed bullies, while being a disgraceful bully herself. Not that anyone had the nerve to say so – least of all my father. We lived by her bizarre codes of practice. Questioning her wisdom, doubting her decisions, was not an option. She was part monster, part magic. I have felt comfortable in the company of bullies, monsters and madness ever since.

2

New Money

A set of beautiful blond pig-skin luggage rested in the attic at home. It had been bought for the honeymoon in the South of France. In the first few years after the war it had gone with my parents to Switzerland, a 'safe' haven while Europe was sorting itself out. The trips were a good practice run on how to 'manage' on a £25 budget for a fortnight, for several years the amount of money permitted to be taken abroad.

My mother's personalised method for overcoming this irritating restriction was to place wads of notes, usually an additional £200, in either pocket of both her and my father's raincoats and hope for the best.

Standing in line for one trip through customs, she noticed that every third person was being called out for a search. Quick arithmetic told her she was likely to be included. In fact she wasn't. No matter, because by the time it was her turn she had switched her money to my father's pocket – who, true to form, neither questioned what was going on, nor looked in the slightest hassled, as smilingly he proceeded through with his illegal booty. His geniality and sunny nature remained his passport through life.

By the time we children understood the times of the year, we realised that summer holidays meant the rest of Blundellsands

disappeared. My brother and I looked on gloomily as great gaggles of playmates went missing. The bulk of our friends seemed
to decamp to Abersoch in North Wales. The prosperous old
families had houses there. Others made for their second homes
in the Lake District. Sadly, from the age of four and six we had
been declared old enough for abroad. We were therefore destined for nothing more than each other's company on the
Riviera. There would be the journey to Ringway Airport outside
Manchester. A plane to London. Often another one to Paris and
then on to Nice. After which we would hang on to our seats for
a fast ride along to the coast to Cannes. The last part of our trip
was punctuated by my mother either imploring my father to
slow down, even though he wasn't driving, or worrying out loud
that yet again he had failed to establish clearly enough the price
of the journey.

Once or twice we went all the way by car. This was memorable for the long avenues of trees, unlike anything at home,
and the rather pleasing sight of French children and adults, on
seeing a car from Great Britain, giving us Churchillian victory
signs. Occasionally, in northern France, lorries would hog the
narrow roads. My mother would call the drivers communists.
She also included Gregory Peck and Charlie Chaplin in this category. Naturally no one argued with these sweeping assessments.
(It was years before it dawned on me that the misinformation of
the McCarthy era was the reason why Gregory Peck in particular, who often turned up in Liverpool for the Grand National,
was considered by her to be a Russian spy.)

En route we would eat cautiously at recommended restaurants. In the back of the car – variously a Bentley, a Rover or a
Daimler – we would have packets of tea to scatter as tips. This
was in place of the usual currency for easing our lives, the offer
of the delivery of a fresh roasting chicken.

To overcome the boredom Peter and I developed a game. One
or other would spread their hands out. Each finger would represent a radio station. So as I tugged on my brother's forefinger,

he would break into song. His thumb would be the Home Service. From the front of the car our parents would join in.

Any sort of performing was a neat way of diverting my mother from worrying out loud and/or pestering my father – otherwise her chief occupation. Instead, before long, both parents would become like children demanding to 'tune in'. 'Abou Ben Adhem, may his tribe increase' was one of my father's favourite bits of poetry. His jokes were wonderful. His taking off of dotty army officers a joy.

It wasn't surprising we chose to be pretend broadcasters. The radio and the BBC was our friend. Listening to it was much encouraged by our parents. *Dick Barton, Special Agent* and *Two-Way Family Favourites* were musts with Sunday lunch. *Round the Horne* and *Beyond Our Ken* were never missed. *Mrs Dale's Diary* and Jack De Manio in the mornings, Uncle Mac at teatime.

At one point my father rigged up the radiogram in the dining room. He'd then 'transmit' to us from the morning room. Our own studio! Eagerly, we took it in turns. My brother would play the part of Cliff Michelmore. I was Jean Metcalfe. We did endless 'requests' and pretended to be listeners in BFPO Germany and Cyprus. The postcards read out by Cliff and Jean, or whoever broadcast from the other end, talked about families looking forward to being home again in three, four or five years. A lifetime away to two fervent young listeners still under ten.

Unappreciated by either child was the fact that while our mother was tirelessly gearing us up to be traders our father was subversively ensuring that in their children a love of show business would overrule.

Our destination in Cannes was sometimes the Savoy Hotel, since demolished, or the Carlton – the very grandest of several very grand hotels that overlook the bay – distinguished by the small black towers at its corners. The entrance hall would be busy and bustling. The bedrooms – we would have three with adjoining doors – huge and airy. The bath towels far larger than anything we had at home from George Henry Lee's. The reception staff impossibly courteous. Even to us.

All sorts of people swept in and out of the doors of the Carlton. Few missed my mother's beady eye. As far as she was concerned it was part of our education to be able to recognise a swarthy, tubby man as ex-King Farouk. And the tall, handsome black man as the boxer Sugar Ray Robinson.

In the rue d'Antibes we would make for M'sieur René, who cut my mother's hair and famously one year tore into mine after it had been given a perm. Most importantly at M'sieur René's there were more opportunities to star spot. My mother would do her trick of pointing with her nose. This meant, Clock the person over there; I'll tell you later who she is.

'Merle Oberon,' whispered my mother after the American lady who'd been having her nails done departed. I had no idea who Miss Oberon was. Except that she had connections with a Tyrone Power – which sounded like one of the Irish radio stations my uncle Pat listened to. But those names resonate like headlines fifty years later because, from one summer till the next, once back home my mother would be repeating them to everyone.

Perversely, as far as my mother was concerned, the main aim of our annual over-the-top, massively expensive vacation was to broaden our education through travel. But given the plan's director and producer it had not the slightest chance of paying off. Since, for those four to six summer weeks, we existed as if in an isolated bubble, untouched and untainted by anything that smacked of 'foreign'.

For anyone looking on we must have appeared comically British and very new money indeed. Our continental breakfast, delivered to our bedrooms, was enhanced with boiled eggs. Then we would be off to the beach. Every year the first day was fraught, for it involved the 'negotiation'. This entailed my mother agreeing a price for the mattresses, the parasols, the changing cubicle. We looked on embarrassed and irritated that now we were on holiday there was still all that talking about money to do.

Eventually she and the beach boss would shake on a deal. After that the daily ritual of the holiday hardly altered. Early breakfast. Early swim. On the beach our fair skin and red hair were dead give-aways. For some reason my mother decided that Nivea cream would protect us. We would become sunburnt, horribly so in the case of my brother.

On the dot of eleven o'clock each morning we were summoned off the beach and made to eat a full breakfast at one of the cafés on the Croisette. Less than two hours later it was back to the hotel for our three-course lunch. Another trial. Not for us horrid foreign food, thank you. The maître d' would politely translate. Anything sounding suspiciously French would be replaced with 'jambon' or 'omelette'. Two bits of the language we knew. At the end of the meal my mother would eat peach after peach while we sat waiting.

An hour's rest in our room followed lunch. Then back to the beach. Then dinner at the hotel. Not a restaurant ever visited, except for our ham and eggs. Occasionally there would be a walk along the harbour. To look out for the Dockers. And their yacht the *Shemara*, moored alongside the gold-plated Bentley.

Another daily trial was slogging along the busy, noisy rue d'Antibes, checking the exchange rate. It has produced in me a life-long loathing of going a mile to save an inch. But it was part of my mother's religion: never paying over the odds for petrol, for car repairs, for stationery. The fact that you exhausted yourself in the process of seeking out the bargain was beside the point. The same thinking was behind the bulk-buying of fruit, coffee, sugar, HP sauce. In the larder at home, boxes of grapefruit would grow mouldy, the coffee become too dried up to use, the sugar weevil-logged and only good for throwing away, so, ultimately, anything but prudent housekeeping.

As our holiday drew to a close, another negotiation. The currency restriction would hardly cover a handful of days of breakfasts and sun-loungers. My mother, therefore, would lock herself in with the manager and another deal would be done. The account was, in effect, settled back home. But each year the transaction assumed the importance of the Treaty of Versailles. Secrecy, whispers, nose-tapping, looks and the encouragement to regard the manager as some sort of shadowy figure in whose hands our future rested.

Once the deed was done, my mother would smile and announce that in life there was always more than one way to skin a rabbit!

The dawn of the sixties. The Black Swan, in Helmsley, Yorkshire, a coaching inn much gentrified and extended by Trust House Hotels. With good reason. It is Mecca for parents visiting Ampleforth, then ranked as one of the three top Catholic public schools (Downside and Stonyhurst being the others). It is the long-awaited weekend of the opening of the newly completed Abbey.

It would be easier to book a suite with a sea view at the Carlton in Cannes on Film Festival week than to land one of the two bedrooms 'with bath' at the Black Swan for this prize occasion. Naturally we have both of them.

For dinner, my mother is in one of her elegant Dorville suits. She is determined to look her best. That in itself shows her up. The Old School parents have no use for fashion. The fathers are often in their fathers' suits. The mothers quite comfortable in what my mother would class as gardening clothes. Said with a sneer.

In the same way, Old School, Old Money sons stand out on the platform waiting for the school train. The trousers they have grown out of are embarrassingly short. Their blazers similarly are ill-fitting 'hand-me-downs'. Naturally, New Money puts its sons in shiny new shoes. New Money sons have neatly cut hair. New Money is at sea with the concept that Old Money sees no need to show off its wealth or worry that its children might feel disadvantaged in old clothes. Even more disturbing for New Money is the fact that it ends up not really knowing which Old Money still actually *has* money and which has no choice about the hand-me-downs.

The dining room of the Black Swan is packed. My mother variously surveys the scene, talks in a whisper and uses her eyes and her body to indicate we must pull up our shoulders and not slouch. Every so often she menacingly taps her manicured fingers on the table to express her wish for us to be silent.

Brave is the member of the family prepared to question this instruction, however illogical it might seem.

Across the room in the hotel's new extension there is a noisy table with probably twenty-five on it. Including the Abbot of Ampleforth. These diners are not eating from the hotel menu. Their meal has come with them from their estate in Scotland. Their laughter is loud and exuberant. Nobody is monitoring their behaviour. They are enviably at ease with themselves. My mother's expression switches to one of despair. 'How can children do anything but well when they have conversation like that at table?' she announces. The families at the big table on the far side of the room are, according to Mrs Shaw the hotel manager, the Pakenhams, and their relatives by marriage the Frasers. Headed by Lord Lovat, famous for courageously leading his troops on to the shores of Normandy on D-Day.

Lord Lovat would probably have had to lie down in a darkened room if he'd known of our family's 'war effort'.

No matter. My mother has faced her own battles. She's worked on her market stall. She has braved the cold. Taken risks. Allowed us to reach a level of luxury unknown to her family. Peter is now at one of the finest Catholic public schools. Our family has hijacked the keys to the most coveted hotel rooms (1 and 6) for the weekend, courtesy of Miss Denning, the Black Swan's formidable and all-powerful receptionist. Miss Denning doesn't know it but she has been seduced in precisely the same way as has the woman on the ticket desk of the Playhouse

Theatre in Liverpool. Ditto the old biddy in charge of bookings at the Royal Court (who provides my parents with permanently reserved front row seats), ditto the alterations lady at Marshall and Snelgrove in Southport or anyone else whom my mother requires to bend the rules so her needs can be satisfied. The routine, a combination of flattery and willingness to invest time in listening to the minutiae of the person's life, rarely fails. Plus – leaving the favour-maker in no doubt that a satisfactory result is expected – the promise of the arrival on their home doorstep of a fresh roasting chicken. 'Write down your address. Will anyone be there to take in a chicken?' is my mother's war cry.

By such stealth the unobtainable becomes available. But beyond my mother's grasp is the wherewithal to provide us with 'the conversation' that goes on across the room.

The real distinction of the Pakenham–Fraser group that evening was that it was entirely comfortable with what it stood for. Those people knew that they belonged.

Whereas for us, belonging and not belonging was a daily worry. We didn't fit in a lot of the time with middle-class Blundellsands. Equally, we looked odd and prissy going to my aunt Liz's. She was nearly always in bed, although, as far as we knew, she was as fit as a fiddle. Often there was a perilously full chamber pot standing close by. Her son, my mother's first cousin Pat, had worked for a time as a driver on the green corporation buses. His local government career had ceased when he was discovered taking an unauthorised route through Bootle with his mother on board and dropping her outside her home.

Young Peter should take up law, declared Aunt Liz from her huge throne-like bed, on one of our regular visits. Another Flanagan sister with ideas above her station. 'Thank you,' Aunt Liz would say when she wished a child in her presence to be silent. 'Goodbye,' when she'd had enough of her visitors and wanted them to get up and leave.

My mother's boarding-school friend, whom we called Auntie

Barbara, loved retelling the tale of how, when Cousin Pat was still at school, Aunt Liz had received a home visit from the bishop who was doing the rounds. 'What do you have planned for the boy?' asked His Grace. 'We think the civil service or banking,' responded Aunt Liz, as if it were merely a puzzle which of these two respected professions to choose. The bishop was gravely nodding his approval, according to Auntie Barbara, when 'young Patrick' piped up, 'Oh hey der, Ma, I wanner be a docker like me dar . . .'

My mother's ambitions for *her* precious son were based on more solid foundations and needed no encouragement from Aunt Liz. She had resolved at the moment of his birth that only the best would do, and on leaving Park House Nursing Home almost her first task was to put his name down for Stonyhurst, run by the Jesuits. The plan was derailed when a Benedictine monk who regularly visited her stall insisted Ampleforth was far superior. The guidance came dangerously late. Peter was by now six. Only persistence of the highest order achieved the switch – and at a price.

In the post-war years Ampleforth was full and had an enviable waiting list. So was Gilling Castle, its prep school, a few miles away. Undaunted by a postal refusal, my mother journeyed uninvited up to Yorkshire and Gilling for six consecutive weekends to beg the head, Fr Hilary, to take Peter. Father Hilary relented, provided Peter came the very next term.

So off went my brother in his brand-new grey uniform, a blazer with a royal blue badge and short trousers. His clothes all name-taped. His trunk and everything else bearing his newly allotted number, 547. He was three weeks past his seventh birthday. I felt we were waving him goodbye for ever. In a way we were. School, he reflected later, became his home. Home became a dim memory.

The first time we were allowed to visit him – a month later – our depleted family swept up the drive of the castle and saw a gaggle of boys playing rugby. One of them came running towards us, tears in his eyes, his nose bleeding. It was my brother.

What had my mother done? For the month since he left she had sat not at the front of the church at Sunday Mass as was usually her custom, but at the back, weeping. The worry had caused great clumps of her hair to fall out. Now her worst suspicions were confirmed. Her son, for whom she wanted only the best, was dreadfully unhappy.

The puzzle is why she allowed him to stay. What instinct for his future compelled her to force-feed him this superior and traumatising education?

Years later, if asked, and of course no one demanded that she account for her sin, she would probably have fallen back on that most bogus of parental excuses: 'I was doing it for you.'

Back at the table at the Black Swan, my father is behaving himself. In that he is saying very little except occasionally to attempt a joke. The joke when it arrives can go either way. Both children look on anxiously to see if we are to be given permission by our mother to find it funny. Or whether we must stifle our giggles, ask to be excused and fly outside to laugh.

In between, our mother is being extraordinarily and embarrassingly gushing to the waitress. This works unfailingly to increase the amount of vegetables and meat we will be served. Towards the end of the table d'hôte meal there is a ritual about the pudding. I probably will not want one. My mother will be on another of her diets. But you have to order anyway. 'Find out what your father wants,' my mother would say. Not wasting something you've paid for was another theme of our upbringing. It headed an infinite number of contradictions. What was funny and what was not. What was a necessary economy. What you blew a fortune on and what you watched like a hawk.

In the same topsy-turvy way, the oh so solemn meal at the Black Swan would be the subject of huge family laughter once it was over. Later we would be allowed to mock, to mimic the waiter, the waitress, the hotel manager. Lady this. Lord that. It had been painful at the time but now no one was spared our ridicule.

3

Nose Against the Window

Thirteen and 14 Market Street, the cellars below St John's Market, had originally been rented out as storage space. But as the street market became increasingly popular, the city councillors sanctioned traders opening them as stalls.

A. Wilson became tenants of numbers 13 and 14, having moved from inside the market in the early fifties. At the back there was a huge walk-in fridge and an office. At the front, the stall with a cash register. Underfoot was concrete. Standing, for hours, selling in the icy cold was an ordeal suffered in silence.

'You need to see how the money is made,' ordered my mother. So by the time we could be relied upon to count, and for half the school holidays, we were there in over-large, laundry-starched white coats flogging chickens.

'Only takes an hour to cook,' was the sales patter, which for some reason was delivered in a Scouse accent. Also, I've often reflected since, most chickens actually take longer than an hour to roast.

There were strict rules about selling. Not least about announcing in a loud voice the receipt of a five-pound or a ten-pound note. It had to stay on top of the cash register until the change was counted out to the customer. This way the amount of the original note handed over could not be disputed.

You failed to carry out this routine at your peril. Miss Wilson, as her customers so often referred to her, saw no need to admonish in private.

The customers were royalty. They were to be treated as such. They were there to buy and if in the process they chose to boast of their holidays, their new car, their sister's cousin's baby, so be it.

Notable were the wives of the consultants who lived in Rodney Street, the city's equivalent to Harley Street. They came for a brace of pheasant or ducklings and talked endlessly about their children, their dinner parties, their cars, their holidays, while a humble Miss Wilson nodded in apparent admiration. (How were they to know that after the surgeon's wife had left she would remark: 'She was his nurse, you know.') One of the wives, almost certainly a nurse in an earlier life, once explained to my mother how her son was just leaving for a boarding school. 'Of course, Miss Wilson, you won't have heard of it. It's called Ampleforth.' My mother said not a word.

My brother, who was inches away when this conversation took place, was happy to stay out of it. He hated the idea that Ampleforth, being in the next county, had plenty of pupils who lived in Liverpool or on the Wirral. Peter became skilled at jumping behind the stall or feigning a coughing fit each time he thought he spotted someone from school in the distance.

My school was in Hampshire, a much safer distance away. Only a handful of girls came from the north-west. But it would have been unwise in the extreme for either of us to indicate we were ashamed.

Often, I would trail around after my mother as she bought her chickens, haggled over a price for putting them into cold storage, haggled over the transport costs, haggled over the weight. Haggle, haggle, haggle! Nothing missed her sharp eye. Worry, haggle, worry, haggle, spend, spend, spend! None of it made sense but our mother was determined to teach us the code of conduct for operating as an A. Wilson employee. Sometimes one of us would be sent to accompany a driver on deliveries to the hotels and restaurants. To come away without a signed invoice was unforgivable. If a chef asked to weigh the consignment we must stand close to the scales to ensure no monkey business was taking place. The same slavish devotion to detail and 'not being taken for a ride' formed the backbone of every operation.

What did the chefs and cooks make of a twelve-year-old in charge? What did a burly Scouse van driver, already sinking from the shock of having a woman give him orders, think of the woman's prissy kids being sent to monitor him?

Who cared? In any case, each order, every delivery, was an ongoing soap opera.

The top talent we dealt with was the head chef of the Adelphi Hotel. In the days when the only places to eat well outside London were the restaurants in the Victorian railway hotels in Manchester, Glasgow, Liverpool, etc., the Adelphi's French Room was one of the finest. Its reputation for quality cuisine and elegant, rich patronage was world famous. The job as chef of this empire was regarded as every bit as important as that in a top-class London Establishment.

For Miss Wilson's children, who had been taken the other side of the kitchen walls to dine at the French since they were in carrycots, the kitchens were as exciting as the Christmas pantomime at the Royal Court.

Chef Gianni was usually in his office. I never saw him cooking. His number two was a Liverpudlian called Jack Allen, with the language of a trooper. He hurled it at young commis chefs, at waitresses, at porters. The yelling and screaming, the tears, the rages were relentless. It was particularly impressive that the waitresses, middle-aged women, who ran around looking as though they were on the verge of a breakdown, were exactly the same ones who emerged serene, on the other side of the doors, to serve the diners.

Chef Gianni had come from the famous Gleneagles Hotel in

Scotland. His mistress still lived in Edinburgh. He would turn up at Market Street one weekend in every four – elegant, if over-weight – to collect two capons and then catch the evening train up north. My mother's natural sense of curiosity and abiding interest in the lives of others far outweighed any disapproval of his domestic arrangements. Did the chef's wife know where he was going? we would ponder between the four of us. Peter and I, who had only come across 'mistresses' in movies, were inordi-nately excited actually to know someone who had one. My mother's conclusion was that the chef's wife in her massive house on the Wirral was probably quite happy with her lot. My mother naturally regarding anyone whose husband kept them as 'on to a good thing'.

At the other end of the scale from the elegant Chef Gianni was Chef Jones of the Lime Street station cafeteria. Chef Jones had an elderly mother and a bullet nose and no noticeable talent for cooking. Sweetly, he would turn up at the stall with boxes of rock cakes. Aptly named. We fed them to the pigeons.

Every chef wise enough to order his supplies through my mother got his reward in the shape of a brown envelope. The '5 per cents' – their cash cut of the monthly bill – was the estab-lished method for keeping these important men sweet. The chefs would often also receive 'tips' from the butcher, the grocer and so on.

It was normal business practice and a monthly headache as our parents would sit in the morning room at home, my father relying on the Ready Reckoner to calculate, my mother shouting him down for being too slow. 'I've got it worked out in my head before he's found the right page,' she would complain.

The main source of the chickens was Northern Ireland and two farmers in particular: Mr O'Hagan and Mr Carson. It was to my mother's credit and theirs that neither side had any idea about the other's religious bent until we made an Easter visit to Lurgan and Dungannon one year and found Mr O'Hagan had Catholicky statues everywhere in his home, while the centrepiece of Mr Carson's grand dining table was a box containing a Union Jack.

The chickens, in stout wooden boxes, arrived each morning on the overnight boats, the *Ulster Monarch* and the *Ulster Princess*, and we would help my father collect them. As we bumped along the still cobbled Lower Dock Road, my father would say for the umpteenth time, 'He came home with his thumbnail in the tramline,' referring to drunks who steered themselves back from the pub on the tram routes.

This would be followed by the joke of the guy taking the tramcar to the Pier Head and then proclaiming the worst bit of the journey was over. 'Where are you going?' asks the conductor. 'To China' was the answer.

China loomed large in our lives. Grandad Wilson was forever going round the house saying: 'Never trust a Chinaman.' He had been in San Francisco at the turn of the century and had adopted the prevailing attitude. Yet post-war my mother was building an entire section of her business on trusting Chinamen. After the fall of Chiang Kai-shek, their ranks swelled in Liverpool.

As children we knew dozens of them. There was Harry with the Four Ways restaurants, who weighed everything twice but paid cash immediately. There was Gloria at the Tai Ping, who never seemed to pay when you wanted and complained she couldn't because 'all the customers were on holiday'. And there was the Golden Fleece where they had three fierce Alsatian dogs that made delivering a nightmare.

But although we grew up going in and out of these places, we never ate Chinese food. We distrusted it because my father insisted that one of the restaurants we delivered to had pork, duck, lamb and beef on the menu but the only meat they ever bought was ropey old boiling fowl from us.

Beyond the market, Peter and I enjoyed a special bizarre relationship with the local department stores, Bon Marché, George

Henry Lee's, and Owen Owen's. The heads of many of the sections within them knew us well. 'Miss Wilson' (or Mrs Robinson) was the local equivalent of royalty. The staff rushed forward to greet her. They allowed her to take 'on appro' whatever she wished. Cloths, tableclothes, bed linen, rugs, crockery. They certainly knew and respected the fact that the same woman with the cold hands who could be seen on her market stall selling chickens was one of their best customers. She bought in bulk. Her children by the age of ten and twelve regarded the stores as an extension of the family empire.

'Green knickers for the new school,' Miss Winn, the huge woman in charge of school uniforms, would cry as we came into sight. 'Clear the brides' changing room. Mrs Robinson is here to try on,' Miss Bamber in women's fashions would order as she spotted us.

Naturally Miss Winn and Miss Bamber were on the chicken run. As was Mrs Ball in the shoe department and Miss Murphy on the Elizabeth Arden counter.

Even without their mother, Mrs Robinson's children, when home from school, would lunch in either the Bon Marché or George Henry Lee restaurant. A. Wilson supplied both with chickens, ducks, eggs and bacon and in return sent two precious little customers to dine there.

Sometimes, when her brother was away, the little sister would sit and eat all on her own. My mother's arrangements for childcare were, like everything else, distinctive.

Back in Blundellsands, for the other half of our school holidays, our teenage lives centred on the tennis clubs (Blundellsands and Hightown), the rugby club (Waterloo) and our various friends. Mostly, other people's parents were professionals: doctors, consultants, accountants, lawyers. A few owned family businesses of a kind that meant the parents had been away to school and in truth were a different 'class'. For them, however, the distinction was between those of us who went away to school and those at the local grammar school. We were accepted and acceptable. My mother quietly knew we were different. Her way of coping was to make sure, and constantly remind us, that we 'wanted for nothing'. She saw to it that we had the best tennis racquets, the best holidays, we gave the best dances, we had no restrictions on the time we came home. Once we could drive, we could have whatever sort of car we wished.

It didn't make me feel we belonged. I still imagined the others looked down on us, because we didn't gather together and eat our evening meal with the same finesse. Our home was either spick and span because there had been another blitz, another cleaning lady. Or it was such a terrible tip there would be strict instructions: 'Don't let anyone upstairs.'

Other people's mothers, who had gone to university, for goodness' sake, were always busy in the kitchen or sewing or playing golf. When these mothers went out shopping they had dainty little brown wicker shopping baskets and a neat little pad and pencil. It was hard to gauge their circumstances – financially, that is – because it was not their habit to boast or display the sort of profligacy that we at home took as normal.

My mother looked upon most stay-at-home women with a mixture of envy and contempt. The ones who were not 'empty' she would declare had been clever enough to find a man to keep them. That notwithstanding, my mother would also insist she could buy and sell any man in Blundellsands without waking up.

Money was our yardstick. We were taught to regard it as the finest form of oneupmanship. It excused everything else, breeding, class, manners, social standing; except, secretly, we children knew it didn't.

It didn't make up for a working mother. An untidy house, an empty house, parents who rowed. A mother who was always tired and too often when at home remained in her bed. A presentless Christmas.

Christmas meant worry with a big W. There was the worry

over which orders my mother might lose and which she could get. The price of turkeys was another. In the absence of fore-casters and market research my mother would smell the air through October and November and decree: 'Turkeys will be on the floor,' or 'Turkeys are going to be scarce.' I never knew her to be wrong.

Christmas itself was a grim affair. By Christmas Eve, after a fortnight of my parents working until late into the night, check-ing orders, doing the books, there was nothing left for the family. The tree, if it had been bought at all, would still be without its lights. Our presents would be cash. Our Christmas dinner a goose. By Christmas Day all of us were sick of the sight of turkey. In any case, my mother would say turkey had no taste.

Like a child from an orphanage, I would metaphorically press my nose against the windows of our friends in Blundellsands. Their mothers in smart little black Austins – most families' second car – would have spent weeks haring around Crosby village, buying presents, wrapping paper, collecting the ingredients for the Christmas pudding, assisting with the church. Doing Mummy things. Our mummy never did Mummy things, unless you counted hugging you and telling you you were greater than anyone else in the whole wide world. In that bit of being a mummy my mother excelled. As far as I knew no one else's mummy said 'have both' when you were in a dress shop, or could juggle eight oranges with her eyes shut. But this was as far as her skills seemed to extend.

Come the end of the holidays it was back to school. Peter heading for Yorkshire. Me to Farnborough Hill Convent. We could share with our friends our Blundellsands life. The tennis club, the rugby club, even our trips to the South of France. But Christmas and our market lives we never mentioned.

I had been desperate to be sent to Farnborough Hill Convent, my boarding school, once I had enjoyed the excitement of visit-ing Ampleforth and read every single word of Enid Blyton and

Angela Brazil. I chose Farnborough for no better reason than that I liked the uniform. It didn't occur to me that being able to make the selection myself without anyone appearing to be too fussed was the very opposite of what had gone on with my brother. The building was the former home of the Empress Eugenie. The nuns, many of the teaching staff old girls themselves, were a relatively new order called the Sisters of Christian Education. Within the convent, class distinctions were observed. The teachers were Mothers; the nuns who worked in the kitchens and in the gardens were Sisters.

Memorable was Mother O'Toole, the maths teacher, who ridiculed me in about lesson two in Algebra. I didn't get it. Not, I believe, because I was slow, but because I had been brought up in a world where nothing just happened. I had been brought up by a father who explained why things happened.

So somewhere in 1957, a child is put down. And relinquishes all ambition in a subject.

Not surprisingly, I insisted on leaving at sixteen and my mother made no great fuss except continually and embarrassingly to tell people that the Reverend Mother had said, 'Your daughter is perfectly capable of making Oxford but she's had enough of us.'

I had. I loathed the pettiness of the nuns and the endless small-minded rules that taught you to conform. Surely if you were to make it in the world you needed to do exactly the opposite?

Thirty-odd years later, I return to Farnborough Hill. The school has invited me to speak to the parents. They have sold tickets for the event. The hall is packed; according to the headmistress there are 380 in the audience. Three hundred and eighty × £10. Not a bad gate. Nearly four thousand pounds, I say. Adding that I have calculated it especially for Mother O'Toole, who had told me with crushing certainty that I wouldn't make anything of myself.

Mother O'Toole aside, it is possible that the only skill I

acquired at Farnborough before I skipped out was the knack of how to curtsey elegantly while carrying a pile of books. It was a school rule that for visitors, the Reverend Mother and the Headmistress we must bob down when we passed them.

Footnote: It would be hard to think of a singularly more useless talent to take into grown-up life. So much so that when unexpectedly, at a BBC dinner, I was once placed next to Prince Edward, I insisted, against his protestations, on curtseying before we sat down.

'It cost my mother about thirty grand for me to get the hang of it,' I told him, 'and I long to be able to tell her it was not wasted.'

To be fair to the nuns, which they rarely were to us, the rat-like cunning I practised in ducking the system was invaluable when I became a news reporter. That, and an early opportunity to become accustomed to performing in public. To limit my trouble-making during our annual retreat, the headmistress chose me to read aloud to the school during mealtimes. Anyone who has stood on a chair, green gym knickers on show, narrating from a holy book for the benefit of an unappreciative, giggling young audience, is later likely to find no terror in facing a 'telly-prompter' and live broadcasting.

My mother appeared to be entirely sanguine about my leaving school. In contrast, Peter's future education was a matter of desperation. Poor Peter.

I believe you can spot a first child, especially a boy, from the other end of a sales conference or a business seminar. He is over-conscientious, he cries and sulks at the drop of a hat; he likes to be the centre of attention. He rarely has the carefree cheekiness of his less cosseted younger brothers and sisters. He is prone to marry his mother all over again. His chances of being, if political correctness allowed us to say so, 'a terrible old woman', a 'big girl's blouse', are depressingly higher than average. Ironic, since he is the one who will most likely have benefited from the expert advice. The one who has been breastfed, pampered and had his temperature checked so often he thinks the thermometer is part of his anatomy.

If he has two or three brothers or sisters they will have been cared for with less and less anxiety. So much for the fad of excess parenting.

Peter remembers the year before his A levels. No one from Ampleforth had been in contact with my mother about his future. Unknown to her, Peter had been steered towards the idea that he should modestly aim for a redbrick university. When he eventually told my mother she looked puzzled. She hadn't heard the term 'redbrick'. However, once the words Manchester, Nottingham and Birmingham were added to the explanation, there was no need for anyone to draw diagrams. She was very sure indeed that redbrick was entirely unsuitable for her beloved son. In simple trader fashion she argued that she had paid out a great deal of money and as far as she was concerned that meant Oxford or Cambridge.

Peter recalls her visit to see the Ampleforth headmaster, Fr William. Headmasters of public schools, being on a par with doctors and parish priests, were people you respected and looked up to. You unquestioningly accepted their counsel.

An unsuspecting Fr William – a remote, unworldly, monastic figure who appeared only very occasionally to concern himself with the day-to-day running of the school – had ushered Mrs Robinson into his beautiful, panelled, book-lined study. She had announced her name and the name of her son. At which point Fr William, a faraway look in his eyes (and very possibly facing the twentieth parent of the morning), began to fiddle around on his desk for some notes to help him.

'What are you shuffling papers for, Father William?' my mother demanded. 'Don't you know who I am and who my son is?' According to my mother, Fr William had quickly 'pulled himself together' (always a satisfying thing for my mother to witness). Whether or not Fr William had any more idea by the end of the conversation who my brother was, we know not. But he got the message, which was: 'Don't mess with me. I want Oxbridge and you had better deliver.'

The lesson to be learnt: never be afraid or intimidated. Being unapproachable is often someone's way of avoiding confrontation. Make sure you get what you've paid for. Customers have a right to service.

4

A Permanent Dull Ache

W hat is a mother for? Why is so much of what makes her tick unfathomable and unchanged through centuries of change?

At holiday time, I hear the wails of daughters: 'My mother is coming to stay,' or 'We have to go and see my mother.' (Sons in my view do not suffer anything like the same degrees of torment, guilt and conflicting loyalties.)

What causes the hand that rocks the cradle to become a burden? Or, rather, what ugly dynamic means that so often, secretly, a daughter has always regarded her mother as more of an enemy than a friend?

Once free from her mother's clutches and maybe with a family of her own, she wrestles with the guilt. But however good the intentions, however firm the resolve, often each side comes away from time spent together with a heavy heart, because whatever is simmering just below the surface has risen up yet again.

We are meant to love our mothers, for goodness' sake. That's the rub. No one tells us what to do when they turn out to be unlovable, devious, controlling, scheming, unfair, alcoholics or nymphomaniacs (or maybe a nightmare combination of all these things). When they favour one child above another. When they have no time for their children because they are more concerned about their careers or finding a new boyfriend.

Why do we adopt unrealistic expectations of a relationship that might have been doomed from the start? Doomed, not because one or other is 'bad' but because maybe all those years ago a baby daughter innocently arrived at a lousy time in her mother's life. 'Timing', as every wise old actor advises, 'is all.'

Look around. In the new century there are captainesses of industry, executives in sharp suits who run multi-million-pound businesses, who dominate boardrooms and wield undreamt-of power, but who, when faced with a little old lady who watches afternoon game shows and gives the vicar tea, can still be terrorised and made to cry.

The resentment between a mother and daughter, built up and unspoken of for years, alas, culminates in bitter disappointment and regret, beaming forcefully and cruelly from one side, countered by seething, unresolved anger from the other.

'I've just about come to terms with what she did/didn't do,' says a daughter of an ageing mother – having hung on until almost the end waiting for this lonely, frightened, confused old lady to say 'Sorry,' and 'I didn't mean it,' and 'It was all my fault.'

Whenever I describe my mother I am surprised that people see her as more monster than magic. Her moods were ugly, unexpected and to a child unjust. Sickness was the easiest way to curb her anger. She would drop all charges and willingly nurse you, cosset you, feed you, stay up all night with you. She believed that her kids were the most important thing in the world.

You haven't grown up until your parents stop embarrassing you, Alan Brien, the journalist and film critic, once famously said. I've never forgotten it.

My mother embarrassed me. But whose didn't?

Viewed from afar, we were sufficiently different to appear enviable. But behind the wealth and the small-town importance we were granted there was a more complicated and sadder truth.

I don't remember when or how I first realised my mother drank, but I imagine I was about seven or eight. I would see her lying in her bed, long after she should have gone to the market. 'I'm not well,' she would say. And she would probably also cry. I would try to comfort her. Not realising, although it hardly required much of a leap of reason, that the more whisky she'd had the more maudlin she became. Her speech would be slurred. She would sleep fitfully. Awake, she would berate my father on the phone.

One morning, when I was no more than eight or nine, she and I walked along to buy chickens at one of the depots on the edge of the wholesale fruit market. There was the usual bartering and dealing – if the price couldn't be reduced, she invariably insisted on free storage in the local cold stores for six to eight weeks. Business concluded, she began to sway. One of the men, receiving a waft of her whisky-soaked breath, shook his head in startled response. I watched with indignation. His reaction might have been unconscious. But I doubted it. I knew he would not have dared insult her in this way in normal times. Thankfully, she failed to notice. Or was it thankfully? If she had, might she have been more aware of her condition? Of course not, but how was I to know? I worried and worried on her behalf. When the bender had ceased, I mentioned the incident, uncertain, as so often, how the information would play. She took the account placidly. 'Always tell me about things like that,' she said, without any of the wrath I'd imagined. Discussion over. Line drawn.

When the benders were in-house, they were more controllable. Then there was only the vital business of being on phone watch. Of grabbing the receiver before she did, when the phone rang. If she got there first, it was excruciating to hover and eavesdrop. Who was on the other end? Hard to say, since the way she addressed them could change several times during the conversation, from Christian name to surname to another name. If that didn't convince them of her drunken state, there must have been the surprise of a stern, unbending, snooty Miss Wilson sounding like their equal. Or, if it was a social call, someone she hardly knew, she would be dramatically gushing. I, listening, would squirm in embarrassment. How could they fail to notice her bizarre chumminess and her slurred words?

As we got older my brother and I would attempt to pour the whisky down the sink. Why did my father buy it for her? In the odd moment of truth she asked herself and me the same question. I had no idea of the answer. A child in the fifties was not versed in the ways of dysfunctional families. The answer, more obvious now, is that she had not chosen to marry a man who was going to say, 'No whisky for you. It doesn't work for any of us when you drink.' She had in fact married a man programmed to do what she said. To take the line of least resistance. The possibility that whisky for her meant whisky for him might also have played a part.

Either way, her drinking shaped my childhood. Any child of an alcoholic parent, if they remember the experience, will tell of the constant dread of waiting for the other shoe to drop. There is the secret relief when the early signs of another bender turn out to have been misread, and the mother or father is happy, smiling and normal. Or when the bender arrives without telltale signs being entirely obvious, so a puzzling conversation on the telephone makes perfect sense a few hours later, when there is no mistaking the dreaded turn of events. The worst times were when my mother had not reached the stay-in-bed stage and would still be up and partly functioning.

One holiday, when my brother had a friend to stay from school, I recall my mother reeling around as she served breakfast. Then, minutes later, agreeing to drive the two boys to the station so they could catch the train to Liverpool. What could a child do to stop her?

Mostly my memory is of a permanent dull ache. The ongoing worry. Was it about to happen? The fear while we were in the midst of a bender was who was in the doghouse? Inevitably one of us was.

'Perversely, whoever hid the whisky bottle was the goody-goody for the day and out of the frame,' my brother once observed. He was right. It was a tacit acknowledgement by my mother that something had been done to help her. She never said this but the result was that she did not attack her rescuer. But now my brother doesn't remember the benders. He doesn't remember the rows. He doesn't remember the edgy days after, when the hangover was at its worst.

He can't recall a single day of upset or worry on the matter.

I believe him. Children accommodate what they can. So he blocked out my mother's drinking. While I was only too aware of it.

Nobody ever mentioned any of the strange behaviour to her, as far as I knew, except my auntie Barbara, although it must have been much discussed. Surely indeed, a source of satisfaction to those envious of her, to know that her arrogance and her wealth went alongside an anti-social, shameful habit about which they could endlessly sneer. A secret drinker, tut, tut, jeer, jeer. (Then again, maybe I judged others by our own uncharitable standards.) It was a bewildering, ongoing burden. Worried about, and never to be shared.

Once at boarding school, I dreaded being told there was a telephone call for me. Typically my mother would phone on a whim, often during mealtimes. The nuns, imagining it was an emergency, would allow me to take the call. The phone she called on was behind the main stair of the grand house. My mother's words would be slurred. Her questions incomprehensible. She might be happy or sad. Often it was difficult to gauge which.

Whatever her state, I fretted about who had taken her call. And, even more, what I could do to make her happy.

Above all else, I resolved never to drink. Not when it could have such an awful effect on one's children.

5

Wandering Hands

'Is it Oxford or Cambridge you are going to, Peter?' my father had asked my brother one day, weeks after the matter had finally been settled. Given the agonies we'd endured over Peter's uncertain university plans, the idea that my father couldn't remember the main detail was astonishing. Like someone walking down the street in 1945 and saying: 'Remind me, was it us or the Germans who won the war?'

The family crisis of my brother failing to be offered a place at either university, despite applying to several colleges, was unforgettable. My mother demanded of Ampleforth that he retook his A levels and at her insistence try several more colleges.

It worked. Fitzwilliam at Cambridge said yes. We heaved a sigh of relief. This had been our daily worry for more than a year. As far as my mother was concerned, Peter not making Oxbridge would have been the equivalent of being struck down with polio. A disease still much feared.

My father's apathy was remarkable in view of the explosive anguish that surrounded him. His desire to be popular and admired for his good humour allowed him to absent himself emotionally and thus be charming to my mother's sworn enemies, cheerful and unconcerned in the face of disagreement and jovial when the rest of us were in despair. Very little got to him.

Had I then appreciated that the look on his face which I frequently assumed to be deep pain was in fact a magnificent state of indifference, I might not have been so troubled at what I saw as the daily humiliating blows dealt to him by his wife.

My brother, on the other hand, remained unmoved by his father's plight and felt very little goodwill towards him. Peter was his mother's son. For Peter to have shown any sympathy towards her target would have been an act of gross disloyalty. His upbringing left him as confused as I was.

Cambridge increased his already solid devotion to literature and the theatre. He dreamt of remaining at university to teach. But he was torn. One bit of him was pulled towards dusty cloisters, spilling egg on his tie, drinking sherry and passing his knowledge on to another generation. Another bit of him was propelled towards aping the mother he adored and gaining her approval by attempting moneymaking schemes. Temperamentally he was ill suited for chicanery.

In any case, the openings for academic con men were thin on the ground.

Had Oxbridge been my goal, would heaven and earth have been moved likewise? I doubt it. But the issue didn't arise. I had forfeited any chance of higher learning by failing to turn up at school for half my exams, and my mother had not so much as blinked in opposition to my rampant self-will.

The conventional mothers of Blundellsands who cooked and sewed and played golf were training their daughters to carry out the same role. The goal was a good marriage. And on this count my mother's ambitions for me appeared shockingly similar to the local women she claimed to despise.

After Farnborough Hill, having just turned seventeen, I announced I fancied a finishing school in Paris. That was fine with my mother. We wrote away for brochures and after making a tour of several chose an establishment called Les Ambassadrices in Boulevard Berthier in the seventeenth arrondissement. The fees were colossal. The school list required you to have ball gowns, suits, ski wear, casual wear, church wear, cookery wear, painting wear and goodness knows what else. The new recruits were invited to meet for a get-together at the Dorchester Hotel before leaving on the train for Paris the following morning. We were an ill-assorted bunch. A collection of seventeen- and eighteen-year-olds. Some planned to 'come out' as debutants and 'do the season'. Others were exceedingly rich Jewish princesses from north London. There were one or two lumpy girls from Harrogate.

The north London contingent had wonderful wardrobes and one was engaged to be married. I, from Lancashire, was lumpy too and felt out of place since I neither spoke French as well as the debs nor had any interest in or knowledge of the Yorkshire society the Harrogate brigade prattled on about.

An elderly mother and her bad-tempered menopausal spinster daughter ran the school. The mornings were lessons. The afternoons were improvement classes of one sort or another: cordon bleu cookery, fashion shows, the Louvre for instruction on art, and more instruction on French architecture. We were only allowed to travel first class on the Métro. We had dances at Versailles with the young men from the military Académie française.

It was all wasted on me. Once I learnt where I could buy English newspapers I'd sit out the day's expedition and read until they were finished. No one minded.

I left after a term, although my mother had paid for the year. She didn't object to my decision. Or the next one, when I enrolled at the Gregg College in the centre of Liverpool. Learning how to type seemed to me to be the fastest route out of the suburbs and beyond my home city. But I still felt entirely unqualified. Also, what else was I suited for? What skills I had acquired from school were hopeless to pursue a professional career. Even teaching, which naturally, since I valued my life, I would not have dreamt of suggesting. As a starter, a secretarial job seemed the only option.

1962 A. Robinson curriculum vitae

O levels in Geography, English, Cookery and Religious Instruction.

Mentally suited for openings as a full-time Princess (and, although she doesn't know it, alternatively a future captain of industry).

What I failed to realise was that almost every day of my life I had been learning something, with my mother as the sole teacher.

'Do you remember the burglary?' I say to my brother when he comes to visit. A tall, imposing man, intelligent, thoughtful, gentle, charmingly awkward and shy, with salt and pepper hair and not far off his sixtieth birthday. The day we came home and found robbers had broken into St Michael's Road and ransacked it. Jewellery, silver, two mink coats and several of my father's suits had vanished. 'They targeted us and they were professionals,' my mother told people. (Burglars, like everyone we dealt with, had to be the best.)

Whatever the quality of the robbers, this was one case where the man from the Pru put up a good fight and came second.

With no sign of the robbers or their swag, the insurance company had issued a cheque to cover the loss – when news came that the police had recovered my father's suits. The Pru gave my mother a choice: the value of the suits, or the suits returned. My mother opted for the pay-off. Once that was agreed she asked what the insurance company intended to do with the recovered suits. The man from the Pru said they would be sold. My mother asked the price. She promptly said she would buy them. Which she did – at a fraction of their original cost.

Peter doesn't remember the transaction. I say it has stayed with me ever since. It seemed to illustrate a talent for business that couldn't be taught.

The Harvard Business School prefers what it calls the

win–win situation. The art of negotiating a deal in such a way that both sides believe they have come out with something. My mother's approach left no room for the other side to feel it had done well.

The lesson learnt? No demand is too outrageous. It can only be refused. Sometimes, to your astonishment, the other side says yes. The worst they can do is say no.

But at eighteen I was unaware that such unconsciously learnt beliefs were precious. I imagined because I had ignored university and rejected drama school (I had been offered the chance of a scholarship to the Guildhall School of Music and Drama) that I would have to tackle the job market from another angle. My ambition was (a) to be famous (b) to act (c) to write (d) never, never to run a business. Above all else, I was determined not to be like the other girls in Blundellsands, marking time before they found a husband.

My mother meanwhile was going backwards. In her crystal ball she saw a titled barrister for my husband. A large income and a big house. In her book, perhaps understandably, a good marriage was preferable to the slog and worry of being the chief breadwinner.

For a teenager the message was so mixed as to be heartless. For what she had taught by example was an independence so fierce as to scupper any chance of my being able to participate in an equal, harmonious emotional partnership.

Instead of compromise, of giving way, of turning the other cheek, all handy starting points for married life, indelibly printed on my subconscious were the very opposite values.

'Be wary' was another of my mother's mottoes. At all times she carried with her and practised a natural suspicion. Be it of men, traders, relatives or cleaning ladies. So for me to have the ability or willingness to conduct a relationship based on love and mutual dependence would have required a miracle.

Yet repeated over and over again was her expectation that a man should keep you. You shouldn't, you mustn't work and slave like she had had to do. With all her heart she wanted me to have an easier time.

So another irony: as Germaine Greer in Britain and Gloria Steinem, Marilyn French, Betty Friedan and the rest in the States were waking up to the shocking realisation that inequality existed, my mother had gone into reverse.

I fear a younger generation think that those of us who came of age in the early sixties often exaggerate the plight of women at the start of what was to become the most revolutionary of decades.

But when I turned eighteen in 1962 we were still in a world where a child born out of wedlock was a bastard. 'She's illegitimate', it was whispered of girls at my school and before I knew what it meant I knew it wasn't nice.

A young woman who found herself pregnant was on the horns of a devastating dilemma. Since an abortion was virtually unobtainable except for the rich and knowledgeable, there were few options. In most cases parents thought it perfectly acceptable to take over the decision-making. A confused mother would be persuaded to part with a baby a few days old and let nothing more be said. (Difficult to imagine at the dawn of a new century, when there is talk of two men being able to create their own child.)

Those who hung on to their babies were referred to as unmarried mothers. In middle-class Britain this was a shame a daughter was unlikely to recover from. She would be looked upon with pity. She could not expect any man to want her now.

That so many women became pregnant was hardly surprising: the pill was intended for married women. That left the unreliable, haphazard, alternative ways of practising birth control. Sex, sex, sex! You thought about it. You talked with awe about the odd girl at school who claimed to have had it. But for the vast majority of us the decade began with it being regarded as out of touch for single girls – you waited until you married.

On the other hand, if you were a man you were encouraged and admired for grabbing it at every opportunity.

I can hardly think of a girlfriend at this time who wasn't subjected to a rape or an attempted rape. The usual method of dealing with it was to say not a word. Rape was something that happened if you were stupid enough to allow the opportunity to arise. Being pawed, being leered at, the size of your breasts being remarked upon, your bum being patted was, well, normal.

My friend Olivia, who had just graduated from the LSE in the mid-sixties and was due to be married, innocently went to her doctor to ask for some birth-control advice. The doctor examined her and declared her vagina was altogether too tiny. He advised her to go to John Bell and Croyden – the large chemist in Wigmore Street off Harley Street – and invest in a vibrator. She was, he ordered, to bring it back to the surgery and he would instruct her. The vibrator was bought and the instruction had begun before it dawned on Olivia that the doctor was actually a dirty old man.

1969. Geraldine, in her first job after university, was in the local BBC newsroom in Newcastle. One senior male boss was notorious for sticking his hands up and along where they were not wanted. Those on the receiving end suffered in silence. One morning, the boss crept up behind Geraldine and grabbed her breasts and juggled them in his hands. Geraldine, startled and carrying a scalding cup of black coffee, threw it in panic at the offending dirty paws. A shriek followed as the hot liquid found its target. Geraldine rushed out of the building in fear. She went back the next day fully expecting to be fired. But as she made her way through the newsroom, women came up timidly to congratulate her. The male boss meanwhile had put in an official complaint. His hands, he told the personnel department, had been scarred, possibly for life.

No wonder they marched!

It was the same prevailing wind that meant a woman couldn't hire a television set without a man's signature. It mattered not that she might be on the first ladder of a career and the man whose signature she got was some no-hoper poet without a pot to piss in.

As late as 1971 I recall my bank manager apologetically telling me that as I was a woman he had to read the conditions to me out loud before he could grant me a bridging loan. Women in the sixties assumed their pay would be less than men's. In the same way, a pregnant woman did not expect to be treated well at work. Maternity leave was unheard of in newspaper offices when I was pregnant in 1970.

At seven months pregnant, and a news reporter on the *Sunday Times*, my news editor sent me to cover the crowds at the Wembley Cup Final. 'What happens if I faint?' I asked him. 'File your copy before you do,' he ordered.

For my part, the inequality passed me by. Save a mild irritation that for women to wear trousers in offices was out of the question. I assumed that the reason I was treated with derision and sneered at was because I was inexperienced and as soon as I earned my spurs I could move up the ladder. Not for one single second, even despite the most glaring examples, did I imagine that being a woman was a disadvantage.

As George Orwell put it, we didn't know how bad it was until they told us.

As a guide to the typical attitude of men towards women in the early sixties we need look no further than the redoubtable Commander. He was, as his title suggests, a former naval officer: tall, broad and elegant with silver hair, a signet ring, a Bentley and a suspect way of pronouncing his As that suggested a more humble start in life.

I was summoned to be interviewed by him after answering an advertisement in *The Times*. The paper's front page was then uncluttered by news. The ad had its own spacious box and was for a secretary to the chairman of a company with offices in Mayfair. Languages were an advantage. Superb secretarial skills were taken for granted. There was use of a car. Foreign travel and dealing with international clients were other carrots dangled. What I lacked in skills I made up with *folie de grandeur*. I wanted to be famous. That meant London, and the idea of a job with a car and in Mayfair looked like a step in the geographical direction of my dreams. I was nineteen. My languages amounted to slightly above-average French. There were two O levels – English and geography. (I discounted my passes in cookery and religious instruction, since I would have scoffed at anyone who thought these were proper qualifications for anything.) My degree of competence in shorthand and typing was what you might expect from someone who had dispensed with attending classes as soon as she had a rudimentary grasp of both; that, plus a smattering of temping jobs in Liverpool over the previous year.

The office was pleasingly in Upper Brook Street, off Park Lane, on the top two floors of a Georgian house, the rest of which was used as a corporate headquarters by Guinness. The address was comfortingly near to where my mother had ordered all her made-to-measure, cost-a-fortune fitted bedroom furniture after a visit to the Ideal Home Exhibition a few years earlier. The furniture showroom in Davies Street was called Chippendale, and since she knew nothing of the original Chippendale she saw no irony in mentioning frequently around Blundellsands that 'Chippendale's do all our furniture'.

Mayfair for me also meant nightingales singing in Berkeley Square, Anna Neagle, ball gowns and the home of high society as depicted in the films we had been taken to see. The company specialised in electronics and had bought up a number of disparate small factories scattered around the south of England that variously made ultrasound and hi-fi equipment, microphones, parts for depth charges, etc.

The Commander took about thirty seconds to eye me up and suggest that I was not old enough or experienced enough for the advertised job. But, as my mother would observe admiringly later, he used his head to save his legs and one ad to catch several applicants, and invited me to consider a lesser secretarial post, seeing to the needs of the sales director and the sales manager.

I agreed to think about it. The Commander, standing in his grand office filled with highly polished antique furniture, then asked where I was heading. I told him I was catching a train at Euston to Tring to join my mother at her health farm, Champneys. Like a shot he offered to drive me there in his silver Bentley. Just like that. He appeared not to have to cancel meetings or make other arrangements. I was bowled over.

My mother's visits to Tring were as many as four times a year. They were her muddled way of coping with her drinking. The health farm at least called a halt to a bender if she was on one. It also gave her breathing space and a change of scene. At Champneys she formed friendships with men (platonic, no sex, naturally) that expressed her longing for a strong, capable, successful partner. One was a charming Scottish rough diamond called Willie Logan, who had founded Logan Air and was sadly killed years later in one of his own aircraft. Another was a famed financier, Julian Hodge. They clearly enjoyed her company as much as she did theirs.

She struggled with her booze problem in secret. She never shared her shame but she was unabashed in boasting of how attractive men like Logan and Hodge found her. My father never so much as raised an eyebrow. His cosy world was rarely threatened. Was he the only well-adjusted member of the family? The voice of sanity amid the madness? My brother, with a degree of contempt, insists he was. But my mother's natural liking for 'strong males' explained why the sight of the impressive Commander in his silver Bentley neither appalled nor worried her.

Of course, I didn't tell her in detail about the journey. As I sat beside the Commander, he stroked my knee on and off for a couple of hours. I was embarrassed, flattered, bemused. Nothing else happened. It must have been pleasure enough, for, as far as

I knew, he turned tail and went back to London once he had waved me off.

Was I naive, stupid, inexperienced? All three, I suppose. It sounds like a limp excuse several decades on, but the Commander had no reason to believe he was behaving unacceptably. Nobody had told him not to paw young girls. It would take a president of the United States, nearly half a century later, unwittingly to reveal the problems of the 'sex addict' and diminish the status of the overactive Lothario to one of a man to be pitied rather than admired.

The Commander's approach can't have bothered me unduly. I accepted the job and moved to London. Well, sort of. The Commander arranged for me to share a flat with the woman he had appointed to the main secretarial post advertised. The flat was in Kew. Not quite Chelsea. Barbara Harrison was at least five years older than me. Her sister, a former air hostess, shared too. We had nothing in common. It hardly mattered. Barbara lasted in the job less than six months. She was angered and outraged by the Commander's behaviour. (He also had a very short fuse.)

I remained in Upper Brook Street for the best part of a year and sat in for Barbara's replacement during her lunch hour. Almost as soon as the Commander knew the change of shift had taken place he would buzz for me to come in to take dictation. I would sit there with a silly grin on my face as a hand went towards my bra or on to my knee, with the aim of moving up my skirt. If the Commander sensed he was about to be rebuffed – I would usually shift position out of range – the dictation would restart in earnest. He could turn in seconds from lecher to angry tyrant. After a while, it emerged that everyone put up with this treatment. I suspected another secretary, who was French, had a deal of her own with him. She would shrug her shoulders and grin whenever I raised his behaviour. Who knows what went on?

Apparently one of the Commander's earlier secretaries, a jolly Home Counties woman, who had married late, used to emerge from his office squealing with laughter, saying, 'Oh, isn't he a case.'

'Were you cross, outraged, terrified?' Emma, my daughter, asks now. No. My secretarial skills were so limited that my greatest fear was not coping with the work. The Commander's straying hands were a side issue. They didn't keep me awake at night. Also the office had in it several charming males, including two young sales managers who were only ever polite and well mannered to the women. And there was a delightful middle-aged adviser who was lovely to me. He never complained about my smudgy typing, my spelling errors or my non-existent shorthand. He would scrawl his letters in ink himself rather than bother me. He always called me Miss Robinson and practised old-world courtesy that meant he treated me as an equal. The two young sales managers similarly made very little fuss about my lack of office experience.

1963 made news. Some of the *London Evening Standard* front pages remain as vividly in my mind now as the day I first saw them.

The BBC withdrew its ban on the mention of sex, religion, politics and royalty in comedy shows. Too late for the satirists who had created the wonderful *That Was The Week That Was* we had loved in cosy Crosby. It, and they, had been banished.

By the end of the year the President of the United States had been shot dead. Kim Philby, an MI6 officer, had turned up in Moscow as a Soviet spy. Most exotic of all, Britain's Minister for War, John Profumo, resigned after sleeping with a call girl who had also slept with a Russian naval attaché. The Profumo scandal had it all. A government minister married to a famous actress, Valerie Hobson. Christine Keeler, a call girl, who was a bit of an Eliza Doolittle, in that she acquired some of the manners and elegance of a society girl; and a go-between and 'friend to the stars', an osteopath called Stephen Ward. Ward achieved the sympathy vote. He was charged with living off immoral earnings. On the final day of his trial, he was found unconscious, having taken an overdose, in a friend's flat in Chelsea. He never regained consciousness. At his trial the public gallery was overflowing with those eager for details of two-way mirrors and black magic rituals. Who says the national disease of double standards, which allows tabloid newspapers to thrive, is a new one?

While I was still struggling to be a secretary Barbara Harrison, my flatmate but no longer my workmate, invited me to see a live transmission of the BBC *Tonight* programme. She had been a PA at the BBC on the show that starred Derek Hart, Cliff Michelmore, Fyfe Robertson and, briefly, a wonderful Canadian called Jacqueline Mackenzie. These people were my mother's heroes. She adored *Tonight*. She heard about the invitation and announced: 'Your father and I will be in London that week and would like to join you.' We trooped along, quietly standing in the studio as the programme went out live.

That evening out ensured that any glamour attached to working in a Mayfair office was over. Several of my friends and my flatmates were employed by a temping agency off Berkeley Square. I begged a nice woman there to find me a job in television. Months later she rang with the offer of 'secretary to an editor of outside broadcasts'. I couldn't have been more eager to make the appointment.

6

Fantastically Delicious

Associated-Rediffusion, a fledgling commercial television company, was housed in a grey office block in Kingsway opposite BBC Bush House, a few yards from the Law Courts and at the top of Fleet Street. It too was run by ranks of former commanders or former captains still using their titles, and female personnel officers in dirndl skirts. Yet somewhere beneath this Ministry of Defence-type atmosphere, run by small men with grand wars behind them, a string of innovative programmes was emerging.

The personnel officer warned me that my prospective boss had lost four secretaries in as many months. I couldn't see that being a problem. No one was more qualified to work for a despot.

Frank Keating was summoned and given the personnel officer's room to assess me. He had black hair. A wonderful smile. A gap in his teeth. He was wearing a black corduroy suit. A red V-neck sweater. He smoked. Sticking out of his pocket was a newspaper. He looked at my carefully exaggerated CV. He picked on the 'finishing school in Paris', finding it incredibly funny, all the more since I'd added 'cordon bleu cookery course' to the description. 'Cordon bleu, cordon bleu,' he kept saying. I blushed, rightly so. He told me that several earlier applicants had found him difficult and that the personnel officer was getting a bit short of patience. I accepted the job.

My first morning working in television I sat for what seemed like hours in an empty office. At eleven Keating telephoned to say he had been 'held up' but was on his way. I quickly learnt that this was his habit. He rang when he woke up, which was never early. When he eventually left his flat he would buy the newspapers, travel to work on the Tube, make a brief appearance, then go and have his breakfast at the Kardomah café on the corner of Kingsway. He was always surrounded by newspapers.

Frank had lots of chums. He took more phone calls from them than he ever did from anybody connected with outside broadcasting. I had never before met anyone so exciting. He ignored every petty rule of office life. He found the departments run by ex-commanders and ex-captains hilarious. He would roar with laughter as he replaced the receiver after taking an instruction from one of them. Cleverly, he would somehow ingratiate himself with his stern, inflexible bosses while at the same time talking the sort of language they found utterly incomprehensible. Banter would be exchanged amid winks and eyebrow-raising to me across the desk. Having successfully tied them in knots, he would finalise the deal: 'We'll make sure it's shipshape and all guns blazing,' he would end reassuringly.

The Director of Programmes at Rediffusion was Commander Robert Everett, a small man who puffed on a pipe and still spoke as if he was in charge of a ship. Commander Everett became so convinced by his outside broadcast editor's awareness of all things maritime that one day, unexpectedly, he presented Keating with a manuscript of a proposed book of great naval battles – a tour de force by the Commander himself. With much ceremony he invited Keating to contribute a thought or two for the preface.

No sooner had the request been made than Keating, without

hesitation, pulled out his fountain pen and wrote several lines, adding with a flourish, 'Nelson, 1798'.

Only years later did I learn the words credited to Nelson were as phoney as Keating's knowledge of the sea.

The discovery of a boss who found authority in any form absurd and worthy of ridicule was refreshing. Frank's wickedness was wholly in keeping with my mother's approach to those who thought they were better and more important.

His newly created job was to think up afternoon programmes to be covered by the outside broadcast unit that until then had confined itself to sports events and major state occasions. He serviced three directors, all of whom were ex-cameramen. And they, like the commanders and captains, rarely had a clue what he was on about.

I was astonished by Keating's ability to contact major stars he'd never met and persuade them to come on a programme we were putting together. One day he called Peter Sellers and the next we knew Sellers was joining us. Frank would say to the 'star': 'Darling, it's a tiny programme, no money but it will be enormous fun!' Agents would melt. When the star arrived, Frank treated him or her with a combination of servility and equality as if he and the star were both a cut above what was happening, but were decent and nice enough to go along with it all.

Frank never left me behind in the office but would take me on whatever job we were doing. I was his willing slave. The son of devout Catholics and Labour Party supporters, members of the post-war Catholic Land Movement, Frank had been brought up in Gloucestershire, educated at Douai, a minor Catholic public school, and had worked in local newspapers. His devotion to cricket and the theatre was matched by his interest in politics. I told him when we met that I voted Conservative. 'Why?' he asked, as if someone had just announced they preferred cod to caviar.

His circle of friends was huge. He gathered people. He was a natural, easygoing host who thought nothing of inviting newly acquired chums to have supper. Or he would throw a party. He saw no class divisions. Either up or down. I marvelled at the way he moved around with a social ease I'd never seen in Crosby. After one memorable outside broadcast at Fulham or Chelsea football ground I found myself 'hosting' – at the flat I briefly shared with some girlfriends in Queen's Gate, South Kensington – a dinner for Jimmy Greaves and Johnny Haynes, both former England internationals, and Ben Parkin, the then Labour MP for Paddington, whom Frank had helped at election time. It was quite unlike the close-knit circles of middle-class Blundellsands that my mother abhorred but that she had failed to replace with anything more unconventional.

Frank seemed able to pick up women as well without the slightest difficulty. There was always one in residence at his flat. Women adored him. I adored him. Even though he would mock me constantly. After a year he urged me to apply for a better job as a researcher on a children's programme called *Five O'Clock Club*. I got it. Within weeks, no longer working for him, our relationship changed. He and I became girlfriend and boyfriend. I describe it so quaintly because quaint it was.

My mother lost her virginity on her honeymoon at the age of twenty-seven. I was her Catholic daughter with an attitude to sex which, roughly summed up, meant it was wrong before marriage, not something you talked about and if you enjoyed it . . . well, that didn't seem right.

I duly took Frank home to meet my mother. He arrived in Blundellsands with his pyjamas in a brown carrier bag. On the Sunday morning, he insisted on me driving him to the village shop. As usual, he bought all the papers and spread them out in front of the fire. My mother wasn't quite sure. But he charmed her.

Within weeks we had become engaged. I refused to acknowledge it until the announcement appeared in the *Telegraph* and *The Times*. He thought that as preposterous and inappropriate as I would now. 'Why are we being controlled by some sub-editor on a national paper?' he kept asking. He was talking a foreign language. I was a middle-class provincial girl who wanted a proper engagement, a wedding list, a three-piece suite, a home and the chance to give dinner parties. The more plans I drew up, the more, unknown to me, he began to take small but firm steps in the opposite direction.

Ring on my finger, and unaware of the impending doom, I finally lost my virginity.

Sex. It was fantastically delicious! It happened in Frank's flat above a shop in the Fulham Road one night after we had been out to dinner. My virginal state was in no doubt because, as is the tradition, I bled. He was very tender about it. I imagine we made love several times more in the coming weeks. Each time we did, I would leave early the next morning and confess my sins at Brompton Oratory. It was there that I always went to Mass on a Sunday. Like almost everything else connected with our relationship and wedding plans, Frank looked upon my church-going, my sense of guilt over sex, with amusement and puzzlement.

No matter. We fixed a date for the wedding. June 1966. The invitations were printed. We looked for a better flat to rent. We had no money. Frank was a spender. He ate out, and would pick up any tab. He had no furniture. He loved his books. I wanted all that my mother had taught me to expect. But I had chosen the wrong man. I didn't realise it until it was too late. At first, Frank registered his unease by making his objections to my wishes more obvious. A row would ensue. One day, before posting the invitations, I suggested we put off the wedding. I didn't expect my offer to be accepted. Alas, my fiancé clutched at the idea with enthusiasm. I knew the game was up. A yellowing newspaper cutting tells the tale. The *Liverpool Daily Post* ran a picture of us but with the news that our wedding had been postponed because of Frank's commitment to the 1966 World Cup.

The invitations, embossed and expensive, were never posted.

The wedding plans were abandoned. The relationship staggered on. It got bleaker by the day.

I tried to make matters better by doing things to please my man. I bought him a book on cricket by Robertson Glasgow that he tells me thirty-five years on he still treasures. But playing the subservient obedient slave was not my forte. So, while I also bought him a cricket bat, within a week, in a fit of temper, I hurled it out of the flat window. It landed in the Fulham Road. A passing cabby stopped, picked it up and drove on.

One weekend, after I had shouted the odds and left in a temper, I returned late at night to find Frank with another woman. I remember driving away, devastated by the unfairness of life. I had experienced a new world, one that involved working in television. I had found the man I wanted to spend the rest of my life married to. Someone who loved books, politics, and made me laugh and had introduced me to sex. But now, as quickly as this had come my way, it was about to vanish. Socially, emotionally and to a large extent professionally – for Frank was my mentor – I was convinced I was washed up. Finished!

Without us noticing, the decade was moving from the constriction of the conventional fifties to the sixties. At *Five O'Clock Club*, pop stars turning up were two a penny. Lulu and Gerry and the Pacemakers would line up alongside Cleo Laine and Johnny Dankworth. The Beatles had arrived. So had the Kinks, the Animals, the Rolling Stones.

Five O'Clock Club had a middle-aged presenter called Muriel Young (Auntie Mu) and a couple of puppets called Olly and Fred who were voiced and worked by Wally Whyton and Ivan Owen – the genius behind Basil Brush. The programme consisted of a music spot, a bit of banter, Olly and Fred and instructions from Auntie Mu on how – say – to make a house out of a packet of cornflakes. I was one of two researchers required on programme days to sit behind a desk on set and say not a word. Who cared? I was appearing on the telly. It was an eye-opener in the ways of show business. An elderly bandleader called Ambrose frequently used to arrive with a new female star. One lunchtime I caught him, in a state of undress, in a dressing room allotted to one of his protégées, and could barely wait to phone my mother so she and I could marvel at the horror of it all.

On Tuesdays we journeyed to the Wembley studios, the very same that now record *Ready, Steady, Cook* and *Have I Got News for You*. One programme went out live. The second was recorded for Thursday. They were in black and white. Colour television was still a few years off. But for me, finally, the roar of the grease-paint, the smell of the crowd was within my grasp.

Then not long after Frank and I parted Rediffusion failed to renew my contract. New brooms replaced old. There was no longer to be a club. Auntie Mu staggered on for a while, but I was out on my ear. Couldn't I move on to current affairs? I begged the head of the department. Go away and get some Fleet Street experience first, he said kindly.

I had adored the magical world of journalism that Frank had introduced me to. The opportunity to meet politicians and artists and sportsmen and make them your friends, who came to your home for dinner. Or joined you for supper.

Here was a career that with luck meant I could become someone but with the added bonus of being famous for being intelligent and able to write.

But how? There was a small problem.

I had no real qualifications or experience to enter print journalism and television did not want me back until I had.

7

'We're sending the bird down'

I'd spotted the advert for North London News Agency in a long since defunct magazine, *World's Press News*. 'A prestigious London-based news agency' was seeking reporters with experience. Must own car. I qualified only on the last bit. My mother had provided me with a brand-new British racing green soft-top MG. 'Pet, here is £800 to buy a car, love Mummy' was one of the few letters she ever wrote to me. I also had a dog. Brandy was a Labrador/retriever, who disappointingly never grew the long furry coat I had expected. Even more distressing, she died of liver disease within a year. But then and almost always since, I've never been without a pet, feeling, quite rightly, that they at least never abandon you.

Car and dog and I turned up for the interview. It was held in a former butcher's shop at the Holloway end of the Hornsey Road in north London. There was pegboard in the window. Behind the dilapidated front were three or four metal desks, half a dozen phones and some ancient typewriters. Out back there was a lavatory and a smaller office with a kettle in the corner. I wore a Courrèges-style suit, a black dress with a green horizontal top to it and a matching jacket. Green boots in the same material, made for me by Annello and Davide the theatrical shoemakers, completed the look.

The owner of the agency, John Rodgers, sifted through a tray, gave me three cuttings and asked me to 'follow up' the stories and return the finished articles to him within the week. Crikey! I rang Frank, by then back at the *Guardian* as a sub. He entered into the spirit. I sailed off to chat to people living in slum conditions in Bethnal Green and Limehouse in the East End of London. It was my first experience of discovering that the more desperate the dwelling, the bigger the television set in the corner is likely to be.

Frank helped me to compose the stories with his usual enthusiasm. When Rodgers inspected the completed work he declared my writing to be a bit 'twee' but hired me anyway. It turned out to be a reasonable deal all round. True, I had never written a story in my life. I didn't know how to. But my mother had trained me to be unafraid, so I didn't balk at the awful jobs they sent me on. I was told each story, when written up, had to be 'snappy' and entertaining in the first sentence. Otherwise no one read the second one. It was my earliest lesson in appealing to a mass audience. Although, to be fair to St John's Market, I had already got used to meeting the audience to whom I must appeal.

The agency was the bargain basement of journalism, and then as now news agencies were used to carry out unpleasant tasks newspapers found time-consuming and distasteful. The worst, by far, was being dispatched to a home where a child had tragically died. The *Daily Mail*, the *Daily Mirror*, or whoever, 'ordered' a picture of the recently dead loved one. The order bit was important. It meant you got paid for going anyway, even if you came away empty-handed.

I hated the idea of disturbing a home rocked by devastating news. But I learnt if you visit a family soon enough after the news you rarely offend and if you ask for a photograph they are generally delighted to think that a child/loved one's death is going to be properly acknowledged.

We were a motley bunch behind the pegboard in the Hornsey

Road. A small, chirpy little man called Peter Game, the news editor, was a genius at interviewing people on the phone and turning the most mundane and innocuous tale into a money-earning exclusive. Peter Atkinson, an elegant, serious, bespectacled young man, almost always in a pinstripe suit, was the only one like myself who had gone to public school. His mother was a legendary woman's editor and he would later become Tory MP for Hexham. If it interests his constituents, he was as up to the tricks of the trade as the rest of us.

Almost every evening a young lad would appear. He worked on the local *Islington Gazette*, but did shifts through the night with the agency. He had a Triumph Herald, was rather well turned out and everyone loved him. He seemed strangely mature for nineteen. His name was John Penrose.

From the time I had innocently gone out with boys in Blundellsands, and throughout the early and mid-sixties, I rarely drank. My mother saw no contradiction in warning us of the perils of drink, while neither she nor any other member of the family had the nerve to bring up her own track record. When I arrived in London, alcohol remained unimportant. Even having reached the outer limits of Fleet Street at the agency, where we would frequently repair over the road to the Tollington Arms, my tipple was pineapple juice. A stupid choice for someone per-manently worried about gaining pounds and inches. But there it was. None of the hard drinking going on around me seemed to matter, and hard drinkers I was certainly among. The young lad from the *Gazette*, John Penrose, liked copious gin and tonics and would often spend a week's wages, reluctantly provided in advance by Rodgers, in a matter of hours. The others drank whisky or beer. The Tollington was a rough sort of place, with old biddies supping in the corner and only the barest of carpets.

Penrose turned out to be a gregarious sort and often after work he would coax me to join him for a few on the way home. I stuck to my pineapple juice. He to his double gins. We were firm enough friends for me to lend him my MG when I went home for the weekend. But on the understanding that he didn't drive it at night and he washed it inside and out. My reservations were reasonable, given his social life. It was hardly surprising that around this time he was done for drunken driving. He was caught crawling down King Street, Hammersmith, at four in the morning, doing five miles an hour in his Triumph Herald convertible with the top down. If the police hadn't clocked the speed of the car they could hardly have failed to notice his front-seat passenger was wearing a lampshade on his head. The ban was for a year. A setback for Penrose's journalistic career (mobility was important), but otherwise the sentence held no particular shame. Tales of drivers returning home three sheets to the wind were common. The art of getting away with it was recognised as an admirable act of cunning and style. Political correctness, keeping fit, not smoking and despising anyone 'out of control' was decades away. For now drinking too much or having a hangover could easily have been mistaken for something that required brains and talent, so familiar was it to hear men boast about both.

Along with the MG and Brandy, I had a rented flat by Sloane Square, a posh accent (according to the lads), a large pair of thighs, flaming red hair and a fearlessness that both amused and delighted them. North London News Agency was the equivalent of a cruel, in-at-the-deep-end run at a northern working men's club for a young comedian. Rougher, and more intense and risk-prone than drama school. Or, in my case, a local newspaper. We took no prisoners. If we didn't get there first we didn't get paid. I once covered a coroner's court in Finchley where one of our team dismantled the handsets in the telephone boxes outside to prevent the opposition from making contact with their offices. After our 'colleagues' had driven off to search for a working phone, we reassembled the equipment and filed the story. We lived by our wits.

My mother couldn't get enough of the gossip I would pass on from my new workplace. It thoroughly appealed to her. She adored the idea of a small, unconventional set-up run on a shoe-string, where being 'up at six and out at five' was as important as in her own trade. She longed to meet John Rodgers and Peter Game and a strange mysterious man called Elgar, who would turn up in the office to monitor the police radio and let us know if it looked as though a story was taking place. Elgar could impersonate officialdom with a talent that deserved a wider audience. One night he heard the police racing to north London where pieces of body had been found scattered on a road. The police were setting up roadblocks. But there was no mention of which road. Elgar was only stumped for a moment. He knew which borough the drama was unfolding in. He put a call in to the local police station. 'Kilburn Council, Highways Department here, gov'nor. Where do you want these barriers?' he demanded. The address was his. We raced over and got exclusive pictures. Sadly, the body parts were not of a dismembered murder victim but had been dumped by some medical students as a jape.

For my mother, whose belief that there was always more than one way to skin a rabbit still held true, the tale was to be enjoyed. I could repeat it and similar tales as often as I liked. 'Tell me again about the night . . .' she would start, as I sat on her bed on a weekend home.

While the police radio was a source of profitable stories, monitoring communications held risks. Peter Game and a photographer were one day arrested after arriving to cover a bank robbery *before* it had taken place. (The agency had overheard the police arranging a stakeout in anticipation of a robbery.)

Hampstead Magistrates' Court at this time too was becoming the fashionable venue for convictions for possessing cannabis. Ideal for us if the person in the dock was famous. We'd have the court list first and be able to sell the story to the newspapers. At worst, we would 'tip' the newspapers and they would send their own reporters and we would be paid for our information. Police officers, ambulance drivers, fire officers, fire assessors, all were on the agency payroll. None of this seemed alien to a trader's daughter. In fact it made perfect sense.

Rodgers' rules, which to the rest of the North London News Agency team appeared draconian and Scrooge-like, were made with an eye on economy that was much the same as my mother had taught me to respect and accept as normal. We were ordered always to transfer the charge of a call by saying the phone box was broken. This way the charge to Rodgers was half of what it would otherwise have been. We typed our stories on old calendars or on notepaper headed 'The People'. (The newspaper Rodgers worked for on Saturdays.) Rodgers' auntie used to come and clean once a week. If she couldn't make it we'd often find Rodgers vacuuming himself. 'Have you written your story?' the news editor would scream at me. 'I can't,' I'd yell back, 'someone else is using the pencil.' (a line unashamedly stolen from Dorothy Parker).

I learnt my trade. I would be sent to 'sell' a recently acquired photo to the picture editors on the national newspapers. It was thought that my youth, mini-skirt and accent might clinch an otherwise uncertain deal. 'We're sending the bird down,' the news editor would say. Off I would go, blissfully unaware of sexism or sisterhood. Happy to use my body for commercial purposes. It held no shame.

Indeed, in the spring of 1967 London was moving towards full swing. I couldn't have been nearer the epicentre of fashion and sexual freedom. I came from the same city as the by then mega-famous Beatles. I had rubbed shoulders with several pop stars on *Five O'Clock Club*. I saw more at Hampstead Magistrates' Court. I had a sports car and a modest private income. Yet I did not regard myself as part of the 'happening scene'. Instead I felt detached, repressed, old-fashioned and out of place. I vividly recall walking down the King's Road on a balmy summer's day that year, feeling completely alien and apart from the exotic sights I passed.

I thought, at the time, it was because I wasn't thin. At least not thin in the way Twiggy, Britain's first 'supermodel', then at her peak, was thin. I was probably a generous size twelve. Too big for most of the Biba dresses I would try on on a Saturday.

I wasn't the only one to feel she was looking in on another world. The old and the new were grappling with each other in most people's minds. Rodgers at the time had a deal with a couple of German magazines and for one of them he was commissioned to get an interview with Marianne Faithfull, a young middle-class girl, daughter of an aristocratic European mother. She'd had a number one hit although she was hardly an accomplished singer. She came out of the Rolling Stones' stable, which was enough. I interviewed her one morning at the Mayfair Hotel. Days later she admitted she was pregnant. She was single. It was considered quite shocking. She quickly married and quietened public disapproval. Even at the height of the age of promiscuity and free love, pregnancy outside of marriage somehow remained a no-no.

No one seemed to question the contradiction. Least of all me. I was still a Catholic Crosby girl at heart. And when one day I was put to the test, I treated the episode exactly as a nice Crosby girl could be relied on to do. I hardly knew Ned and couldn't imagine how he had got my phone number. He was an American who had lived above a gang of us when we briefly shared the furnished flat in Queen's Gate. An area then awash with girls like me, who wore Hermès scarves tied under their chins and could be seen with their battered boarding-school weekend cases on a Friday night, heading home to Mummy and Daddy. Ned was a voice coach on an American movie being made in Britain. In the call he fixed a date with me. I imagined we were going out to dinner and dressed accordingly. He sailed into my flat in Sloane Square and within seconds he had dropped his trousers and asked me to 'pull him off'.

I had no idea what was happening. I held on to his anatomy like I would an old piece of piping. He came, hauled up his trousers and announced he had another appointment. After he left I wasn't entirely sure I hadn't imagined it all. A few years later I discovered he'd pulled much the same trick on the other girls in the flat whose phone numbers he'd managed to get hold of.

It never occurred to any of us to make a fuss. Mistaking the intentions of the Neds of this world was our own stupid fault.

The visits to the newspaper offices only deepened my resolve to get a job in Fleet Street. I heard that casual shifts were available for young reporters and I applied to the *Daily Mail*. I was due to be interviewed by the news editor and his deputy. But when I arrived they were nowhere to be seen. Someone else fobbed me off, insultingly telling me to get some provincial experience.

You have to work at being lucky, my mother would say. She never supposed that unexpected good fortune could be relied upon. But there is such a thing as serendipity. There is a god!

Shortly after the ill-fated interview, I met a *Daily Mail* reporter. He asked me out. He was the paper's education correspondent. He took me to join his newspaper chums in a nightclub called the Cromwellian in South Kensington. And lo! There was the very man I should have met the week before, Charles Wilson, deputy news editor of the *Daily Mail*.

He reminded me that we had been introduced by Keating the year before at Lingfield Races. Charlie and Keating and a young Czechoslovakian-born would-be playwright, Tom Stoppard, had been reporters in the West Country on the *Bristol Evening World* in the late fifties.

Charlie and Stoppard shared a flat, but eventually Stoppard returned to London to try his luck at becoming a full-time writer. But not before he attempted to get a job as a political reporter on the *Evening Standard*. The interview was his last attempt to make a life in newspapers. 'You're interested in politics,' Charles Wintour, the editor, had apparently said to the man destined to be world famous, 'so, perhaps you could tell me, who's the Home Secretary?' There was a silence before Tom retorted with some feeling: 'I said I was interested in politics, not *obsessed* by them.'

In the dim light of the Cromwellian was a wiry Scot of thirty-two, with blond curly hair, who gazed into my eyes in a way I found very flattering. Also, here was the man who represented a career opportunity. I had yet to be told how unacceptable it was to flirt with a male who had the power to give you a job. I wasted no time. He agreed to get in touch if there were any casual shifts available. Yippee!

On my first casual shift for the *Daily Mail*, courtesy of Mr Wilson, the newsroom was a sea of male faces. Almost all in shirtsleeves. I didn't have much time to take it in. Within minutes of arriving, I was sent with a photographer to cover a job at the Kensington Gardens Hotel. 'I hope you don't have to go for a pee all the time like Olga Franklin,' he said as we made our way there. Ms Franklin was a long-serving features writer, near retirement, who wore her hair in a bun and clearly had a bladder problem I can only now wholly sympathise with.

The story was about the stay at the hotel by a pop group called the Monkees. There wasn't the remotest chance of getting through the paid bodyguards who stood outside their suites. 'Behind every strong man there stands a Monkee,' I wrote. Since we could not photograph the group, only their security, it didn't make the paper.

The next try-out the *Daily Mail* gave me on August Bank Holiday weekend 1967 was more successful. Brian Epstein, the manager of the Beatles, was found dead at his home in Chapel Street, Belgravia. The circumstances were mysterious. He was rumoured to be a depressive, and he was a known homosexual. His friends thought he might have accidentally overdosed. The press was convinced he had taken his own life. The Beatles were reported to be shocked, although they had been known to be having trouble with their mercurial boss.

I left my Sloane Square flat in my trusty MG and drove the

less than half a mile to Chapel Street. There was a familiar pack of photographers and reporters loitering on the pavement opposite the house. It was quiet all morning except for the odd comings or goings of people who would say nothing.

Around midday a taxi drew up and I recognised Rex Makin, a well-known Liverpool solicitor. He was let into the house. Lunchtime arrived and the thirst and appetites of the pack overtook their enthusiasm. They departed to the pub, leaving me behind, comfortable with the idea that the youngest among them, and a 'girl', would obediently come and get help if something happened. Or dutifully record all in her notebook and share it around later. Working with the pack was, and remains, a tradition of newspaper reporters. It gives individuals the reassurance of a peaceful night's sleep when away from home on a job, secure in the knowledge that if something happens in their absence they will get to hear about it from a colleague. But it almost guarantees no exclusives. The loner takes high risks in being kept out of the loop, but has the satisfaction of being able to hang on to the best for themselves when they get it. What the pack didn't know was that by nature I was a loner. I had been brought up by a loner, reared in journalism in the puppy farm of loners.

A little later Rex Makin emerged and looked apprehensively for a taxi. There weren't any. It was a bank holiday in the middle of Belgravia. 'I've got to get to Euston station,' he said. 'Jump into my car and I'll take you,' I offered. He did.

On the way he told me that Clive Epstein, Brian's brother and still running the family furniture business, would be the likely successor to run Apple (Epstein's company that looked after the Beatles). Also that Brian Epstein had choked on his own vomit. I had a scoop. An exclusive.

Clive never did take over Apple. But for the next day's paper I had the story. I filed a breathless, probably grammar-free account over the telephone.

I didn't share my knowledge when the rest of the pack came back from the pub. I wasn't even there.

The following morning I rushed out to buy the newspapers. I had no byline on the front-page story. But it was mine and it was good enough for the *Daily Mail* to start taking me seriously. I had arrived.

8

The Office Catch

In the late summer of 1967, in the few short weeks between my triumphant day on the Brian Epstein story and my being officially hired by the *Daily Mail*, Charlie Wilson asked me on a trip to France. It was a first date. I was thrilled. For he was not only my potential boss but also a bachelor with a reputation as a man about town, who loved horse racing, drove a sports car and generally cut an attractive dash. He did not have Keating's handsome features or artistic temperament, but he had intelligence and a charm that bowled me over. Also his ability to secure my first Fleet Street job must have held some sway over how I saw him. The French trip was an office jaunt. Several of Charlie's *Daily Mail* colleagues were on it and it was one of the few occasions before I married when I threw my pineapple-juice tipple to the winds.

By the end of the day, as we piled on to the ferry home, everyone was the worse for French wine and brandy. In my sodden state I pestered Charlie's boss, the news editor Jack Crossley, for a job with a relentlessness that embarrassed my date. The next day Charlie rang and said he had been appalled by my behaviour. He wanted me to promise and assure him I would never behave like that again.

Which of us was the more naive? Me for thinking it was any

of his business and not asking if he was any less sober? (Unlikely.) Or him for supposing you can promise such a thing as never getting drunk again?

Charlie's attitude spelt out the norm. Women couldn't drink themselves senseless and expect to be viewed with the same tolerance or amusement as their male colleagues. Girl power, with gaggles of them going off for hen nights to clubs to enjoy a male striptease act and throwing up in public, was a long way off.

Now, as then, nobody knows what causes someone to become a drunk. Theories abound. Some doctors would have it that there is no such thing as an alcoholic and that it is merely about discipline. Others see it as a psychological dependency rather than a genetic or physical problem. Alcoholics Anonymous programmes ask for it to be looked at sympathetically as a disease that the sufferer did not cause and cannot control and therefore the only solution is to cease to drink altogether. Medics, who privately consider the disease theory questionable, nevertheless concede that the AA twelve-step programme salvages and saves lives.

I am largely indifferent to what particular factors marked my card, except I know the result of getting together with alcohol during the next decade was, for me, to prove catastrophic.

For what it's worth, I believe I was born with the capacity for excess circling my veins. It goes with my Irish background, with the sins of my mother, grandmother and paternal grandfather. I had inherited my mother's ability to be fearless while inwardly being full of the fear of failure. I shared her natural belief that nothing was ever enough.

None of this was obvious in my early twenties. The impression I gave was of a sunny, outgoing, fearless, bright girl. But I suppose I suffered from the same affliction as the Princess of Wales – what *Private Eye* would years later mockingly refer to as 'low sofa esteem'. (The sense best comes out if you say it in a clipped accent, aloud, after several drinks.) Yet no one ever had me down as a loser or a victim.

'How do you go broke?' someone once asked Scott Fitzgerald. 'Slowly and then very quickly,' he replied. My drinking followed the same pattern. Infrequent bouts before my marriage, then many more that for a time ran alongside my professional success without causing alarm. Who would have had the wit to spot in those early days a young woman with a dangerous propensity to drink badly?

But knowing what I know now, I reckon I would recognise a young me today.

Charlie, however, overcame his misgivings about our first date enough to endorse me joining the staff. I worried for longer about how I appeared to others when I had drunk more than was wise. Shades of my mother.

A few weeks after the French trip, clearly in a similar condition, I crashed my car near my Sloane Square flat. I ended up in St George's Hospital casualty department, in Knightsbridge. A huge gash had appeared in my knee and had to be sewn up. The nagging thought that I was not quite right persisted. No matter, the concern, barely articulated in my own head, remained secret.

As things stood, I was on the brink of a wonderful career. 'How much do you want?' Crossley asked me at the meeting to clinch my deal as a Fleet Street reporter. 'Thirty-two pounds a week,' I said. This was nearly double what I was earning. 'We'll pay you thirty-six pounds,' he said.

I was to be the statutory girl. Traditionally the one sent to cover the Chelsea Flower Show and Princess Margaret opening the Ideal Home Exhibition. My predecessor had come straight from Cambridge University as part of a now abandoned graduate trainee scheme at the *Daily Mail*. She was a tough act to follow. 'There are only three natural journalists I have ever come across,' Charlie would say for years after. 'I'm one. Jack Crossley [his boss] and Celia Haddon are the others.'

He reckoned he saw in me, though, the potential to be a proper reporter. I defy any woman not to be attracted by a man who rates her talent and admires her brain.

Sexism, ribbing, merciless joshing by the male workforce were common parts of newspaper life. Apart from the woman's page, the odd feature writer (Olga Franklin of the frequent pit stops, Lynda Lee-Potter, a new arrival) and a couple of reporters on the then Charles Greville Diary, there were no other female journalists there.

Further along the vast newspaper floor was the backbench and the sub-editors. The backbench team was a highly skilled bunch working in shirtsleeves who between them shaped and moulded the next day's edition. One of them used to yell, 'Loaded pad,' every few minutes. (This was a big white pad, with several carbons, to draw rough layouts of the paper.) 'Loaded Pad', as I called him, was fond of summoning me over by waving my copy as if with a query. Then, as I approached, he would 'accidentally' let the paper fall to the floor and allow me to pick it up, thus letting everyone have a good look up my skirt. Even when I cottoned on, I wasn't particularly upset. At the time, desperate to serve, I continued to rush to help when summoned.

In my mother's book, being sexually attractive, being sexually aware, considering oneself sexy didn't feature. I had no idea that a twenty-three-year-old with little more than a pelmet at the top of her legs and with bright red hair and freckles could make men's loins feel twitchy. 'She's a goer,' one of the elderly district reporters up in London for a couple of days said to another reporter in my hearing in the pub one night. I was appalled lest it implied something lacking in my journalistic ability. No, it was explained, it meant I was sexy, up for it . . . 'Oh,' I said, losing interest.

Twice a week I was put on the evening shift. By seven at night the news-desk day staff had been replaced by a night news editor and his team. The night news editor, another Scot, so profoundly believed that women should only be out at night with a husband (and not in a newspaper office) that he would call back from the pub a male reporter, who had finished for the day, to cover a breaking story, rather than send me.

I would watch silently, feeling underused and cross. Charlie, who had no doubt of my use, would meanwhile insist that I take my car to work, whatever it cost in parking, so I was ready to be dispatched.

On the morning shift, in on time, papers read – even the minutiae of the incomprehensible business reports of the *Financial Times* – I would wait to be summoned and given my first assignment of the day. Often it was no more than captioning a picture.

Thirty-two, as Charlie was then, now appears to me to be on the nursery slopes of life. Our daughter Emma is not far off that age.

To an impressionable twenty-three-year-old, he was a real adult. He had a Glaswegian accent, a winning smile, warmth and a dedication to journalism equal to that of my mother's for business.

He had been brought up in Shettleston, Glasgow. An area not quite as bleak as the Gorbals but not much better. His mother Ruth was English, his father a Scot. Ruth had married first one brother, and when he died married the second, Adam, a miner. Life had been no picnic for the family. Ruth, a courageous woman, had one night without warning bundled up her three children and fled back to her family in Kingston, in Surrey. It meant Charlie, a natural scholar, had his education cut short. Several of his schoolfriends went on to become leading surgeons, engineers and academics. Charlie was obliged to help keep his mother and younger brother. He took a job as a tea boy at the *People* and progressed to training as a reporter in Bristol. He would end up as editor of *The Times*.

He was a flattering suitor. His chauvinism – which I didn't then know to be chauvinism – was not in doubt. Yet he wooed me by displaying uninhibited adoration.

He was a strong man, and he was like a person possessed when it came to horses. He regarded jockeys as one of the highest forms of life. He was in awe of their courage.

My knowledge of horses stretched no further than the odd childhood attendance at the Grand National at Aintree. (That plus the annual headache of whether my mother would secure enough poussins at the right price to satisfy the Adelphi chef, who always wanted them top of the menu for the celebration dinner. It was at the dinner that the winning owner, trainer and jockey would be presented with a chocolate horse in their stable colours for dessert. Four horses were made. We got the fourth – always. The rest of the world might reasonably have asked why. We merely regarded it as normal.)

But now, just as I had absorbed Keating's hobbies and adopted his passions as mine, I was to be dragged into the world of racing and jockeys and form. It never held much interest for me, beyond people-watching at race meetings.

Otherwise, as journalists, we lived for the job. Politics were for students, who either dodged the draft to fight in Vietnam, or marched for CND here. Equally, we stayed aloof from flower power, and the gaudy images it invoked. Save for my mini-skirt and Charlie's flowery ties, we were a breed apart from those parading down the King's Road, or Janet Street Porter, the broadcaster and editor of the *Independent on Sunday*, who joined the *Daily Mail* almost the same time as me to work on its woman's page. One morning Janet turned up in an Afghan coat and hat, looking like a yeti, according to Charlie. 'You wouldn't know whether to shoot it or fuck it,' he remarked poetically to Jack Crossley.

I was differently dressed. Unlike possibly any other mother in Blundellsands, mine did not view the prospect of her twenty-three-year-old daughter in the snake pit of Fleet Street as either scary or threatening, any more than she had my job at the news agency. Untypical as ever, our family were good customers of the industry. Newspapers had always been an essential part of keeping up with events at 47 St Michael's Road. She was an avowed reader of columnists, particularly political ones. (Anthony Howard being her out and out favourite.) So she celebrated my arrival on the

Daily Mail, her only concern being a practical one. Standing on doorsteps, being out in the cold, needed sensible equipment. She ordered a mink coat for me.

Her own was one of a small fur collection she held at a time when fur was a normal part of a well-off woman's wardrobe. Ankle-length, it was made up of narrow wild pelts (farmed mink, if it existed at this time, would have been out of the question) and rusty in colour. There was also in the wardrobe, and smelling of mothballs, a blue ocelot – blue apparently being the important bit of this description – two jackets, one fox, one mink and several mink wraps. All were used regularly, the full-length mink particularly in the evening. The shorter fur coats were 'day wear'. Fox was not an evening option, she advised.

It was decided my mink should be a darker colour. The pelts had to be specially selected. In order that 'the child isn't catching her death in the meantime,' I was lent a coat.

Charlie had no mortgage, no commitments. He took me out to dinner – wherever I wanted to go. He travelled exotically. Most captivating of all, he was regarded as the dashing office catch. 'Charlie Wilson will never get cornered,' they said.

No one had told me to think before automatically rising to a challenge. No one said, 'Will it be what you want when you grow up?'

Charlie and I had the same speed of thought and quick wit. It might have meant that when on form we presented ourselves as a couple of natural comic talents. It didn't alas mean we were mature adults, able to see the dangerous waters we were entering. The side of us that clashed would have made a marriage guidance counsellor's hair stand on end.

Here was a middle-class girl tutored to disobey men, to disregard them, to find them a joke. A daughter reared to see her father pushed into the background, to regard doing housework as a sign of failure. Clever women paid others to do their dirty work. Your brain was your biggest asset. Your grooming and appearance were important. Sex was never mentioned. This automatically reduced it to an activity connected with shame and secrecy, never enjoyment. A girl, too, who thought there was nothing odd in the privilege money could bring – be it a chocolate horse in the winning stable's racing colours on Grand National night or the finest rooms in the Black Swan Hotel. And nothing odd that this should be made possible and paid for by sleight of hand and slippery practice.

And here was a man whose father's behaviour had caused his mother to flee. In those days we had no knowledge of the inner child, co-dependency, the sins of the father inherited by the children. The possibility that a broken home is no place to learn compassion and sensitivity. Charlie didn't know about my mother's problems with alcohol, and if he ever had known he was unlikely to have realised that an alcoholic mother has every chance of passing on her drinking skills to her children.

Neither of us considered that a daughter brought up to regard career and money as important will not a subservient wife make. The insights, now so clear, were decades away.

A few weeks after my twenty-third birthday, Charlie took me to Lingfield Races and a belated birthday dinner at a trendy new restaurant in Battersea called 555. We returned to Sloane Square and made love.

I'd committed myself again. The next morning before he left at eight o'clock to start up the news desk on the *Daily Mail*, Charlie asked for breakfast. I promptly went out and bought bacon and eggs and cooked them. He went off to work. I cleared up. Getting ready for work myself meant I was about twenty minutes late for the start of my 10 a.m. shift.

A voice bawled over the glass partitions as I made my way into the newsroom. 'Robinson . . .' Charlie dressed me down and sent me to doorstep Downing Street for the rest of the day as a punishment for being late. Even then, no degree of self-protection moved in to play. Looking back, the shouting at me was a private joke – but also his way of putting out the message that I was not going to be treated differently from any other member of staff. Except he never explained that to me.

My mother had taught me the importance of professionalism. I never doubted or questioned Charlie's motives or his right to behave as he did. We were infatuated with each other. He would sometimes take Friday off to go racing and work on the Sunday. He fixed my shifts so I could do the same. I hardly noticed that he gambled, or his unquestioning assumption that men were men and women should know their place. I did notice that at the races we would bump into the editor of the *Daily Mail* and Charlie would act with a sensible degree of respect towards his boss. But because subservience had never been part of my upbringing I thought him unnecessarily humble.

What I saw in Charlie, of course, was the same uncrushable determination that my mother displayed. In both there was an absolute refusal to be beaten. And with both it was to prove ugly. In other ways he was her opposite. In time, he came to abhor her moral code. Her ducking and diving. She to loathe what she saw as his part in causing the unhappiness of her daughter. One of her most precious possessions. Their worlds might have been different. But the hardship and struggles of their early years were remarkably similar.

For now, my mother's attitude towards my new boyfriend was blunt. She recognised his strengths and weaknesses quicker than anyone else did. 'Be careful,' she warned. 'He's not kind enough for you . . .'

In 1967 the fear of most of my generation – and me – was not about whether a prospective husband was kind enough. It was whether you had one. My biggest dread was to become a fading female journalist, who held on to the bar and had had affairs with most of the men in the office. Then there was sex and my mother. She would have been appalled by the idea that I was 'sleeping' with a man. When I had been with Frank she had phoned early in the morning to check where I was. With Charlie it was less of a problem since I lived alone and that is where he stayed. But I was uncomfortable about the sex bit myself.

Worse, the pill was not easily obtainable. Charlie never seemed to feel the need to provide condoms. So we took our chances. It was, to say the least, unsatisfactory. I lived in permanent fear of accidentally getting pregnant.

I had barely settled in to the job when I was ordered by Charlie to Essex to cover the wedding of Christine Truman, darling of the Centre Court at Wimbledon. She was about to become Mrs Janes, the wife of a well-known rugby player. It was a topper and tails job, with the sports world well represented.

I filed my copy and checked in with Charlie. 'Does the idea of getting married appeal to *you*?' he asked. 'Could do,' I said. We went to lunch next day at the chic Forum restaurant in Chancery Lane and agreed to spend the rest of our lives together.

I wanted no more of wedding invitations and a long run-up to the day. Neither did Charlie. I had been abandoned once. I suggested we kept the whole thing a secret, and got spliced with the minimum of fuss.

I did, however, want a Catholic wedding. Charlie hardly blinked, which was astonishing, considering his background. I insisted that as a Protestant he had better be tutored by an intelligent priest. I chose the Church of the Immaculate Conception in Mayfair, run by the Jesuits. 'My father would turn in his grave,' said Charlie. It went over my head. Northern Ireland was yet to come. Religious bigotry was a working-class experience. I'd remembered my mother saying that in Bootle in her youth the Orange marchers would break ranks and bang on the dustbins at my grandmother's house. But that was all.

In the end it barely mattered. Charlie's instruction lasted twenty minutes. The priest at Farm Street said it was enough. Wise man. They had a drink and parted.

The date set for our wedding was 19 January 1968. My brother was to be best man. Liz Hunter, who was working as a croupier and hadn't been to bed the night before, was my

matron of honour. The only others present were Charlie's
mother and my parents.

On the morning of the wedding I was convinced I was pregnant, which, I decided, overrode all my other reservations. What
were my reservations? I did not really know because I refused to
consider them, lest I fled in terror. My thoughts were about the
need to get this thing done. To tick it off my list. To close the
outstanding account. My impatience – still with me today – is
neither wise nor admirable. The equivalent of jumping into a
cold sea rather than dithering at the edge. Was Charlie the right
husband? Was I a suitable wife? No, no, no. But I didn't allow
myself the luxury of thinking either thought.

The service was scheduled for 11 a.m. The groom arrived in
the editor's office Jaguar. We had thrown a surprise party at
the White Swan, the office pub known as the Mucky Duck, the
night before. It was the first most of the journalists we worked
with knew of our relationship. My parents had turned up, so
had Keating. Charlie, full of champagne, had danced several
times with an old girlfriend. My mother could scarcely believe
it. Her future son-in-law in the clutches of another woman,
one with very few clothes on, who looked to her like a hooker,
sealed her conviction that nothing good would come of her
daughter's nuptials. It was a long, disappointing way from the
titled barrister she had always had in mind.

Our little wedding party gathered at the church in Farm
Street. During the service, Charlie dropped the ring. The priest
whispered to us not to worry because we were 'married'. We
posed for pictures outside. They were taken by two *Daily Mail*
photographers. The *Daily Mail* news desk provided us with the
news-desk driver to take us to our overnight hotel.

Charlie and the driver, another betting man, were desperate to
hear the racing results on the car radio. To this end we toured the
one-way system at East Grinstead several times before moving
on. At Gravetye Manor Hotel the manager looked up and greeted
Charlie: 'Nice to see you both again,' he said. Whoops.

We left for the Canary Isles from Gatwick Airport the next morning. Small shafts of memory remain from the fortnight that followed. First, I had never been to Gatwick Airport before. As a family we knew Ringway, as Manchester Airport was then called. We knew Heathrow. That is how we had gone to Cannes. We even knew about travelling from Lydd in Kent to Le Touquet, with the family Rover being carried on to the plane through a huge bulkhead opening, a form of transport that lasted only briefly as an option for tourists. Naturally, while it did, my mother insisted we experience it. But, please, nobody would think of our family in the same breath as a package holiday.

Or indeed Charlie, who until now had only ever taken himself off for money-no-object luxury jaunts.

In fact, it was my brother who had arranged the honeymoon, free of charge, via an advertising agency he was working for. The deal was that later on one of us would pen a piece about the resort and the tour operator for the *Daily Mail*. The free trip, along with the *Daily Mail* photographers at the wedding and the news-desk driver taking us to the honeymoon hotel, gave me the feeling that we weren't so much experiencing a new beginning for two young people deeply in love but that we were part of some office freebie.

Small surprise that the feature remained unwritten. The experience was too grisly to translate easily into the jolly prose required for the travel page.

In Tenerife, our first discovery was to find our resort was on the side of the island where the beaches were black and there didn't seem to be much sunshine. We didn't know either, until the next day, that package holidays were about Germans bagging the best deckchairs, the English queuing at five-thirty in the evening for their supper. Or that my mother's song and dance in the Carlton Hotel all those years ago about not eating foreign food had miraculously travelled ahead of us. The meals were a combination of British boarding-school lunches and the odd bit of Viennese canteen fare. To ease our disappointment,

Charlie hired a car and we set off in search of better beaches and more sunshine.

There was a sheer drop to the sea as we took bends at breakneck speed on the mountainous roads. Apart from a reasonably based fear for my safety, my suspicions about my pregnancy were heightened. The nausea was too awful for me to go on denying my condition to myself but I said nothing to Charlie.

As I gripped the seat I began to feel like St Paul on his eye-opening journey to Damascus. For here was a new Charlie, one I had never met before. One who found his wife's objections to his driving to be beyond the pale. Each time I begged, demanded, pleaded with him to go slower, far from being concerned or conciliatory his foot pressed ever harder on the accelerator. I could do no more than sob helplessly. I wanted this awful experience to stop. I longed to be cosseted, loved, cared for. I wanted my mummy!

Time, age and experience teach you many things. These days, if anyone persists in driving in a manner I find unpleasant I demand to know why they must go so fast when it is clearly causing discomfort to a passenger. I also know there is a choice. I can get out.

(That said, thirty-five years on I wouldn't recommend that anyone drive with Charlie or persuade him to drive differently. He remains as intolerant of his passengers as he has always been.)

But I didn't know any tricks at twenty-three. My wisdom was almost non-existent.

So was Charlie's. He saw only a new wife criticising his behaviour. His automatic response was to retaliate. I viewed next to me, in the driving seat, an unfeeling, insensitive husband.

Charlie's initial attraction had been that like my mother he was strong and masterly. But suddenly he was responding in a way she never did. How the hell was I meant to cope with what was confronting me? With her, you only had to sniffle for a full-blown medical crisis to be announced. She would dispatch my father to the chemist with a warning, 'Don't be wasting time chatting to people with this child so sick,' while my brother, to his intense annoyance, would be ordered to play quietly so as not to upset his sister.

A honeymoon is not the ideal place to find you have mis-judged a husband on a grand scale.

Charlie must have felt the same about his new wife. Nothing was said. We slept, we sunbathed. We drank. I threw up before breakfast each day. The combination of morning sickness and hangovers was grim. A joyless trip all round.

We returned home, our fears unspoken. I had neither the will nor the sense to analyse what was going on. Instead trenches were dug on both sides. Charlie expected me to fit in with what he wanted – a devoted and adoring wife. I wanted to be looked after as my mother had taught me a princess of my standing deserved. Both of us reverted even more firmly to the people we had been brought up to be. Each day would start with fresh hopes, new res-olutions, good intentions, but a battle of wills before nightfall became the norm. I dreaded the confrontations.

Meanwhile, the mink coat ordered by my mother was ready, and when the furrier rang to ask what initials were to be embroi-dered in the silk lining, I requested 'A. W'. It turned out to be the only voluntary acknowledgement by me, apart from wearing a wedding ring, that I had changed my status. Like my mother, I have continued to use my maiden name, opting for it from con-venience and a pride and a habit learnt from her, rather than a deliberate step to mark my independence.

Once we returned to work there were dark whispers that 'the husband and wife rule' that existed in newspapers would see me gone. No married couples were then allowed to work together in the same office. The edict was in force over the road at Express Newspapers where the *Mail*'s editor, Arthur Brittenden, earlier had been an executive.

Noticing me back in the newsroom, suntanned, Brittenden

buzzed through to the news editor on the famous internal 'squawk box' and asked what I was still doing there. Jack Crossley, who had hoped we had got away with it, ordered his deputy, my new husband, to pass on the news. Charlie duly obeyed when we both got home that night.

Did I rage at the unfairness of it all? I don't recall doing so. Charlie added the comforting crumb that the diary on the *Evening News*, a paper owned by Associated Newspapers, proprietors of the *Mail*, and now defunct, was a possible alternative. 'Why on earth', I yelled, coming to life for the first time, 'would I want to work as a diary reporter?' Charlie looked horror struck and told me that to object would be to jeopardise *his* career.

So I did as he ordered. I made the call, went for the interview and sat looking at the diary editor. He in turn glanced at my CV and said disdainfully: 'You don't appear to have any diary experience.' To accuse a news reporter of not having diary experience was like telling someone from the Royal Ballet School that they were unsuitable for an amateur production of *Cats*.

Two things became clear. The memo telling this man to hire me to save embarrassment had got stuck in the endless overhead pipe system. Secondly, I had no intention of begging for a job well below my capabilities. 'You're absolutely right,' I said as I stormed out. Charlie was very concerned. Phrases like 'rocking the boat' and 'putting our futures on the line' came out.

He need not have worried. I went quietly, unaware of the full injustice. We had rented a cottage in Claygate, near Esher in Surrey, to see if we wanted to live out of town. I went there with the luxury of endless, lonely days to ponder my fate.

Charlie made no changes to his work pattern. After a long day at the office he would go for a session in the pub. I washed away the horrible feelings of fear, of failure, of despair, by having a drink round about the time I considered he should arrive home. A downhill turn was shaping up nicely.

Did I feel miserable? Did I wonder whether this was it? Yes and yes. For me there was little magic about this marriage. But my childhood had been a pattern of struggle and worry so I suppose I saw the situation merely as another version of my parents' own daily lives.

That said, I took my mother's phone calls and assured her that Charlie was cooking every meal, washing up, taking care of me, getting me plenty of help in the house. Paying the bills. Alone, I would wander round my old haunts of Kensington and Chelsea where my friends were still having a fun time in their flats. I didn't tell a soul how desperate I felt.

A month after we returned from honeymoon there were no doubts left about my pregnancy. I also knew that for me the marriage was already looking too shaky to contemplate a baby. At the back of my mind and overriding everything was the thought that unless I continued to establish my credentials in Fleet Street I would be washed up, dependent on a man who frightened me.

But for the moment we had to make decisions about my condition.

The way we did was proof enough of the growing uncertainty we felt. In a new marriage, we barely disagreed over the decision to seek an abortion. The only detail to be worked out was how to gather the cash we needed to pay for it. Abortion had only recently been decriminalised by the 1967 Abortion Act but a woman required the permission of two independent doctors to obtain a termination. It took no more than money to arrange the appointments, answer a few questions and get the pieces of paper.

We booked into the Avenue Clinic. I blocked what I was doing from my mind. How could I, in a few short years, have moved from being guilt-ridden about sex before marriage to committing the mortal sin of killing another human being?

The operation over, I returned home. No one had warned me that a woman's hormones are tossed around by pregnancy. Even more so by it being abruptly ended.

I was sunk by a depression I had never known before. I

avoided sharing my dilemma with my Catholic mother. I was loath to admit failure to my girlfriends, or anyone else for that matter. Help. Again.

From a girl who hardly touched a drop my drinking increased. When Charlie came home I would be a couple of stiff gins ahead. The verbal fights would start. One night he raged about the state of the cottage. He wanted a wife. His mother had never left a bed unmade all day. His mother, he said, had always cleaned his shoes. I raged back, my sarcastic wit at its most cutting. The row continued up the tiny stairs and into the bedroom. Charlie says I bit him on the arm. We hit out at each other. It was very ugly. The next morning I lay in bed unable to move. My face was swollen. My mouth cut. Charlie left for the day. I stayed under the blankets, feigning sleep when the cleaning woman came.

I believed then, and I still do, that the end of a drunken night, when both sides have swallowed more than is wise, is no basis for a woman to start deciding the man has physically taken advantage of her.

'Why didn't you take yourself off to the hospital?' my solicitor demanded a few years later. But then I didn't think about collecting evidence for what had happened, only about what was to become of us.

Not so my husband. Alone in the cottage one night, waiting yet again for Charlie to come home, I was suspicious enough to go through his suit pockets. In one I found a letter from a solicitor that said he was sorry the marriage was not working out and Charlie should come for further guidance should he need it.

My shock was not so much about the state of the marriage being acknowledged but that Charlie's fears were as real as mine and he was even seeking legal help. Alarm bells sufficient to waken the whole of Surrey should have rung.

They didn't.

It would take a far bigger crisis to learn that, by instinct, Charlie faced adversity by planning his campaign and covering his back, marshalling troops, securing defences. His strategy versus my ignorance of the growing force of the enemy was later to prove no contest.

Charlie was the product of a broken home. I was the daughter of an alcoholic who, like it or not, was heading in the same direction.

Did I provoke him? Almost certainly. Was he cruel? Yes.

Whose fault was it? His father's? My mother's? Fate bringing together, like some bad joke, two people, clever, quick, ambitious, essentially decent, yet from their backgrounds profoundly unsuited emotionally? The morning after the fight Charlie and I didn't speak. Later in the day he sent me flowers. Part of me believed, as he said, that my attitude was to blame. Another part kept rerunning the bit about cleaning his shoes.

I had a husband who felt cheated, caged and disillusioned by what had overtaken him. He had enjoyed a mother who had waited on him hand and foot. A previous long-term girlfriend who adored him, a woman with whom he had had a relationship for nearly ten years. The night before the wedding she had begged him to change the name on the wedding banns and marry her. I'd no idea that she had sat in the back pews of the church at our wedding. She did not think Charlie and I were suited. She was right. But neither of us would have been persuaded at the time.

I had come from a home where it had been drummed into me on a daily basis that housework, looking after men, sewing was out, out, out! Yet here I was failing in marriage because I was not doing any of these things. Who was right?

The new Mrs Wilson's mother hadn't spent all that money on an education to have her daughter clean floors, iron shirts, behave like a wife. While Mr Wilson, who had always been looked after by adoring women, took clean shirts, hot meals, a tidy home for granted.

Oh for the wisdom of an old head. How obvious it all seems now. Not then. I didn't know how to share my troubles and try to seek a solution. I did the only thing I knew, I threw myself into my work.

Out of the blue a call came asking if I would like to do some shifts on the *Sun*. It had replaced the *Daily Herald*, but was still a left-wing broadsheet. I leapt at a chance to get back to work. For a few months I toiled with pieces on diets and home furnishing.

I was busy at the Ideal Home Exhibition (how ironic was that?), interviewing an up-and-coming interior designer called David Hicks who had married the daughter of Lord Mountbatten. Elsewhere I was reporting on the latest trends in household cleaning products. Was there a reporter less qualified?

1968 was another historic year. The gentleness of flower power was replaced by the sight of angry protestors in London's Grosvenor Square, demonstrating against US military involvement in Vietnam. In Paris, students and workers vented their anger not just about America's foreign policy but also their own government's censorship, discrimination and low salaries. Martin Luther King and Robert Kennedy were gunned down. Regardless of the public reaction to King's assassination, Enoch Powell in the same month made a speech in which he expressed his despair over immigration policy. 'Like the Roman, I seem to see the River Tiber foaming with much blood' was his forecast. By the summer, Soviet tanks had rolled into Prague and crushed the Czechoslovaks' bid for freedom.

Foreign news, sadly, was of little professional importance to me on the Pacesetter pages of the *Sun*. The depression following my abortion was made worse by the knowledge that I had ended up doing the sort of jobs that were even more silly than the diary position on the *Evening News*, which I had so arrogantly rejected.

Quite unexpectedly one day, the *Sun*'s grand woman's editor Amy Landreth, mother of Peter Atkinson, with whom I had worked at North London News Agency, called me into her office. (It was a puzzle what she did in there, for she never appeared to involve herself in the running of the Pacesetter pages that were under her official charge but were actually organised by the Pacesetter editor, Unity Hall.) 'You ought not to be here, dear,' she said kindly. 'The *Sunday Times* is looking for a reporter. Go for it.'

I did. There were sixty applicants. I was, said the news editor, the only one without a degree and I was married. Another drawback. 'But I see you've got good enough A levels to have taken a university place if you'd wanted,' he added. No, actually, I hadn't. But yes, it did say so on my application. Who was to know? Ten of us got a week's trial. I might not have had a 2.1 in Politics and Economics from Cambridge, but I knew how to report. Finding stories, getting to stories, seeing the point of stories held no fear for me.

I was sent to the north-east to investigate the fishing industry. Despite my mother, I'd yet to learn how to use my head to save my legs and I doubt there was a person left in Hull or Grimsby that I hadn't interviewed by Thursday of that week. But my report made the paper.

The editor of the *Sunday Times* was Harry Evans. His reputation as a campaigning journalist was already well known. He had fought for and eventually won a pardon for Timothy Evans, who had been hanged for the murders committed by John Christie. The pardon, when it came, was accompanied by the abolition of hanging. Harry was the son of a Manchester train driver and had none of the chic Oxbridge credentials of those who surrounded him. After I was recommended by the news editor Harry did no more than take a quick glance at my cuttings, and declare: 'Well, you can obviously do the job.'

I was in. I could barely conceal my joy as the cabby dropped me off back at the *Sun*. I tipped him five pounds. A fortune.

9

Not So Cosy Canonbury

The *Sunday Times*, despite its deserved reputation for investigative reporting, lacked the permanent warlike atmosphere of traditional Fleet Street. It was much gentler. Even if the leisurely pace was the despair of the chief sub and his team who were required to get the paper out.

Harry Evans' deputy was the graceful, urbane Frank Giles, a history scholar at Brasenose, who had been in the Foreign Office and served in Moscow. His office, and presumably his home, had pictures of him and world leaders fighting for space. I'd rarely met anyone so grand.

The Tuesday conference for the heads of departments that kicked off the week was held in the suite of offices Harry had inherited from his predecessor, C. D. Hamilton. It was book-lined and had sofas, silk cushions and an Eames chair. The roll-call of staff writers and contributors contained some of the most glittering names on the literary and journalistic scenes. Lord Snowdon took pictures for the *Sunday Times* magazine. Cyril Connolly was a book reviewer and could be seen most Tuesdays, when he arrived at about midday to deliver his copy. Nick Tomalin, who was killed by a Syrian tank during the Yom Kippur War, was a foreign reporter, along with Murray Sayle, David Blundy (who was killed in San Salvador in 1989) and

David Holden, later murdered in Cairo by espionage agents and acknowledged after his death as being a British agent himself.

There was also the legendary Insight team, which in the years to come would bring justice to bear on the huge Distillers organisation – whose marketing of the drug thalidomide as a cure for morning sickness had caused hundreds of mothers to give birth to deformed babies – and pursue countless other award-winning investigations. The four-man, one-female-researcher, one-female-secretary operation appeared to work independently of the rest of the newspaper. Their routine varied from staying in the office night after night and subsequently filling half the paper to doing nothing much except wandering around having lunch and enjoying themselves.

Bruce Chatwin was a permanently suntanned member of the magazine staff, another bunch who led a life every bit as exotic and free from interference as the Insight boys. The fashion editor was Ernestine Carter, an elderly American who dressed like a petite Chanel or Dior model. She was never without a velvet bow in her immaculate hair. Pity any man, casually dressed, particularly if dark-skinned, who might be unfortunate enough to be standing in the front hall as Ernestine came to leave at night. She would automatically assume it was her cab driver.

'We've booked you on a train with a restaurant car,' the news-desk secretary said as she arranged my transport in my first week when I was being sent on an out-of-town job. This was refreshingly modern and accommodating compared to the *Daily Mail* regime, where Crossley and Wilson would have been quite happy if you'd walked to save them money; this was altogether more civilised. Throughout the editorial floor there was the air of a senior common room. No one appeared to have to clock in at a certain time. The photographers were different too – freelancers who didn't wear ties and actually read books.

The jobs they sent me on at the *Sunday Times* were great fun. But I would be terrified each Friday going into the office to write up my story. For now there was no question of stringing together a few facts for the sub-editors to rewrite. This was a paper that expected its reporters to *write*. Composing my essay was in turn tortuous and rewarding. The fear of not writing well enough was replaced by the joy of seeing my name bylined and my words in the paper early every Saturday evening when the first edition dropped. But the drama of getting my story sorted was secondary to the headache of dealing with a husband who I felt continued to treat me like one of his reporters.

In the early weeks of my arrival I had been sent to investigate the milk and butter and cream-making industry. The government had declared war on the unhygienic methods of dairy farmers. It was early summer and wonderfully warm. We began in Southampton. My husband expected me to ring in three or four times a day.

Mike Ward, the photographer, was a former actor and trained classical pianist who owned and only ever travelled in a magnificent Rolls-Royce. He was charming, urbane, irresistibly funny and good-natured and found it difficult to take any story very seriously. He simply liked taking good pictures. Also he made it clear he regarded my phone calls to Charlie about my hotel arrangements as a joke. 'How are you doing, number one?' Ward would demand at breakfast as we toured the West Country. 'Has hubby been assured I'm not ravishing you?'

Ward, of course, was about as far removed from the ruthless, savage, highly professional world of journalism as practised by Charlie Wilson and those at the *Daily Mail* as it was possible to be. And while Ward was a wandering husband (he'd been married several times), it struck him as inappropriate that I should have what to him appeared like a suspicious one.

Back home, the atmosphere of scholarship and sophistication in Gray's Inn Road was much derided by Charlie. He was wary of the people I worked with. They weren't his sort of Fleet Street warriors. After a few drinks I would taunt him by boasting of the *Sunday Times*' superior strengths in reporting. Charlie's occasional forays to the Blue Lion pub opposite my office only increased his belief that I was mixing with a bunch of people many of whom were unwisely educated beyond their intelligence. He had a point with some of them.

Memorably, when Ian Jack, now editor of *Granta*, was hired as a young deputy chief sub from the *Daily Express* in Glasgow I invited him, out of pity for a young man alone in London, to Sunday lunch. Charlie shared with him his often-stated view that the *Sunday Times* was 'full of long-haired intellectuals who wouldn't know a story if it bit them in the balls'. Ian Jack agreed. 'Aye, Charlie, it's no so much a newspaper. More an adventure playground for journalists.'

A thankful break from the divisions at home came in the summer. Charlie was sent to New York by the *Daily Mail* to assist in the coverage of the American elections. For me it was a blessed breathing space from the daily scrutiny of my domestic failings and my new working life. Towards the end of the period I joined him in New York. One afternoon, after he had had lunch at the 21 Club with his newspaper colleagues, he returned to our hotel room and an almighty row took place. The fight was horrible but familiar.

We dusted ourselves down and agreed it was both our faults. We were so busy fighting the fire we didn't think to stop to ask ourselves what had caused the blaze in the first place and whether it wouldn't be wiser to cut our losses and leave the mess to burn away without us. Or seek help. To seek help, of course, we would have had to admit to the outside world that there was a problem. This was 1968. You didn't do that sort of thing. Let people know your business. It could only get worse – and it did.

I didn't tell anyone. I was miles from home. I thought I was largely to blame. We left for a holiday in Antigua. It was a spectacular setting. Much more in keeping with my childhood idea of a luxury resort. We slept, we drank, we made love, we sunbathed. We pretended we didn't have a care in the world. We didn't acknowledge our fears. My biggest one was that my new husband seemed to have taken over from my mother in being in charge of me. Of controlling me, of being critical one minute and intensely proud of me the next. I felt like a naughty child. Not a newish bride. Charlie for his part saw a wife who didn't conform to his standards. A bright, bouncy girl who within seconds could change into a harridan who belittled him. A woman who, when accused of behaving badly, put up two fingers and stormed off. Our values were different. No one had taught me to consider the feelings of a husband. To be kind. My training was all about not being taken for a ride. Not giving in. Always winning. Charlie, so keen on appearances, was aghast at my lack of respect.

Nothing my mother had taught me seemed useful now. There was no question of going to her to seek advice. Her response would have been all too obvious. Then again, if it was my fault, as Charlie told me, surely it was within my power to put it right.

I wrestled with the worry alone. Charlie returned to New York for the last couple of weeks of his assignment. For me there was the chance to see history in the making.

It was the autumn of 1968 and the *Sunday Times* dispatched me to Londonderry. The week before had seen a civil rights march take place that, although we didn't know it, was to change the face of the politics of Northern Ireland for the rest of the century and on.

After two days of bloody battles, riot police broke up a demonstration of nearly a thousand Catholics and sympathisers. The protest, memorably illustrated with pictures of a young student, Bernadette Devlin, brick in hand, had been a long time coming. Once you knew the background you could only marvel that the issues had been kept at bay for so long. When it came to housing, jobs, votes, Catholics had been discriminated against in a way that took your breath away, but that was and had been accepted as the status quo.

The students and trade unionists were determined to wipe out the sectarianism that penalised the poor and most deserving.

The ferocity with which they made their case was at first only understood by Mary Holland of the *Observer*. An Irish journalist of outstanding ability, her account of that first display of frustration and anger by Catholics and students alike was impressive for its background knowledge. I was ordered to follow up the story. I was twenty-four years of age.

To call me inexperienced, no matter what I might have learnt from my days in a tough agency and under the tutelage of a husband-come-news editor, was an understatement. My only visits to Ireland, north or south, before 1968 had been as a child when my mother had taken us to meet her main suppliers. I had no idea of the bigotry and hostility that existed between Catholics and Protestants. Admittedly I was a Catholic but a middle-class one, and it showed. I arrived in Londonderry in an emerald green pure wool coat and a matching dress, topped off by my then powerfully bright red hair. It's a wonder I survived the week.

The headquarters for the press was the City Hotel. There I arranged to meet a teacher, who was working part time in a smoked-salmon factory. He had dirty fingernails and a mass of curly black hair, a gentle manner and an indignation about the plight of ordinary Catholics that was to make him into one of the most important political figures of the decade. He was John Hume.

At the City Hotel too was a young man called Eammon McCann, a firebrand leader of the Catholic community. McCann and I went off to the Bogside, where he called a local factory out on strike for an hour.

On the Unionist side, a major and his cronies took me to the Unionist Club. It was shocking enough for the other members to spot a young girl in there, but one in a bright emerald green coat. I went along with their sarcasm, their threats about what might happen to me if I dared to print an unfair account of events. I presumed the bullying was because I was young and female and this was bound to irritate old farts. Not for a moment did I imagine any of it was prompted by my appearance. But I might just as well have been draped in a tricolour.

Even by the following Sunday I was unaware of the impact of how I looked. Before flying home, I pitched up with another reporter at a church service in Belfast, where the sermon was to be delivered by the Reverend Ian Paisley, again wearing my stupid emerald green outfit.

During the next decade I would witness countless tragic events in Ireland. Or at least I would arrive to report on the devastation they brought with them. The distressing part was driving around the city and its outskirts with a local *A–Z* and realising you were not only in a road you had visited before but calling again on the same family because they had lost yet another member to the Troubles.

There was the eleven-year-old robbed of both hands. A young Catholic couple whose eighteen-month-old baby Angela was killed in the crossfire between the army and the IRA and whom one member of the IRA called 'an unfortunate casualty of war'. A young woman lost her sight, her arms, her legs when the Abercorn café in the centre of Belfast was wiped out by a bomb. The compensation for these innocents was less than a few hundred pounds for the children and a few thousand for the adults, facing a lifetime with their disabilities.

In Belfast a few years later, I narrowly missed being blown up in the Europa Hotel. The bomb was discovered in the Ladies on the first floor. Remarkably, until then the hotel had a policy of searching only the baggage and the men going in. Not the women.

Apart from what became regular trips to Ireland, I cut my teeth on reporting politics at the round of major autumn seaside conferences. They began with the Trades Union Congress conference and progressed to the Tory and Labour meetings. Blackpool or Brighton was always the venue.

My first year at the Labour Party conference in Brighton, I had been seconded to Atticus, the gossip column begun by Ian

Fleming and at that time written by Hunter Davies. The brief was to report on the way the political correspondents operated in the lobby system, which had its own special rules. I wandered around asking this and that, again innocently unaware of stepping on toes. The lobby men were the bane of every news desk. They could not be ordered around in the same way. They produced political reports, but were not in the business of following up anything that took the fancy of the news desk. So when a story broke about a famous politician philandering or buggering little boys, it would invariably turn out that the paper's parliamentary team had known about it for years: 'No story there, old boy. It happens every day.' But, since the knowledge came to them from within the House of Commons, it was, they claimed, privileged.

To those of us brought up as firemen, covering a different territory every week, not worrying about meeting the same people ever again, the restrictive practices of the lobby journalists were difficult to admire. (It is now a much more open arrangement.) The political correspondents I approached at Brighton found my questions unsettling. Enough for three of them to join me in a lift at the Grand Hotel and make their views crystal clear. They bullied, they threatened, just like the old farts at the Unionist Club in Derry. As I saw it, any story that forced men to act in such a shameful way must surely be worth having. I persisted. But the words were never printed. Too much else was happening at Brighton for Hunter to use my copy.

The stimulating working routine of the *Sunday Times* and my enthusiasm for it did nothing to improve things at home. I was often away from Wednesday to Friday. Friday lunchtime I would write my main story. Saturday in the newsroom was for covering the stories of the day. At 6 p.m. when the first edition of the paper appeared, the place would be filled with the business news reporters, foreign correspondents and any members of the Insight team who happened to be in town. Chuckling and patting each other on the back, we would make for home. One

Saturday in four would mean staying in the office until the early hours of Sunday morning. What chance did Mr and Mrs Wilson have for their marriage?

In desperation, and without either of us saying how bad things were, we moved back to London. There, we assured each other, everything would be fine.

We couldn't afford Chelsea. Houses in SW3 were nearly twenty thousand pounds. But Unity Hall from the *Sun*, whose husband Owen Summers was the *Daily Mail*'s crime reporter, urged us to look at a property a few doors down from their house in Canonbury, Islington. Both were on a neo-Georgian development in Alwyne Square. Number 13 had, like Owen and Unity's, four bedrooms, two bathrooms, a study and a dining room. And a garage. A snip at £13,500. We jumped at the idea.

Charlie, Owen and Unity and their local friends were much older than me. They liked pubs and good food and going to France but seemed not in the least interested in books or politics or art, although Charlie had been a regular theatre-goer before we married. I obediently joined in. Unity was an excellent and sophisticated cook who deepened my own interest in cooking, although she was quietly astonished by my lack of household skills. Somewhere in the archives of the old broadsheet *Sun* is an article written by her about her young friend who had asked: 'How do I learn about housework? Who teaches you to dust and polish and iron?' I felt strangely alone and isolated in the Canonbury set. Our marriage lurched along, galvanised by socialising and drinking.

Our life together was continually throwing up examples of our different and diverse approaches to things. His to me was comically conventional. Mine to him was exasperatingly anti-Establishment.

There had been the panic in the middle of the night when the oysters my husband had eaten were reacting violently in his stomach and his cries of pain had alarmed me so much I insisted we took him off to hospital there and then. He agreed. I presented myself in jeans and T-shirt in our hall three minutes later. 'You are not going looking like that,' he said, and he went upstairs to put on a suit, shirt and tie. Reluctantly, I changed into a skirt, blouse, tights and heels. But as I presented myself for inspection the second time, he announced that the pain had stopped. It was four in the morning. 'Now you've made us both dress up, we're going anyway,' I insisted.

There was the famous Monday when we were both off work and Charlie wanted to buy a new hat for our next visit to the races. We were at odds again over what each of us considered suitable attire for the shopping trip to Moss Bros, the outfitters in Covent Garden. Except this time I held my ground. I had grown wise. He could dress how he liked. I wasn't changing.

We arrived at the door of the store. Me in a skimpy white T-shirt, Charlie in a dark suit, white shirt and dark tie. 'Hats?' asked my husband of the commissionaire on the door. 'Chauffeurs on the second floor . . .' said the doorman. He apparently added that leisurewear was on the fourth. I didn't hear the last bit. Me and my T-shirt were doubled up with mirth.

Our drinking affected us in different ways. Charlie seemed to be able to put away gallons of the stuff at weekends. But he would still rise early each morning, tapping his watch impatiently on, say, a Sunday when we were both off, and asking if I was 'having another lie-in'.

I would feel sick, hung-over, depressed. The house was only half furnished. I didn't know where to begin. Oh, now for Chippendales of Dover Street. We had carpeted and bought sofas and curtains for a couple of the rooms. We had a new fitted kitchen installed. Another feature in the archives of the pre-Murdoch-owned *Sun*. A treat for Pacesetter readers: Mrs Wilson in an apron, frying at her new gas hob. We had a cleaning lady we had brought from Surrey. Just as well, as Mrs Wilson spent even less time behind a vacuum cleaner than she did conjuring up new meals.

But the new house wasn't making us happy. What about a

baby? Yes. What a great idea. Oh, dear reader, let us not under-estimate the stupidity and selfishness of this decision. Let us remember how the middle classes would come thoroughly to disapprove of feckless girls in their mid-teens who admitted they had a baby to feel better, to get a council flat, or because they thought it would bring them happiness. What made us any different? Except we did not have the excuse of poverty, or lack of education, or a need for a roof over our heads. For all our smartness and professional skills, which allowed us to cover wars, break stories, beat the opposition, we were no better when it came to life-changing, irresponsible decisions.

To our surprise the pregnancy didn't happen overnight. It didn't happen for quite a few months. The more it didn't happen the more convinced I became that a baby was the answer.

Unknown to me, around this time there was something called the birth of feminism. Even if I had been in early on the news it would not have occurred to me that the concept held any rele-vance to my unhappy marriage.

Feminism arrived on the coat-tails of free love and doing your own thing and a woman having half a dozen lovers in a week if she wished and smoking dope and living in a caravan painted in bright flower-power colours.

Its exact onset was at different times for different women. For the radicals and intellectuals among the female population, feminism dawned in the final years of the sixties. It burst on a larger public in 1970 with Germaine Greer's groundbreaking book *The Female Eunuch*. It urged women almost for the first time since the suffragettes to question their status, to scrutinise the inequality of their daily lives and understand how much they were at the beck and call of men. It was not an unreason-able argument. But in its infancy, to anyone but the most enlightened, the battle appeared undignified, and unnecessary. Particularly as those at the centre seemed, well, so unladylike. They looked to me like rowdy, uncouth sorts, who wanted to declare their love for other women or publicise their belief that men were to be not just despised, but hated.

When it came into my consciousness I took a very aloof view. What, after all, could the movement offer me? Why should I alter the ways taught to me by my mother, who had amassed a small fortune without even knowing how to spell inequality? Let alone complain of it.

So, no, I didn't seize on *The Female Eunuch* and announce it had changed my life, as many of my generation and future generations would do. I didn't need Germaine. As far as I could see, she was banging on about matters that were irrelevant to someone brought up with a career mother who now had a career herself. Who had ever shown me any discrimination? And why on earth should I hate men? They weren't important enough to hate, for goodness' sake.

As for the tyranny of life for a woman, I knew the pit-falls, thank you very much. I'd read Margaret Drabble. Where my mother left off Margaret Drabble had taken over. I've never seen Drabble credited with being a precursor to feminism. But she was my guiding light. I suppose I have merged several of her early books into one in my head. But as I saw it the plots went like this. Two ambitious, intelligent young people meet at university and marry. They move to Hampstead or Kentish Town. He goes to work in some clever profession like publishing. She does too until she becomes pregnant and then she is at home in her stripped-pine kitchen with her little ones and the au pair, while her husband becomes increasingly unreasonable and cruel and, of course, unfaithful. My friend Jilly once remarked wryly that she never had to read a Drabble novel because she was living the life. Her husband had abandoned her. Leaving four children. But not the au pair, who went with him.

For me the message was already crystal clear. Get a job that makes you independent. Whatever you do, do not become reliant on a husband who will wander once he has the opportunity. No surprise that, as the cracks appeared in my marriage, I clung on so desperately to the bit of my life that was working.

To make matters worse at home, out of the blue Charlie was promoted to sports editor at the *Daily Mail*. He now automatically worked every Sunday. There was no sign of a baby. There was every sign the marriage was in an irreversible decline.

In desperation, I asked to see Harry Evans. It was an idea I discussed with no one before I went in. I said I had a problem with my marriage. My husband was working every Sunday in his new job, I was working every Saturday; could he do anything to help? I remember him looking first at his shoes. Then at my shoes. Slowly his eyes travelled up my body and stopped at my neck. Our eyes never met. Here was a man celebrated for his groundbreaking journalism, but a man as out of his depth as the next when it came to the personal dilemmas of his female staff. It was unimaginable that any of his male journalists would have presented him with such a request. I was a woman in 1968, grappling with a career less and less successfully and with an already shaky marriage. Harry promised to 'look into things'. I never heard another word.

There was no useful measuring stick to quantify the dismal state of affairs at home. Only the guilt of knowing that if my mother had been privy to even half of what was going on she would have arrived in the middle of the night and taken me away.

In cosy Canonbury, or not so cosy Canonbury, ignoring Germaine and indeed her sisters in America, our social life continued to revolve around the local, the Canonbury Tavern. We both worked long hours. We would end most days with a bottle of red wine. And roll into bed. What weekends we had were spent with the local friends I somehow never felt at home with.

At the *Sunday Times*, the people I worked with seemed to have fuller lives, more interesting and more carefree than mine. I looked on from the sidelines. It was in the autumn of 1969 that I fell into an affair. I say fell into because typically I didn't sit down and plan it. It was not calculated. He was a member of the

Insight team. Tall and gregarious. If not a titled barrister he was built along the same lines. He was also married. It began with the odd lunch date. We somehow contrived to spend an evening together in Leicester. I prepared myself for the night to come by arriving at the hotel several drinks ahead. That way I wouldn't have to think too long or hard about what I was getting into. I simply wanted someone to hold and cuddle me who wouldn't the next morning be listing my shortcomings. Sex wasn't the point, uncritical companionship was. I didn't realise that my chosen companion was a man unhappy in *his* home life who took his pleasures as they became available. He was gentle, comforting, funny, but not in any way committed to me. Our only common thread was that he too was tired of the endless rows at home. The other thing I didn't realise was that I was already pregnant.

There was never any real question of the occasional lover and me having a future. But the fact that I had so casually moved from virgin to young bride to adulteress in a few short years was pretty shocking. It left no room for denying that the marriage had sunk beyond repair. Once I was sure about the pregnancy, I told no one. Instead I went back to the elderly doctor in Harley Street who had helped arrange my abortion. I asked him to speak to Charlie and tell him that medically it would be unwise for me to give birth. He did as he was asked. Charlie went berserk. It took only a few minutes of vigorous interrogation to establish there were no medical grounds to stop me having the baby and the doctor got off the phone, embarrassed he'd been rumbled. Charlie's second reaction was to argue his legal rights. He said that the baby was as much his as mine and I could not destroy his child without his permission. I thought, quietly, he had a reasonable point. (Thirty-one years on, in March 2001, I note a man goes to court in Coventry to seek an injunction on the same grounds. He fails.) Charlie gave up talk of making legal trouble after a few days. I imagined that maybe he had consulted a solicitor and was told he was wasting his time. Instead, he moved on to alternately bullying and begging me.

In the end, time sorted the outcome. A termination at eight weeks was possible. One at twelve was emotionally and physically far more difficult. I gave up the fight. We bought a bright orange and white rug at Casa Pupo, the Spanish shop in Pimlico, to celebrate the decision and tried to look bravely and optimistically at our soon-to-be roles as parents. Easier said than done.

One night, we came to blows yet again. Once more, having had a few drinks, the anger around the house got worse. It needed very little to spark us off.

It was during this time I remember discovering that if a gin made you feel better facing a husband in the evening, it would work just as well on a Sunday morning. Particularly when Charlie was at work and the even more occasional lover – now he knew I was pregnant – was hardly ever in contact.

It was an appalling start for any baby. I tried not to think too much about the future, except to cling to the absolute knowledge that I needed to continue to work, to allow myself the freedom to leave my husband.

In 1970 it was still tricky beyond bohemian circles to have a child outside marriage. Women didn't become estate agents. They didn't become accountants. They didn't become stockbrokers. They didn't become newspaper editors. There was nothing to say that they couldn't and, true enough, in every profession you could look and find an exception. But these women never talked in public about any problems they encountered – if they had, we might have been more prepared. Those that struggled at home with children, with resentful husbands jealous of their wives' abilities and earning power, kept it a secret. If they had to make compromises to ease the despair and discontentment of a spouse doing less well, they did so silently.

Most of the exceptions didn't have children. Those that did somehow managed to be in two places at once. Or else have no truck with the notion that they needed to contribute 'quality time' at home. My mother, in business, and a young Margaret Thatcher, scaling the heights of the Conservative Party, both being of this school. My mother didn't allow anyone to make her feel guilty. If they had tried she would have assumed they were jealous of her.

In the brief, heady days of my engagement to Frank we had been to a gathering thrown by one of his friends in a large, airy Holland Park flat. Present had been a coterie of wives of journalists on the *Guardian*. The women were different from the wives I knew. They were graduates who were the academic equals of their husbands but now stayed at home with young children. I must have announced my intention to continue to work after I was married and to do so even if I had children. 'A nanny to look after your children?' one of them shrieked, as though I had suggested an axe murderer. The others nodded in agreement, showing varying degrees of pity or puzzlement. Their disapproval largely went over my head. Just as well. It would be three decades or so before I would cotton on to their true feelings. What they were thinking, whether they knew it or not, wasn't 'How dare you do this to your children?' but 'How dare you get away with it?'

The *Sunday Times*, in common with the rest of Fleet Street, had no maternity leave arrangements in place. The BBC had recently introduced eight weeks' paid leave for pregnant women. But it was out on its own.

The managing editor of the paper agreed I too could have eight weeks' paid leave. But I would be excluded from any pay rises until it was seen whether I was capable of giving my full attention to my job as a reporter on my return. The news editor grudgingly conceded to this but made no bones about his determination to get his money's worth before I left. Which is how he ended up sending me, seven months pregnant, to cover the crowds circling the stadium at the Wembley Cup Final. Ironically Charlie, in his capacity as a sports editor, was inside the ground in a VIP seat. He naturally saw nothing odd in my presence outside.

About a month before the baby was due, and by then on maternity leave, I had my first call from the sisterhood. Well, sort of. Unity Hall had long had a thing about not being able to join her husband at El Vino, the wine bar in Fleet Street, because women were forbidden to stand at the front of the Establishment. They could enter only if there were seats available in the back room. I had no beef about it whatsoever. I never used El Vino. But when Unity joined with Anna Coote, a far more politically minded journalist, and others to protest she asked me to join the fray. I was delighted for an excuse to get out.

We marched into El Vino. Geoffrey Van Hay, the tall, emotional and, as I discovered years later, rather kind manager, attempted to eject us. He came off worst. With cuts and bruises and God knows what else. Pictures were taken. The *Evening Standard* reported the fiasco in full. Hugh Cudlipp, then boss at the *Daily Mirror*, who had apparently for years resented the Establishment, gave it a similar show. (Although how it could have interested his working-class readers is another matter.) To my horror and complete surprise, it infuriated Charlie. I had rung him when it was over. Rather than finding the whole thing a hoot, as I had done, he was ranting. How did I think it reflected on him? One of his *Daily Mail* colleagues, a foreign correspondent, had apparently witnessed the scenes and gone back to the office, deploring our action. How did I think the *Sunday Times* would look on a reporter they had had the decency to grant maternity leave? he asked. My fun day had been destroyed. Like my mother, his reactions were impossible to predict. Like her, it seemed one day you were applauded for being you, the next you were being scolded and punished. Could I get anything right?

As if the marriage needed anything more to destabilise it, my mother stepped in to 'rescue and control'. She insisted I had the baby in Liverpool at Park House, the reliable nursing home run by nuns where my brother and I had been born. She arranged for me to see the city's top gynaecologist. And I agreed. Thoughtless but, perhaps, unconsciously relieved.

The gynaecologist had a considerable reputation. But it was long before pregnancy had reached the sacred, hallowed ground of today. I smoked and drank champagne throughout the nine months without anyone raising an eyebrow. In the run-up Charlie and my mother kept their relationship to one of manageable dislike. He was angered by her commandeering events. His distrust of her had heightened after one of his early weekend visits when she had produced a meal of cold chicken and hot sauce for him but cooked me a steak. I had not realised how bad this looked to Charlie or how he would take it amiss – which I should have. If I had, I would have told her to stop. But my mother had always regarded her children as special and different and I suppose I still took it for granted. Only when we got upstairs did Charlie let rip.

My mother couldn't have cared less. She had failed to recover from the news, revealed by my brother, in whom I had confided, that Charlie and I had fought physically more than once. She had also learnt that the Canonbury house for which she had willingly provided the deposit of £2,000 was, at Charlie's insistence, in his name only. It made her furious, and she was little mollified when I received my share when Charlie and I were divorced.

Where could I run? I had a mother and a husband who both expected to be taken notice of, yet saw everything differently. I felt like a bruised volleyball.

Emma was a forceps birth. She arrived at seven o'clock, on the morning of 18 July 1970. You could just see the red hair on the back of her neck. I was up to my eyes in painkillers, for this was before doctors and midwives gave mothers options about their treatment. Or insisted on antenatal classes. I could barely take in my new baby, wonderful, beautiful as she was. Everything surrounding her arrival cried doom and gloom and misery.

Bringing a new baby home to Canonbury was scary too. The nuns at Park House had taught me how to bath her and how to feed her. But their instructions, which I had written down, now seemed very inadequate. I was in charge of a little person. It was hard to believe. Babies had never been part of my Blundellsands childhood. My mother's friends were never other mothers. Babies were things we visited only long enough to hand over for the newborn a couple of crisp white notes 'to start the child's own bank account'.

Nevertheless, as with married life, I knew that Emma and I were somehow separate from the happy-ever-after dreams that a young woman felt she was entitled to. My new baby and I existed in a bubble. I cuddled her, I nursed her. I went prampushing around Canonbury. As always, there were strangers admiring her. I faithfully changed her on her little plastic mattress and talcum-powdered her dozens of times a day. Struggling with big ugly nappy pins. I don't recall disposable nappies being an option. Even if they were, it would have been another rule from Blundellsands that we continued to use the finest-quality towelling nappy and suffered the ugly, giant safety pins. Then there was the ongoing headache of the powdered SMA milk that my mother repeatedly referred to as 'MCC'. Another malapropism had been to tell everyone that Emma had been in an 'incinerator' for the first few days of her life.

In the absence of any maternal guidance in Alwyne Square, or morning television, or literature other than the standard Dr Spock, I continued to get my teaching from the Sheila Kitzinger of Crosby (my mother). This included the order to put Emma outside in her pram 'well wrapped up' and make sure her nighties were hand-washed. We had bought out George Henry Lee's in baby attire. Especially a new kind of towelling romper suit, ranging in colour from navy blue to turquoise. I dressed Emma in them each day. Not appreciating that half the activity required of a new mother was to change her baby's clothes to pretty stuff during daylight hours, even if she was in her pram. Emma was beautifully presented but not in pretty, pretty gear. Maybe that explains her love of party frocks now.

I had at least half a dozen magnificent white christening robes which friends of my mother had given me. They went unused. Emma was never officially christened. (Years later my mother told Emma that she and Auntie Barbara had baptised her as a baby – with a jug of water and a prayer. Rudimentary, but acceptable as the real thing, as far as the Catholic Church was concerned.)

Our home was filled with confusion, suspicion and an ever-present feeling of resentment and loss on both sides. Whatever magic had brought her parents together had gone. Her father was disappointed at how his married life had turned out. Her mother was desperate to be freed from a husband whom she saw as a despot.

Yet, oddly, for all his chauvinism, for all his disgust at me not knowing my place, Charlie turned out to be a doting father. His office hours were no less onerous. The newspaper still had his first call. But when he was home he would change nappies, push the pram, get up for the middle-of-the-night feeds. Rather than help matters it made them worse. Why if he could be so tender with our daughter was he so vile to me?

In any case, playing Mrs Wilson, wife and mother, full time was short-lived. My total maternity leave was three months. Six weeks before the birth and six weeks after. We hired a young girl from Yorkshire as a nanny and I went back to work. I had no option. I had never expected any other outcome. And I refused to allow myself the luxury of contemplating how preferable it would be to stay at home. Some weeks, by working a late Saturday, I had three days in a row with Emma. I persuaded myself it made up for the missing nights of Wednesdays and Thursdays, when I was sometimes away on a story. Returning to work was my only chance of an exit from my marriage. But for a preciously short time I had the uninterrupted joy of a smiling, incredibly well-behaved, weeks-old infant, with her tufts of red hair growing, but not fast. Her little fingers always anxious to grip mine. There was the pleasure of seeing her first smile. Of learning to recognise the difference between a hunger pain, a wind pain, a come-and-get-me-I'm-bored squeal and a come-and-get-me-or-I'll-never-stop squeal.

My mother was of the school that said you left a screaming baby to cry until it exhausted itself. Except I noticed, when I was home with her, having told me this, she went upstairs, or sent my father up to sit with Emma or cuddle her until she stopped.

I remember wondering why there was so little guidance on how to move my baby from milk to solid food. Charlie and I were obliged to work it out as best we could. For once his opinions and decisions sounded no wiser than mine did.

Why did he now berate me not just as a rotten wife but a useless mother? The more he dressed me down the more I gave myself excuses to drink. The more pissed I was the more vicious became my tongue. The more vicious my tongue the more disgusted Charlie became. Somehow we never rationally discussed his lack of feeling or harshness. The rows seemed to revolve around my shortcomings. Why should I put up with it? Why indeed, agreed my mother. She wrote me out a cheque for £4,000. And when Emma was just a little under nine months old I bought a flat at the other end of Islington, hired a new nanny, called the removal people and left.

10

Giving Up Pretences

Thirty-one Noel Road was an upper maisonette that cost me £8,000. It had just enough room. The nanny and Emma shared one bedroom. I had the other. There was a bathroom in the roof space, a small sitting room and a kitchen. The first Sunday after we moved in a young man turned up on the doorstep. He was John Penrose. We had kept in touch since my year at the agency. He had occasionally popped round to Canonbury and shared his excitements, cars, girls, and over-the-top plans for buying and restoring this dilapidated Georgian building or that undiscovered Wapping wharf. He lived with his parents at the top of Noel Road, in Duncan Terrace. Like many pockets of Islington, this part of N1 was now partly gentrified. The grand Georgian houses that had become offices and factories before the war were gradually being brought back into single domestic ownership. Penrose's father was the manager of a shoe-trim manufacturer's. The factory was based in one of these large houses and the Penrose family, his parents and his sister, five years younger, lived rent free on the top two floors.

His mother Anna was Italian. His father Ray had been in the RAF and attached to the Eighth Army that had liberated Naples where they met. Ray had returned, as promised, to claim his bride a year after the war was over. Anna was warm, hospitable and a wonderful cook. Her Sunday lunches were famous because everyone was welcome. Penrose insisted on taking me and my baby along.

Feeling alone and scared and fully pondering for the first time the wisdom of my actions, I felt this kind, funny young man, who had no judgement about what I had chosen to do, was heaven sent. He was a wonderful combination of the obsessive and the easygoing. He adored decent clothes. He was charming and generous even when stony broke, which was often. He also knew everyone. Camden Passage, which in the sixties had developed from a collection of small shops (a newsagent's, an umbrella repairman, a butcher's) into an array of antique shops, was his stamping ground. That and the handful of restaurants and pubs that surrounded it.

As a schoolboy, Penrose had raided his mother's attic and rented a stall in the Saturday antiques market in the Passage held on a vacant piece of land that had been bombed in the war. Anna had taken over her son's stall and now rented a small shop of her own, dealing in silver. Meanwhile, Penrose had progressed from the *Islington Gazette* to work full time for John Rodgers and had then been hired as a *Daily Mirror* reporter where he had been marked out as a star.

Oddly, he had never wanted a journalistic career. He was set for Chelsea Art School, quite rightly for someone with his artistic talent. It was his father, who had an evening hobby job as a props man at Sadler's Wells theatre near by, who unwittingly changed his mind by getting him a holiday position as a tea boy at the local paper. Dressers, scene-shifters, members of the chorus, all gathered in the pub next door to the opera house during lulls in the evening performance. The editor of the *Gazette* was also a regular and a friend of Penrose's father. The deal was done over a pint. Neither of Penrose's parents was in the least bossy with their adored son. When he worked at the agency he would go missing for days and when Rodgers phoned his mother she would say forlornly, in her wonderful Neapolitan

way, 'He wenta-outta-for a-packetta-of-cigarette-on Tuesday-
and-we-never-see-him-since.'

Penrose, of course, was all Charlie was not. Irresponsible,
shocking with money. Hopeless when it came to turning up
anywhere on time. In all, a joy to be with. He was a good two
years younger than me but it mattered less now. Within a few
months he ceased to be the boy playmate he had been before I
married. He became instead lover, best friend, shoulder to cry
on and provider of entertainment.

In contrast to Canonbury, which was only down the road, the
Angel and Barnsbury end of Islington was buzzing and every bit
as fashionable and bohemian as the King's Road. The local pubs,
which included the Island Queen, a hang-out for rock stars, were
packed with a wonderful mixture of musicians, artists, actors,
writers, film-set designers, antique dealers, fruit and veg stall-
owners, market porters, bank robbers and journalists.

Cyril Cusack would stagger in for a pint. His daughter Sinead,
who also lived locally, was making headlines because of her
friendship with a young Georgie Best. Fran and Jay Landesman,
poetess and underground publisher, held court in their magnificent house in Duncan Terrace, a few doors along from the
Penrose household.

Hardly anyone looked to have a 'proper' job. At the Island
Queen, games of chess would take place in corners and lasted for
days. On Sunday mornings the robbers, antique dealers and
stall-owners stood out, for they were in their Sunday best. The
rest of us made sure our suits and day clothes were never seen.

'You're a man of education,' one of the robbers said kindly to
our friend John Grigsby, who had landed himself a job on the
Daily Telegraph, 'wouldn't it help you to get on, son, if you
smartened up a bit?'

I don't suppose our discussions of the arts, politics and literature were any more profound or more in evidence than in
Canonbury, but I felt much more at home. This did not mean I
was settled or content. Far from it. Trying to combine the

rigours of the *Sunday Times* with single motherhood, albeit with a live-in nanny, was confusing and difficult. I'd be there for Emma's breakfast, dash out to the office, rush home at lunchtime if not out of town on a job, stay in at night until she went to sleep, check constantly with the nanny if I was away. On my own, I would nip to the off-licence and buy a quarter of gin to sup at home. It did the trick. I was aware that for all the roistering and sinking of alcohol, it was not the way anyone else around me behaved. Particularly not Penrose, who studiously differentiated between his leisure time, out drinking and being wild and sociable, and his conscientiously sober working days and nights.

By now, the letters from Charlie's solicitors were coming in thick and fast. They accused me of adultery and made it plain that my husband intended to fight for custody of our daughter. Charlie had issued proceedings. Papers were served on my former *Sunday Times* lover and on Penrose, who seemed only proud to be named in such a celebrated couple's divorce.

(There had not been, of course, the slightest chance of my relationship with my lover continuing. After the birth of Emma he had vanished like the proverbial puff of smoke.)

Shortly after I moved out of Alwyne Square, Charlie had accepted the job of deputy editor of the *Daily Mail* in Manchester. To begin with he rented a flat and commuted down at weekends to see Emma. After a while our relationship became less fraught. Somehow I convinced myself I should reconsider what now seemed like a too hasty exit from the marriage.

Let us not imagine that I counted the reasons. Or even voiced them. I acted in the same impetuous, thoughtless, self-willed way I had over getting married in the first place. Let's get it done! Let's tick it off the list! Let us not think too closely about what we are doing lest the noise of thinking scares the horses!

But there were several excuses. The sight of Emma crying as she left her father was distressing. To be fair, she did exactly the same when he collected her and she was leaving me. But I told myself I should reconsider. If I had dug a bit deeper I would have acknowledged that the dread of an embittered court case, which would involve a fight for the custody of Emma, was unnerving to say the least.

The tone of the letters which Charlie's solicitor had been sending me made clear in a bullying manner that there was every reason to suppose a court would look favourably on Charlie's bid to be the more suitable parent to look after our baby daughter. When I was first served with the divorce papers I had sought the help of the *Sunday Times*' solicitors Theodore Goddard. The bills for a few consultations alarmed me. But the man I saw felt confident that all would be well. 'The mother always gets the child', he said.

Then Charlie got to work. His solicitor skilfully wrote the kind of letter guaranteed to rock my confidence and panic me. It didn't take long before the threats and accusations about my unsuitability as a mother on the grounds of my drinking, my adultery, my career ambitions had me believing that I was facing a huge fight. Charlie had sought an affidavit from a nanny we had hired. The girl was an ex-cadet nurse, who had behaved so badly that I did not think her testimony would stand up. But it was the first warning of the depth of feelings of my husband. Also by this time a female member of Theodore Goddard was handling my divorce. At our first meeting she told me she thought things looked ugly. I was appalled. It seemed the reason solicitors said, 'The mother always gets the child,' was simply because fathers rarely contested the idea. A few tough letters from Charlie's side and we looked to be only a move away from the suggestion that I cave in. Yet I knew that however bad on paper my being away from home and at the office, my devotion to journalism and my taste for champagne might look, it was matched by equal absences on Charlie's part. He argued that he always slept and woke up in our house, while I was often out of town. I argued that he arrived home far too late to see Emma. And as for the drinking he had spilt more than I had drunk, although I was aware that the effect of alcohol on me was far worse than it was on him.

In a panic, I shot the messenger. I sacked Theodore Goddard and at the suggestion of a barrister acquaintance, whom I had met at a party and who had taken me to the opera, I moved on to another firm.

The new solicitor, with offices in Park Lane, was a wiry little man, not much older than I was, and he seemed ready for a good old fight. He knew Charlie's solicitor. They had done battle before. He agreed we had an uphill struggle on our hands but one that I could win. Nevertheless, full of fear for the future and the possibility that I would lose my baby, I donned the metaphorical rose-tinted glasses. In no time I was hotfooting it up to the north for weekend visits. With my estranged husband I viewed an enchanting farmhouse on the border of Cheshire and Derbyshire in the Peak District National Park. I urged him to buy it. He did. I told the *Sunday Times* of my plans to try to make a go of things with Charlie.

The news editor, with permission from Harry Evans, offered to allow me to work from my new home and travel from there. I hung on to my Islington flat, just in case. But I ignored the warnings of my mother, my girlfriends, my solicitor. Like a lamb to slaughter I went. Sometimes, against the rules of better journalism, there is no substitute for an old-fashioned cliché to illustrate a point: it was like taking candy from a baby.

Once installed, I started writing the fairy-tale script. We bought a red setter puppy, four unbroken Welsh ponies and agreed to adopt the cat belonging to the previous owners. (Actually a wild one, which like most cats was happy to come indoors if food was provided.) We also bought some chickens. St Francis of Assisi would have approved.

Welcome to the happy home of Mr and Mrs Charles Wilson.

Except you cannot make a script come to life unless you can act convincingly. We were still the same two people we had always been. Only more so. Charlie remained vigilant and suspicious, critical and prone to anger. Did he see my move back as a clever way to get the upper hand in the fight for Emma? Was there ever a time he truly thought we could make it? I never doubted he had been shocked and hurt by the collapse of the marriage and that no one could have convinced him that he had a single thing to reproach himself for. No one knew the way he behaved at home. To the outside world, particularly his male colleagues, he had wed a wild, unruly, wayward, rude girl who showed no signs of being a stay-at-home wife and mother. His solicitor was tailor-made to assist a wronged husband, who felt he'd been humiliated and robbed of happiness.

Charlie said he thought and prayed we could make it work, but my belief was that, as a betting man, he must have worked out there was nothing to lose by giving the marriage a second chance. At best, here was an opportunity to put everything back together again. At worst, I would need no assistance in demonstrating my woeful lack of commitment to a happy home life.

My time in the north is still painful and hard to write about. Like so much of this marriage, it needs to be balanced. Our faults were massive. In times of fear and distress, decent human beings do bad things to each other. I believed then and I believe now that paid legal advisers, the threats these so-called professionals make in an effort to force a victory, the courts and the judges, can cause irreparable damage. We were young parents. We both came to feel cheated, betrayed, fearful and nearly destroyed by the experience – if for different reasons. Our only pride is that we emerged on the other side. We are still parents to a bright, loving, funny and beautiful young woman.

As deputy editor of the *Daily Mail* 'brackets Manchester', as I would add mockingly so many times during that year, Charlie was an important part of the newspaper scene. And very much the boss.

I had no training in toadying to superiors; quite the opposite. I failed to grasp the lengths to which the average person will go to please those in the professional hierarchy. After all, there are mortgages to be paid, rises to seek. So, before long, we had a circle of friends, most of whom worked for Charlie. They were delighted to come to our house with their children. We were generous and lively hosts. Being surrounded by others was easier than facing each other.

For a while, from the outside, it looked cosy and promising.

When he was at home you couldn't fault Charlie's devotion to Emma. He played with her, talked to her, dressed her, bathed her. To watch them together was delightful. But, as I had discovered in Canonbury, this tenderness stopped at Emma. He was one thing as a father, another as a husband. To his wife he was resentful, guarded, sceptical and mistrustful. Always the keeper of his castle. What I had somehow forgotten was his temper. His bullying ways. He was daily appalled by my attitude, by my intransigence, my ridiculing of him. His response of interrogating me reduced me to a shivering wreck. Higher Cliff Farm never felt like *ours*. It was *his* and I was the barely tolerated guest. And again I was lonely. As always, Charlie's first devotion was to his newspaper. Did I feel trapped? You bet I did. Only more so.

But Emma's development was magical. She was always a happy, contented child with, from the earliest age, an enchanting, captivating sense of humour. She was delightfully fearless. She adored the dog, the cat, the horses. Instead of this bringing me joy it made me even more confused. If she was enjoying herself in this fairy-tale setting, how could I take her away again? Then again, how could I live with a man who despised me?

I helped take away the pain by drinking. Without an office to go to, I could start earlier in the day, sleep off the effect and be upright again in the evening if and when Charlie came home in time for dinner. There were also the endlessly long phone calls with Penrose. I missed my cheery mate, who rarely made harsh judgements about me or anybody.

What was to become of me? My only regular companion was the nanny I had in London who had agreed to come north with

Emma and me. Fiona was a middle-class girl, who had dated several of my *Sunday Times* colleagues. She was a godsend because she knew what was going on. She could also sink enough drink at the end of the day's duties to make me look like an amateur. We spent evening after evening together as Charlie worked all the hours available to bring the northern *Daily Mail* up to his exacting standards.

To add to my bag full of woes my mother, now less than a two-hour journey away, began to circle. She distrusted her son-in-law. She recognised the dangers of my predicament and would regularly telephone to warn me that 'he'll end up wiping your eye'.

Meanwhile, the *Sunday Times*' Manchester office would send me on various stories. I made several more visits to Northern Ireland. I took on the Scottish beat as we had no correspondent there.

In Glasgow, a local freelance who supplied stories for the *Sunday Times* would ring me with ideas. In the early part of the week for a Sunday paper, freelances with possible leads are useful to get the news operation up and running. This particular man had, like my brother, been to a Catholic boarding school. He was bright and gentle, and after a while provided another shoulder to cry on. We never had an affair because he wasn't the least interested. Neither, frankly, was I. But he would call me and listen to me for hours. He would travel to meet me. He was another Penrose.

Unknown to me, Charlie was checking my phone calls and had put a private eye on my tail when I went to Scotland. Nothing was proved, because there was nothing *to* prove.

At first I couldn't quite believe that Charlie was back on my case, seriously tracking my movements. But after I switched hotels on a visit – only because of an overbooking and without telling him – he rang in a furious state. Even I began to smell a rat.

Later that same night there was the comical sight of two men in the corner of the Central Hotel in Glasgow. Both were in raincoats. Surely not? I told myself it was ludicrous to suppose they were watching me. But I must have been worried, because I moved from the room and out of the hotel only to find they were behind me. I was with a gang of journalists. We went back into the hotel, ordered another round of drinks and laughed ourselves stupid.

But it wasn't funny. A large noose dangled. I moved effortlessly towards it.

Fiona the nanny announced she was leaving. She had only ever said she would come north as a stop-gap. We hired a local girl from the next village. Within another couple of months Charlie and I had given up all pretences. He was convinced I was having an affair. One weekend he pulled a mattress out of the spare room and insisted in future I slept on it on the floor in our bedroom, instead of in the marital bed.

There was now no question of my fleeing for a second time with Emma. He sought and was granted an injunction to ensure she remained at Higher Cliff Farm. I had never seen him so angry on a daily basis. At least first time round when it had got that bad I had been able to disappear without worrying about the consequences. Now I was a prisoner. As far as I was aware the jolly gang of his newspaper colleagues knew nothing. So they were still arriving to party and enjoy our hospitality.

Charlie remained 100 per cent convinced that I had been the one to cause cracks in the marriage; he was full to the brim with indignation. I had been unfaithful with two men. Not unfaithful once, but twice, he would say over and over again. He unashamedly doted on his daughter. He didn't feel he had behaved badly as a husband. Why should he? No one had witnessed his anger, his moods, his jealousies. On paper, I was the guilty party. For him and his generation unreasonable behaviour, mental cruelty – the less provable, less definable causes of the breakdown of a marriage – didn't exist.

A wife committing adultery, and not just a wife but a *mother*,

My parents' wedding reception. Reece's Café, Liverpool. August Bank Holiday, 1937.

My father in his handmade officer's uniform. He was a captain in the Royal Artillery.

Crowds At Spectacular Bootle Wedding

Miss Anne Wilson Weds Mr. Bernard J. Robinson

TO HONEYMOON ON THE RIVIERA

A SPECTACULAR wedding gown of hammered pewter satin, the material having been specially woven for her, was worn by Miss Anne Josephine Wilson when she was married to Mr Bernard James Robinson at St James' Church on Monday morning.

From the *Bootle Times*, 6 August 1937: 'The wedding attracted crowds of people to the church, and guests had considerable difficulty in walking from their cars to the church door.'

My mother looking elegant – even on the Mersey Ferry.

The Grand National, 1950. My mother's hat was featured on Pathé News.

A Swiss sunhat my parents had brought back from a trip to Geneva. It probably cost a chunk of the £25 allowance then permitted to be taken abroad.

Me, in an early bikini, with Peter and my parents outside the Carlton Hotel.

A Blundellsands princess, aged eight.

With my pony, Princess, at the Formby Show.

Teenage portrait – aged fourteen.

With Rosemary Abbot at Farnborough Hill – someone else who knew how to curtsey.

'Pacesetting' reporter on the old broad-sheet *Sun*. At the Ideal Home Exhibition with David Hicks.

Marriage to Charlie, January 1968.

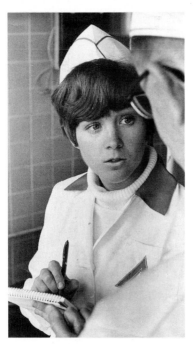

Sunday Times reporter, investigating hygiene in the milk-making process.

The *Daily Mail* Air Race, 1969. London–New York.

With baby Emma.

My mother and father on a cruise on the QEII in the late seventies.

Emma and sunglasses – at St Michael's Road, Blundellsands.

Emma aged two and a half.

Emma, featured in a fashion shoot for the *Evening News*.

Emma and Guinness on the canal holiday. The dog was anxious to get to the car.

'Penrose has broken his leg in three places – the King and Keys, the White Swan and El Vino.' Cartoon by Sallon.

Marriage to Johnny. Finsbury Town Hall, March 1980.

Austria. Skiing during the day and trying to plan the rest of my life in the evenings.

With Robin Day.

With Maxwell at one of his parties.

Emma, the film-maker, on her graduation day from New York University.

At Sissinghurst with Nigel Nicolson, Jill and Michael Foot.

With two husbands: Charlie and Johnny.

My father at Field House, Gloucestershire, in the last year of his life.

A degree – if only honorary.

With Johnny at my surprise fiftieth birthday party.

Emma.

was shocking. The act did not need to be measured against what had precipitated it. Her adultery, particularly if it had taken place in the marital home (mine didn't), came into a quite different and more unacceptable category than, say, a working husband playing away. Having a jolly time screwing a variety of women when at an out-of-town sales conference or a stag night hardly counted, be it a father or just a husband. The fact that men had the chance to commit adultery outside the home while a wife's choice of venue was limited was another example of how equality of opportunity did not exist.

As for the right of a woman, wife and mother to be tried and judged on an equal footing to a man, husband, father. Whoever heard of such nonsense?

The atmosphere was horrible, distressing, and I was more anxious and fearful than ever. Not least when my solicitor rang one Sunday with shattering news. Charlie had returned to the fight, and had also obtained affidavits from our current nanny and from Fiona about my unfitness as a mother.

('Fiona and I only kissed, we never had an affair,' he was to say during our custody battle for Emma. A total shock to me who never knew anything at all had gone on. But perhaps he thought I did. Why else would he admit this?)

Lined up with the nannies were at least half a dozen of the journalists who worked for Charlie. 'Friends' who regularly came to our home, whom I welcomed and cooked for. One had asked me if she could have my job on the *Sunday Times* if I considered giving it up, for Christ's sake. But all of these journalists (in their different ways) had given sworn statements about Charlie's superior talents as a parent. They detailed my absences from home. My ridiculing of my husband. My drinking.

If I had done the same about several of them, cataloguing their drinking and their behaviour – most were high-living, heavy-drinking people – various wives and husbands could have gone to court to plead for their children's welfare. They knew that. I knew that. Without delay, I insisted my solicitor must seek similar testimonies from my colleagues at the *Sunday Times*. The whole circus was horrifying.

But at this stage there were no affidavits on my side. Only the copies of statements from Charlie's friends on my solicitor's desk. He would shake his head at yet another example of the thoroughness of my husband's case. There was no mistaking Charlie's determination to win. Even I gave up on the jokes as I began to grasp the depth of his feeling of indignation. His fight for custody of Emma was to involve all the gritty determination that had been the hallmark of his journalistic career. Getting there first, as my mother had warned me, and 'wiping the eye of the enemy'. His will to succeed was fuelled by his sense of having been wronged.

Charlie says he felt that at this stage of my life I was not capable of looking after Emma, but he was also a husband who felt publicly damaged by this uncontrollable, ridiculing, irresponsible, young no-good wife.

'Lawyers did not perform for Charlie,' one of them would say to me twenty years on. 'Charlie provided us with evidence that would rank among the finest of any Fleet Street investigation.' Not only was every stone turned. The soil was dug, and the earth and the dirt were thrown in increasingly alarming and effective quantities at the enemy.

The enemy tragically was at the time so centred on the awfulness of her husband and her need to escape, she failed for a long time to make a single phone call to mount a counter-offensive.

The line about 'the mother always gets the child' was not ringing in my ears any more. Now my solicitor, who at his urging I had secretly called during a Sunday lunch in Cheshire at some new friends of Charlie's, was saying, 'This is very bad, very worrying news indeed.'

The gloves were off. But it was to be another four or five months before the case came to court. We had to remain at Higher Cliff Farm. For me to leave without Emma was out of the question. The only concession was an agreement by both solicitors that I would not have to tolerate the local nanny who so disapproved of me under my roof. She went the next week. A temporary girl arrived in her place. A man from the local Social Services department was sent to assess us both. I remember his grammar being all over the place. I remember having a few sharp drinks before he turned up. I remember praying like never before that he hadn't noticed my state. How come when it was most important for me to be sober, upright and together, I did exactly the opposite?

How come I would go days without a drink and then, just when it mattered, get plastered? I didn't understand what was happening to me. It was vital I pulled myself together. I knew that. If I hadn't, my mother, now on my case in a major way, was telling me to do so on the phone each morning. She would turn up unexpectedly with my father in tow. She would be horribly pleasant to Charlie, who was not fooled. At one stage, to help, she hired a private eye and a photographer, convinced that Charlie, who was frequently missing in the evenings, was enjoying himself with another woman. He wasn't; he was in his office. I shrugged my shoulders. Unfit for the fight. It was a bleak, desperate, horrible period. I wanted the court case over. Yet I was terrified of the outcome. I lived in dread of the time when the other shoe would drop.

Christmas Day 1972 was cold, cheerless, miserable. Without warning, that night Charlie gathered up Emma and drove off with her to stay with his solicitor. I felt more wretched than ever before. I was left alone at the farmhouse. What was to become of Emma and me?

11

'I do not find her an unfit mother'

The Family Division of the Law Courts. A Monday morning in March 1973. The beginning of a fortnight I can only look back on through deeply etched snapshots.

My mother in the previous week had marched me to George Henry Lee's in Liverpool and bought me two new suits by Mansfield. One was canary yellow with a thick navy blue ribbon on the edge of the jacket, and a skirt with boxed pleats. The other, dark blue, had a similar edging in white. The outfits might have been forgotten for ever had not Mrs Thatcher turned up in an identical yellow one at the start of her first annual party conference as Conservative leader.

From this we eventually learnt two things. First, my mother's choice of the sort of fashion suitable to set a sensible tone was as reliable as ever. Second, Mrs Thatcher hung on to her clothes. She was not to be leader of her party and appear in what became known as my 'divorce outfit' for another two years. More immediately we learnt it would take in excess of a couple of pieces of semi-haute couture to convince the judge of the suitability of a mother to bring up her daughter.

My QC was not the one I had originally chosen. To begin with I had obeyed my mother and grandly ordered my solicitor to send me to 'the finest in his field', someone appropriate to deal with the fight. Then, overnight, he had become unavailable. 'Just like that', as my father, in the hope of lightening the atmosphere, put it, mimicking his favourite comedian, Tommy Cooper.

As always, my father's attempts at jollying along the proceedings, proceedings from which he seemed strangely detached, could go either way. But when it came to the court case there was little hope of his comedy turns being well received. The times when, without notice, the ground was removed from under us became so frequent that after a while even he knew better than to crack a Tommy Cooper joke – or anyone else's. 'Could you make yourself useful, Bernie, and get us a cup of tea; we're not in the mood for a laugh,' my mother would command when my father took his chances with humour. Thus ended any chance of levity.

The loss of 'the best' was an early, depressing sign that the Bar ran on a mysterious and questionable set of rules. Rules that seemed to surprise no one except me and, of course, my mother. The previous autumn, when a degree of optimism still ran alongside our despair, 'the best' meant we had been lined up with James Comyn QC. There was no doubting his reputation and skill. Comyn, like St Jude, the patron saint of lost causes and hopeless cases, was there for those whose lives depended on his talent for swinging a jury in his favour, against all the odds. He was the SAS of advocates, particularly in criminal proceedings. He opened jails, his colleagues would say admiringly.

But as we trekked along to our first conference with him – the cheeky, chirpy solicitor's clerk in a shabby green check suit, the solicitor in a light grey one – I didn't know I might lose him. I was ushered into a huge office and across the room I saw an elderly tubby man who was smoking a Passing Cloud cigarette and who had ash down the white bib of his robes. It was a 4.30 p.m. conference and Mr Comyn was just in from court.

He appeared not in the least shocked at the evidence before him. He had asked only one question, and in a soft, kindly voice:

'Do you, Mrs Wilson, drink in the morning?' I have no idea how I replied. In any case, a drinker who drinks in the morning is as likely to admit to it as a child abuser would tick the box in a survey that asked him if he liked interfering with little boys on a regular basis.

The more detailed, truthful answer would have been that my drinking had got worse at Higher Cliff Farm. There had also been the benders, after which I wouldn't have the remotest idea if it were morning or evening. How much I drank when I woke up depended on whether I was alone in the house. What no one in the room knew was that these were just the early days in my bid to become a sensational success as an all-out soak.

No matter. Mr Comyn's general lack of disapproval registered enough for me to come away more cheerful. Soothingly, too, there were plenty of rumours about Mr Comyn and his drinking and breakdowns. He was said to suffer from severe depression. He didn't *look* as if he had problems but the pertinent question he had asked showed more knowledge and wisdom on the subject of alcoholism than anyone else I was to meet connected with my case. Alas, it would not help. Within a couple of weeks we had 'lost' Mr Comyn to a man who was accused of murdering his wife many years previously. (Then unknown to me, it is a professional obligation for members of the Bar to put defending a client accused of murder before commitments to other clients.)

In what other service industry can one of its number accept a job, listen to the evidence, get his head firmly around the subject matter, then bugger off at a moment's notice? Did I pay for the meeting? I don't know. If I did, I shouldn't have. Do others today put up with the same system in which you waste time and go through the distress of being questioned and quizzed by yet another barrister? – one who might confusingly offer entirely different advice and having done so is likewise entitled to vanish should a more attractive deal come along. Decades on, when George Carman, the most famous of libel lawyers, died of cancer, I heard Ken Dodd, the comedian, explain on the radio how he had been taken by his solicitor on a tour of potential barristers. What is known in the profession now, apparently, as the beauty parade. No such consumer choice was made available to me. Only silently did I puzzle why, since I was the founder of the feast, I had so little say in selecting who would bat on my behalf.

Had my mother been less occupied with my downfall and more acquainted with the legal system, she would have played merry hell. As it was, she insisted forever after that the barristers must surely 'drop' (bribe) solicitors to give them the work.

I could easily see how she arrived at her belief. Barristers were and are dependent on solicitors. If there is no scratching of backs it will be the only profession in which it does not exist.

But for a girl brought up to believe that money let the customer call the shots – money spoke – the experience of not being able to shout my needs or have any part in what was being arranged was just another dismal sign indicating that my life, my future, Emma's life were heading out of my control.

I was twenty-seven. I didn't know legions of influential people who could have explained matters or guided me. Nor did I have the self-confidence to state my concerns. So the second-choice QC came along as if from nowhere. Was he indeed second choice? You might well ask. Perhaps he was actually the sixth choice? How was I to know? Did I ask how many mothers with a growing reputation in the field of alcoholism had retained custody of their young daughters because of his skill? I didn't. I didn't even know that the family courts were not his area of expertise. He was, I later learnt, a good all-rounder. Things were happening to me, I wasn't making them happen.

The replacement QC had a considerably smaller office than that of Mr Comyn. It was in one of the Inns of Court. Another world, entered through an arch, where there were elegant gardens and beautiful architecture and no sign of panic or urgency from those who crossed the lawns. Ironic, I thought each time I

made the journey, since surely the bulk of those seeking the services of the inhabitants are in anything but a peaceful frame of
mind. But then again, since the art of being a barrister is to be
able to bat dispassionately for one side or the other without ever
being part of the distress, I suppose the setting and tranquillity
of the Inns are entirely appropriate.

The replacement QC's desk was neat. The papers on it were
lined up in an orderly fashion in neat bundles wrapped in pink
ribbon. There was no cigarette ash dripping down *his* bib. I
found him far more pompous and remote than the original
favourite. I felt no bond with him. He seemed permanently
pleased with himself. My head swirled with the humiliation of
having to sit silently across the room from him as he pulled his
mouth one way and then the other. With each twitch I caught, I
imagined how tacky and terrible he must think me.

His junior was friendlier. And, once, before we actually went
to court, the junior consented to take a call from me when I
needed guidance on the possibility of taking Emma on a foreign
holiday before the case, to which Charlie's side had raised objections. The negotiations for this call to take place were roughly
akin to what I imagined went on if you wanted personally to
have a word with a home secretary or a Rolling Stone. Such was
the toing and froing to fix the audience, I felt as if I had been
granted some enormous privilege. Imagine being able to speak
directly to counsel.

There were perhaps half a dozen conferences with these men.
Or 'cons' as the solicitor called them. Each one would mean me
being in London, having come by train from Higher Cliff Farm.
Before and after the trips Charlie and I would compete with
'my lawyers are better than your lawyers' jibes. His belief that
there was nothing in the whole wide world that would convince
a judge that I was a suitable mother having a horrible ring of
truth about it. But at least I was living with Emma every day.

Emma, we hoped, never heard us row. She seemed without a
care in the world. Now, of course, I believe it is naive in the

extreme to suppose a child surrounded by unspoken resentment does not feel the chill and the anger.

On one journey from London after a conference, when I had sunk a few miniatures in the buffet car, I got into my Mini-Cooper which I had left at Macclesfield station, a regular stop for the InterCity train from Euston to Manchester, Piccadilly. The road on the way back to Higher Cliff Farm was icy and I skidded. There was no damage. But I was a bit dazed and, without thinking about it, went to a telephone box and called Charlie at home. The next I knew the police had arrived and I was being breathalysed. The test showed green, but only just. I lied and said I had drunk a miniature to soothe my nerves after the skid. Where was the bottle, asked the policeman? I didn't know, I said. We waited and took another breathalyser. It was sufficiently borderline for me to be let off. By this time Charlie had arrived on the scene. He seemed concerned, but I reminded myself that we were in the middle of a deadly battle.

As the date of the hearing got nearer the judge, or rather who was likely to be the judge, became a source of speculation and debate among my legal team.

The 'maybe him, maybe him on the other hand, very worrying indeed for us if it turns out to be him' discussions were remarkably similar to those Charlie would have had about a horse's chances at Aintree or Cheltenham. Whether the going would be soft or hard meant going through the possible pillars of wisdom that might sit and pronounce on our future. Judge A: easier on issues such as who may or may not have jumped into bed with whom. But a shocker if any drinking was involved. Judge B: likely to detest bad language and working women, but would not want to separate a mother and daughter. Judge C: generally considered anti-women. Judge D: female, but unpredictable and single. And so on. None of the names meant anything to me. I merely puzzled, as I still do, over a system that depends on the luck of the draw with a judge; on who has the most money to hire the best lawyers; on the extra energy one side puts into proving the bad behaviour of the other as being a fair way to determine the future of a young child. It can't be. I believe that calling in the legal profession is the last resort of the stubborn. The process sends the children of lawyers to public school; it pays for judges' holiday homes in Portugal and barristers' seats at Covent Garden; for made-to-measure suits, tennis courts, villas in St John's Wood, expensive golf clubs, sports cars, and racehorses and mansions in Middle England. But, in civil cases, does it dispense justice?

How appropriate, indeed, was a courtroom, with men in wigs racking up more than £250,000 in today's prices between them, to decide on what, in effect, was to be the next thirty-odd years of our lives?

Before the start of the case there was yet another nasty surprise. Charlie, it was rumoured, had managed to get legal aid. How could a man who was deputy editor of a national newspaper with a large house, four ponies, a donkey, a nanny, active accounts with William Hill, Tote Investors and Ladbrokes, be regarded as suitable for state assistance? Not one of my expensive, charging-by-the-minute legal team seemed capable of answering that. My mother, more practically, on hearing the news took seconds to demand why, if Charlie had legal aid, couldn't we get it too? We received no good answer. In fact, it turned out to be untrue.

When the ticket was pulled from the hat, or whatever fate decides such things, we got Sir Neville Faulks as our judge. He was sixty-five years old. Uppingham and Cambridge. He had fought in the war. Had been made a QC at the end of the fifties. His expertise had been in the field of defamation and not family law. He had been a judge for ten years when we came before him. His entry in *Who's Who* showed he'd had two wives – he had married the second Lady Faulks in 1967. Under recreations he listed 'the company of his wife'.

His name had not come up as a possibility during the 'runners and riders' discussions. But he had a reputation for being extremely prissy when it came to loose morals and bad language. He had spent a good deal of his working life acting either for or against newspapers. The general opinion, however, was that we could have done worse.

He was known for his own hefty drinking. So, it was reasoned, he was unlikely to be easily shocked by the evidence of heavy drinking he was to hear. For this we heaved a collective sigh. Although I alone knew just how bad my drinking was – I had never had the courage completely to confide in my team. I worried long and hard that whatever the level of Mr Justice Faulks' social drinking it surely would be insufficient for him to disregard my woeful state. Deep inside me I knew this should be the crux of the case. That it wasn't makes me ask again, is this the right way to decide upon a child's future?

We entered the Law Courts that first morning, and every other, by the well-known front entrance of the building. The one still seen almost daily on the television news bulletins. The Family Division was then housed in a newish extension, round at the back. The wood in the court was a light oak. The benches were clad in dark blue leather. The court officials sat below the judge. Our seats were beyond theirs. My team faced the judge's right, Charlie's his left.

The potential roll-call of witnesses was lengthy: those who had made statements on behalf of Charlie and who were willing to testify to my inability as a wife, a mother, a keeper of my home, or, alternatively, to my alarming drinking habits; it was a formidable list.

They included three ex-nannies, half a dozen of his staff from the *Daily Mail* and the publican of the *Mail* pub off Fleet Street. (Some time in the late eighties I bumped into this man at BBC Broadcasting House. He was a shivering, shaking, most unwell old soul, who was then working as a uniformed security guard. I had forgotten he had joined Charlie's band, so greeted him pleasantly.) There was an antiques dealer from whom I had bought half a dozen pieces of furniture. Another was an old friend called Harry. One half of a gay couple we used to drink with in the Canonbury Tavern during our time at Alwyne Square. He was a middle-aged man who worked in the old Covent Garden fruit market and whose capacity for red wine left everyone standing. He was another sign of our hard-drinking environment. Most distressing of all was the sight of Penrose's name on Charlie's list.

Penrose and I had fallen out. He had called at my flat in Noel Road one evening to discover my solicitor, who had taken me out to dinner, drinking coffee. Outraged, he had rung Charlie and offered to give evidence on 'behalf of the child'. He also reported my solicitor to the Law Society. It was to the judge's credit that he dismissed my former lover (and later second husband) from the witness stand, recognising at least the result of a lovers' tiff. The Law Society, likewise, took no action.

The witnesses on my side differed in that there were only three who had worked for me – all at home. Two former nannies and a cleaning lady. There were a handful of *Sunday Times* colleagues, and my *Sunday Times* managing editor Mike Randall, my gynaecologist, our family doctor, my brother, my friend Liz Hunter, my mother. And, most bizarrely, a son of Mr O'Hagan from Lurgan, whom my mother had bought her chickens from for so long. (He, along with the curate at our Catholic church in Crosby, was there to give my mother a character reference.) The nannies aside, the rest of the bunch on both sides should have been rejected. What place did they have in a dispute between a couple both fighting to keep their baby daughter? The one independent witness, the man from Cheshire Social Services, had ended up filing a report that came to no useful conclusion about either of us.

Charlie's QC was a small man who had a tinge of an Antipodean accent and, outside the courtroom, smoked a pipe. His junior was tall, his bald head hidden by his wig. He was, surprisingly, a grammar-school boy but also a former army man who had acquired the accent and manners of the officer class.

Charlie's belligerent solicitor, with whom he and Emma had spent Christmas night and Boxing Day, was there too, of course. Just to add to my confusion, my solicitor professed to know Charlie's junior counsel well and liked him. He was, however, contemptuous about his opposing solicitor. He assured me that in most cases solicitors on opposite sides could discuss things amiably, but in this case it was not possible, explained my man, because of the quarrelsome and unpleasant nature of Charlie's chosen representative.

The judge, when he appeared, was ruddy-faced, almost beetroot in colour, with a crusty, cantankerous demeanour. At some early point he said that he knew one of my witnesses, Mike Randall, from when he had been editor of the *Daily Mail*. The connection was a professional one between a newspaper libel lawyer and a newspaper executive. At this point, and bearing in mind the notion that this judge would be lenient on drinking, my side agreed they were happy with the case continuing. Charlie's side did likewise.

Like my honeymoon, the weeks in court come back only in moments, some comical for members of the legal team. All of them cringingly, distressingly awful for me.

Because my chances were being painted so bleakly, my side agreed to put forward immediately my suggestion that I was prepared to give up working if it meant that I could have Emma living with me. Momentarily, and satisfyingly, this appeared to rattle our opponents. I must, I suppose, have wondered, at least fleetingly, why I was obliged to bend over backwards in a way Charlie would not have dreamt of doing. But the constant warnings of the damning evidence against me were enough to persuade me that drastic steps were needed.

Equally, in the first few days, Charlie's side wished to illustrate how he had found an excellent nanny who could begin immediately and would be there to look after Emma while he, Charlie, continued to work as deputy editor of the *Daily Mail* in Manchester. Finally kick-started into aggressive action my team, led by me, attempted over the following weekend to prove by fair means or foul how unsuitable this woman was. We tracked down her former employers in Cheshire, a wealthy young family with three children, living in a large, well-appointed farmhouse. We obtained records to show the proposed nanny had had periods of mental instability.

The mother of the family who had employed her was obliged by subpoena to turn up in London. 'Don't worry. When I serve the papers their family lawyer will tell them there is no way out,' the solicitor's clerk told me as we arrived in the dead of Sunday night at the family's farmhouse. He was correct. By the Monday afternoon, back in court in London, we managed to damn the nanny's reputation. The judge praised my tenacity. 'The mother has gone to considerable lengths to show this nanny's unsuitability' were his words. Should Charlie win, other arrangements would have to be made, he declared.

If this was a victory, and a taste of the judge praising my efforts and my concern, it was the only one we would enjoy.

For the next however-many days the case continued. People who had been to my house, eaten my food, enjoyed my hospitality, lined up. Outside the courtroom each of them, there for Charlie, avoided my glance as our little group with our counter-stories stood only feet away. Even the one who had asked for my help in getting a job. It wasn't fun. 'Don't imagine how love letters will be received by your lover,' one of the barristers had said at some stage, 'just imagine what they will sound like read out in court.' Whose actions and antics after a night out drinking, described in court, would not appear irresponsible, unattractive, damning? Especially if the person is female.

Most of Charlie's witnesses were anxious to stress my drunken rages, my ridiculing of Charlie and my ambitions as a journalist – as well as Charlie's utter devotion to his daughter. I deny none of this, but it was not by any means the full story.

Charlie saw me as a self-centred, selfish, uncaring wife and mother. I saw him as a bully and a pig.

There was no mention of Charlie's constant ridiculing of *me*. His harshness, his domineering ways, his filthy temper. My side concentrated on excusing the drinking as no more than the standard Fleet Street capacity to down more in one evening than most communities would regard as safe to do in a year. The fact that I was talented, ambitious and keen to be a good journalist didn't strike me as of much importance. Except perhaps to illustrate that I could hardly be the shocking soak people were testifying me to be, since I was still regarded as someone of exceptional capabilities.

Only the evidence of one nanny, the local Derbyshire girl from the nearby village, was truly damaging. She testified truthfully that I would be in a drunken state sometimes by lunchtime. I had read her testimony months before. I was shocked that my drinking was so obvious. And for the brief time she remained at the farm after she had made her statement I saw she carried a diary in the pocket of her jeans. I presumed it was to make a note of the state I was in. (For the weeks after she left, until the court case, I was obliged to stay at the farm if I wanted to be with Emma. But thankfully a temporary nanny from London was found to replace the local girl.)

There were also a couple of sub-plots. In those same weeks leading up to the case my solicitor had declared how much he liked my company and how attracted he felt towards me. He would ring me for long chats on a Sunday if Charlie was out of the way. He was in the process of divorcing his wife, had a daughter the same age as Emma and seemed so sympathetic. Our relationship amounted to me smooching with him in his car when he took me out to dinner in London. I was far too pre-occupied to think of him as anything other than a comforting companion, but after Penrose had gone over to the other side with his information, Charlie was determined to make something of it.

Suddenly my side was immersed in discussion about whether my solicitor would be called to admit to driving me home and coming into my flat in Islington. Since I was innocent of what was being suggested I saw this as no more than a tiresome and irrelevant interruption. But the 'in-joke' was considered hilarious by my legal team – and distracting. My solicitor, and whether he would be called, occupied them greatly. I watched their excitement mount. Big deal! My solicitor *was* called. He acquitted himself without ruining the rest of his life. It turned out the other side saw this as equally amusing.

The more serious sub-plot was my mother's notion to declare herself the most suitable person to bring up Emma. The idea being that if my offer of bringing Emma up on my own was unacceptable she was there to take over. Secretly, I was horrified. I almost felt I would rather our daughter went to Charlie than for Emma and me to attempt to make a home with my mother. I need not have worried. While Charlie's moves to discredit my mother failed, so did her shot at cutting the sort of homely figure who looked as if she might be a suitable replacement for me. She commandeered our local Catholic priest, an elderly Irishman, called Father Noonan. The very same man famed in our family for downing several large brandies whenever he visited our home and for telling my mother, yet again, that he and the other curates laid bets on the colour and shape of the latest designer hat she would be wearing when she came up the aisle to take communion. How often had my mother announced she would feel very unsafe in a room with Father Noonan when he was 'the worse for drink'?

No matter. Father Noonan was doing his best for Mrs Robinson when Charlie's junior counsel jumped to his feet to ask him if he knew that Mrs Robinson's daughter, Anne, whom Father Noonan had known since she was a babe in arms, had had one abortion and had sought a second? Father Noonan's mouth opened without any words emerging. He left the witness box as if in a daze.

Another memory: the morning Charlie's junior pursued a line about my 'drug taking'. The pot-smoking sixties had never been my scene. I had never done drugs. Nor to my knowledge had Charlie. But this was a reference to a prescription for Valium I had received from a doctor. 'Nothing wrong with Valium,' interrupted the judge. 'Had a couple myself this morning . . .' Junior counsel for Charlie withdrew sharpish.

And another: my mother giving evidence. 'I always cook a nice steak for you, don't I, Charles?' my mother was declaring as she leant over the witness box towards my husband. The court-room tittered. The judge reminded my mother that this was not an informal gathering and she must address him or counsel. (The cold chicken for Charlie, steak for Anne scenario in the early days of our marriage on a visit to Blundellsands flashed before me and I thought I'd shaken my head in despair. Later I discovered, fatefully, that I'd grinned like a Cheshire cat.)

Charlie's legal team then opened up the Pandora's box of my mother's '5 per cents' to the chefs who ordered from her. His QC embarked on a lengthy and damning list of 'bribes' she was in the habit of giving out. His smugness at having discredited someone who, until now, had appeared to be a decent grand-mother was short-lived. Again the judge saved the day: 'Normal business practice.' Another avenue closed down.

They were more successful with my brother. Peter alone had witnessed the aftermath of one of the physical battles Charlie and I had had in the early weeks of our marriage while still living in the rented cottage in Claygate. First Charlie's team implied that Peter, at the time an author come teacher come jack of all trades, mostly travelling in America, had claimed for some baggage that had not really been lost. This appeared to make little impact one way or the other. More damagingly, Peter, in a misguided attempt to help, grossly over-gilded the lily on the scene that he discovered at Claygate when his sister had called him in a panic. The exaggerated version was barely recognisable. I was dismayed and alarmed in equal parts and, as I gathered later, again grinned in a maniacal way. Peter's testimony was felt to be sufficiently suspect so that when Charlie was in the witness box and was asked if he had ever hit me and replied, 'I only slapped her,' that was the end of the matter.

One who knew more of the sad tale than most was Fiona, the nanny who had agreed to come with me to Higher Cliff Farm when I had originally returned to Charlie. Fiona was my friend. The one who sat and smoked and drank wine with me in the mornings. The one who sympathised with my plight. However, not only had she moved to Charlie's side, but when one of his barristers asked his client if there had been any intimacy between the nanny and him, Charlie, to my shock, replied: 'I only ever kissed her.'

What the hell was all that about? I had no idea until Fiona's statement came through that she thought any more of Charlie than I did. When did they kiss? Who ever heard of Charlie settling for just a kiss? If a kiss was on offer at the end of an evening, why stop there? Indeed, if he was admitting to kissing her was that because he thought I knew more than I did? I was never to know.

Less to the point, a number of drunken parties were recounted on behalf of both sides. More than once the judge gauged whether a person was a heavy drinker by normal standards, or by 'Fleet Street' standards.

Where did it all lead? The priest, the poor woman who only wanted a job as a nanny, who had been exposed rightly or wrongly as a depressive and a recluse. My mother and her business. The antiques dealer, one who had abandoned his own family, whom I barely knew but who had become Charlie's friend and who claimed I showed no great interest in being a mother. The freelance journalist who relied heavily on Charlie at the *Daily Mail* for work, who likewise gave me a poor character reference. And from my side *Sunday Times* colleagues, anxious to help, who swore blind what a decent, responsible, caring, good person I was.

And that most memorable of moments, much quoted by me and other women to illustrate the times we then lived in. 'Is it true, Mrs Wilson,' asked Charlie's junior barrister when I stood in the witness box, 'that you once said you would rather cover the Vietnam War than Hoover the sitting room?'

'Yes,' I said. And, yes, when Charlie once asked me to cook Sunday lunch, I yelled, 'Fuck that for a game of soldiers.' Adding, by way of amplification, that I often called Charlie 'boring'. In the same way he would call me 'ugly'. We were sharp in our humour. And these pet names had been used in the first couple of years of our marriage when we were still affectionate towards each other. How can any of this be evidence of my unsuitability as a parent? Any more than when during one lively fight Charlie had hurled a plant pot out of the window of our house in Alwyne Square and a neighbour's child had politely knocked on the door to return it.

Another tangent: Charlie's side, we learnt, had my diaries. But not even the finest expert of Gregg shorthand could decipher them. A short attention span and the uncompleted secretarial course of my youth had come up trumps.

Each night after court we would repair to my flat in Noel Road, which I had held on to since I had gone back to Higher Cliff Farm, and which was empty. My mother would satisfy herself that I had eaten then go off to stay at a hotel near my brother in Kensington. I walked around in a daze. Unable to comprehend how it had come to this. The shame was unbearable. Even worse was the horror of losing Emma. Grief, anger, incredulity that any of this nonsense was important to a two-year-old's future.

All in all, the court, the judges and barristers in the wigs, the money poured away by two beleaguered parents, seems now, as then, the most inappropriate place for a situation like ours to be settled.

The final day dawned with my having not the remotest idea what the outcome might be. Not because I didn't realise the evidence against me was damning. I had been painted as a loose, scarlet woman who drank too much and had a horribly sharp tongue. At worst Charlie came across as brusque. But since I had made it clear that in order to have Emma in my care I would willingly forsake work, socialising, London, consider living with my well-meaning but unsuitable mother, maybe, just maybe, the judge would not part me from my daughter.

We adjourned for lunch. The QC and me. He had made his closing speech. His pride in it, and in the son who had turned up from nowhere, was another bit of the black comedy. We trailed back into court. The judge summed up.

The drunkenness on my part, which I was convinced would damn me, was seen by the judge as a hazard of my profession. I could hardly believe it. He seemed to think it worth no more than a passing reference.

My allegations that Charlie had beaten me up went the same way. (A couple of years later Mr Justice Faulks was to make headlines by declaring in court that while it was okay for a miner in South Wales to hit his wife, it was not acceptable behaviour for a husband in Belgravia. As luck would have it, the *Daily Mirror* sent Penrose to the judge's Chelsea home for a comment. The judge was happy to chat. At least he was once he had yelled, 'Wifey, Wifey, give me some money', and when she had done so had taken himself off, still wearing his carpet slippers, to the nearby off-licence for a fresh bottle of gin. Then, with drink in hand, he repeated and stood by his comments that miners in South Wales could be excused violent behaviour towards their womenfolk because they lacked education. Both Faulks' beliefs and his demeanour that day explained a great deal. But we knew none of this as we sat in court.)

The judge went on to give my mother a glowing report, but didn't seem interested in grandmothers looking after children. I don't recall my brother being mentioned.

Then there was the 'mother'. The judge said he had observed

me closely during the case and I appeared to think the whole thing was funny. I had, he said witheringly, his upper lip curling towards his nose, continually sat there with a sneer or a grin on my face.

Ye gods! What had Mother Alexander told my mother more than once when I was at Farnborough Hill? 'Anne only ever thinks it funny when she is chastised.' Why didn't the judge question me about it? I had and still have a nervous sneer. I see it turning up on television programmes whenever I am ill at ease. It no more implies a desire to mock the proceedings now than it did then. But it helped to hang me.

Even worse, and to my complete astonishment, was what the judge called my 'undoubted ambition', adding, without fear of contradiction, that the mother's ambition, in his opinion, was greater than that of her husband.

There was no going back. There was no opportunity to say, 'Hang on a second, if we'd known you were going down that road, we could easily have shown how there was no contest between the mother's ambition and work ethic and the father's.' The father was, and is, a man who has only ever given 110 per cent to whoever was employing him. A man who from an employer's point of view could not be faulted. A man who accepted the responsibility of family life totally in that he expected to provide for his children, to ensure they were properly looked after, educated, given extra tuition if needs be, the best medical care, the finest football boots, a decent horse to learn to ride on. But he was not a man who in terms of hours would put his family first.

I'd never expected the case to turn on ambition and, to be fair, neither had Charlie originally, but once I'd offered to stop working, his side knew it was fine to include it. This was 1973. The mother's ambition damned her. The father's ambition was never questioned. It would not have occurred to anyone from my side to demand of Mr Wilson what choice he would make between Hoovering the sitting room and covering the Vietnam War.

The very fact that he had produced a prospective nanny in the early days of the case meant both sides accepted that if Emma went to live with Charlie he would not be raising her on a full-time basis. He would be working. Had I gone on working, as Charlie expected, I would have had a nanny too.

In 1973 maternity leave in the newspaper world was not an issue. The Sex Discrimination Act and the Equal Pay Act were not to come into force for another three years. Like the woman interviewed by George Orwell, I knew only of the harshness of the judge's logic when they told me about it. At the time, out of ignorance, I colluded in this decision. I, who three years earlier had marched into El Vino as part of the protest about prohibiting women from standing at the bar, because I was bored at home and glad of an afternoon's fun, still knew no better.

'I do not find her an unfit mother,' declared the judge. But my nervous sneer and my ambition had done for me. Charlie was to have sole custody, care and control of Emma. Dazed and bewildered, I only vaguely heard the terms of my access. Alternate weekends from four in the afternoon on Friday until five in the afternoon on Sunday. And two afternoons in the week when there was no weekend access. The judge also ordered me to pay some of Charlie's legal costs: £3000, the equivalent of £22,000 today.

I was helped out of court.

'It was about as good as we could have expected,' one or other member of my legal team was saying. 'With your drinking history, it could have gone the other way. And you could have been denied unsupervised access.'

And there was the rub. My drinking was frighteningly out of control. I needed help. But no one had addressed the problem. Least of all the judge, the expert in libel and not family matters. I did not recognise I had a serious problem with alcohol. Nor, I thought, did Charlie, who regarded me merely as someone who in a short space of time had become a hardened, crass, self-indulgent 'Fleet Street' woman. Nearly thirty years later I learnt from him that while lunching with his solicitor 'three-quarters of the way through the case, the solicitor said, "You do know what the trouble with Anne is, don't you? She is an alcoholic."' Charlie says it was a revelation.

But no one during our weeks in court ever suggested it. Indeed, that huge amounts of money, brains, intellect and the considerable evidence picked over and thrashed out during the course of the hearing failed to establish one of the major causes of our difficulties was both astonishing and lamentable. Today, I would hope a mother with a drink problem would be given the opportunity to seek treatment and an opportunity to re-present her case in, say, a year or two's time.

If I was not an unfit mother then, I was soon to be. Deep down, maybe I knew that. My mother certainly did.

Did Charlie know all along which way to play the judge? I doubt it. But the outcome for him must have been akin to a policeman's squaring his conscience when he sees a criminal go to jail for a crime he did not commit. 'That's okay,' says the cop, 'because he committed a crime, just as bad, that we weren't able to prove.'

My lawyers assured me that we could discuss an appeal, while simultaneously packing up their belongings. They had other conferences to attend. Other clients who would pour out their woes, perhaps, then find their barrister was unavailable to act for them in court at a later date.

Where did my mother and father and brother disappear to? I do not know. I know only that Penrose put me in a car and took me to Marlow to the Compleat Angler Hotel for a night.

I was left with the worst sort of abandonment I could ever have imagined. I rang Emma at Higher Cliff Farm. She was her usual cheery self, happy to hear from Mummy. Happy to hear her daddy would be home later.

In the short term it meant clearing my possessions from the farm and moving back to London to my flat. Emma alone was unchanged by the trauma of the past weeks. Had I gone home to her that night, which I wasn't allowed to, she would have greeted her mummy with hugs and delight. Her father the same. The extent of the loss lodged somewhere in my brain, although not quite at the front. I had permission to have Emma at my mother's. But not until the following weekend.

I feared that if I let the facts sink in I would crumble. So I clung grimly on to the possibility that now my drinking had been dismissed, the Appeal Court would see sense. My lawyers were as non-committal as usual. What did they know? What did anyone know? My mother was barely able to articulate her grief and horror. My father made cups of tea.

I stayed at my parents'. The *Sunday Times* allowed me time off to recover.

As the appeal date loomed I knew in my heart that I was fighting a lost cause. Whatever old Faulks might have thought, three wise men were never going to consider me fit to look after Emma – they would see my drinking for what it was. The warnings from my legal team were grim. I might come off even worse. Three judges might consider me unfit rather than just ambitious. The best plan, they advised, was to argue for greater access.

The lawyers had a point, although I had long since given up respecting their opinions. What if the Appeal Court judgement overturned the only thing I could hang on to: that Mr Justice Faulks had said he had not found me an unfit mother. On the other hand, if, as I had been told, mothers never, ever lose custody of their children, what other conclusion was there to draw?

At the doors of the Appeal Court my side offered to talk. Charlie's side offered to reduce the costs we had been ordered to pay. The QC thought it was a reasonable deal. I nodded out of weariness, hopelessness. The warrior's spirit in me was spent. 'No judgement is for ever,' said somebody from my legal team.

Charlie came over and shook my hand. We took ourselves off down to Fleet Street. The very place that had brought us together. We had a drink. We made a pact that whatever happened we would remain Emma's parents. Neither would do anything to our daughter to damn the other. We had the instinct to know that a child needs to feel the love of both parents and the respect of the two for each other.

12

Rock Bottom

Where did I go from here? A mother without her baby daughter. A daughter I was to be allowed to see only every other weekend. A soon to be three-year-old whom henceforth a hired hand would help bring up.

Within a week of Mr Justice Faulks making his judgement Charlie had produced a nanny for my viewing. I went to meet her at Higher Cliff Farm. She was, I think, by then in her late forties, maybe early fifties. She had been with one family for twenty-odd years. She was as near as you could get to that sketch with Joyce Grenfell sitting on a park bench. A professional nanny, all alone, singing a song about 'other people's children'.

Gwyneth was Welsh by birth, well spoken, Norland trained, a spinster: she couldn't be faulted. She was suntanned, sensibly dressed and looked like just about anyone who had taught me geography or gym at school. I asked her why she had never been married and she said the opportunity hadn't arisen. There were no more useful questions I could raise. I rang Charlie later and said she was fine.

Still on compassionate leave from the *Sunday Times*, I stayed on at my parents' in Blundellsands. To add to my misery I was obliged on a daily basis to face my mother's dramatic outbursts on the matter of our family tragedy. Her mood would swing from tenderness and understanding to anger at the thought of what Charlie had done to us. She was unstoppable in her condemnation of how my drinking was to blame and that I needed to pull myself together.

We never discussed how.

But she took it upon herself to mastermind our weekends of access with Emma. The larder fridge would groan with food. The cash-and-carry outlet she used would be emptied of sweets. If Emma casually mentioned she liked a certain chocolate bar it would be bought in bulk. She discovered that while Emma was not keen on meat, she would eat it smothered in bright green mint jelly from a bottle. So it was mint jelly and bacon. Mint jelly and stew. Mint jelly and ham. I looked on, helpless. Helplessness and despair by now being just about the only feelings I had left.

My mother orchestrating Emma's stays followed on the heels of the trauma of collecting my daughter every fortnight and every alternate mid-week. The pick-up was something else I came to dread.

It had been agreed that for my access Gwyneth would drive Emma in Charlie's car to the car park of the Knutsford Service Station on the M6. A reasonable halfway distance between the farm and my parents' home. Twenty-seven years on I still feel a knot in my stomach every time I pass that service station.

The collections and hand-backs were akin to being mugged and raped. But with no one looking on, aware of the gravity or agony, minute by minute, of the situation.

On the first ever drop-off Gwyneth sprang to undo Emma from her baby chair. As she lifted her out I came face to face with my little girl in a dark blue T-shirt with a huge plastic Mickey Mouse face on it. The T-shirt was foul. But that wasn't really the point. Who knows, in different circumstances it might have been one that my beloved daughter insisted on and one that I would have allowed her to wear to avoid a song and dance? But that afternoon it represented all I had lost. I would no more have chosen it than dye her beautiful red hair.

How Emma was dressed each morning was no longer within my control.

In the coming months the Mickey Mouse T-shirt set-up repeated itself over and over in different guises. There was the 'wee-wee' expression. As in Emma announcing, 'I need a wee-wee.' Obviously one of Gwyneth's phrases. I shrank in disbelief the first time Emma said it. When I admonished her, she rightly looked upset. Even my fuddled, confused brain realised that you couldn't decently chastise a child for using words she had innocently picked up from someone in charge of her. To object on the grounds that Gwyneth's way with the English language tested my snobbery would hardly have been wise. Or rather, not something that would have made the slightest sense to Charlie.

In time, there would be a catalogue of other toe-curling examples. Emma would put her forefinger to her closed lips, open her eyes wide and remark 'let me see' in a conspiratorial sort of way. That too was pure Gwyneth. The fact that someone else was rearing and shaping my daughter was inescapable – and agonising.

When Mr Justice Faulks, a man who had spent a lifetime working and had never been a mother, made his judgement did he know even half the ongoing heartbreak his decision would cause?

The pinpricks, unnoticeable to anyone but me, went on multiplying through the years. So many of those everyday tasks that mothers regard as normal and take for granted, even find thoroughly tiresome, were to be out of my grasp. I would never become properly acquainted with *Blue Peter*. I would never take Emma to a piano lesson, a ballet class, or become friends with the mothers of children she went to school with. I would never buy her school uniform. For years the style of her hair, the colour of her wardrobe were not my prerogative. I would rarely do homework with her. Watch her on the sports field, pick her up from school, or, if I did, I would stand apart from the other mothers because I knew they knew she didn't live with me. And surely I must be seriously, seriously awful to have lost the right to have my daughter under my roof. Even worse, I suppose they thought that I had chosen to abandon her. I felt like a pariah.

Some of these things were beyond my reach because of distance and circumstance. Others because I'd lost the confidence to regard myself as worthy of making a fuss or even voicing an opinion.

Meeting Emma's teachers was a special humiliation mainly because of the story going on in my own head about my ignominy. At parents' evenings, when Charlie and I would make an effort to appear together to discuss Emma's progress, shame and remorse clouded each appointment. (There was, much later, a particularly memorable parents' evening when Emma was at day school in London and I had become assistant editor of the *Daily Mirror*. I had left the office sufficiently early to be at her school on time. Charlie, who was by then editor of *The Times*, arrived in a chauffeur-driven Jag about half an hour late. 'Charles, how wonderful of you to make the effort and get here,' gushed the headmistress.)

Like a barren woman who longs for a baby and sees only pregnant mothers in her path, it was impossible not to be reminded of my plight almost every minute of my waking day. I never shared with anyone my feelings: a mixture of defeat, regret, hopelessness and utter sadness. To do so would have meant voicing the extent of my disgrace out loud. Instead, I used another way to screen the hurt. One at which I was already practised and before long I would make my special area of expertise.

That way would become the enemy of a promising career. It would rob me of living a full and useful life for some years. It had already helped remove my role as a full-time mother. It would now go on to stop in its tracks my chances of exploiting my natural talents. It would dump me with a shame so overpowering it nearly killed me. It would leave me with my nervous system blown to pieces. It would wipe out large tracts of the mid-1970s.

So events, music, people, fashion trends, television programmes, news items from that time are a blur. It would shape the next thirty years of my life.

In the eighties and nineties it became fashionable for Hollywood stars to boast about their new-found sobriety and declare 'the party is over'. I, sadly, hardly had a party. The fun stage of my drinking was short-lived compared to the ugly years. When it reached its worst it meant ending up with my knickers round my neck in a bed I did not recognise, surrounded by vomit and having not the faintest idea where I was. Even alone at home it became familiar to open my eyes and feel fear, uncertain if it was day or night, or Tuesday or Saturday week. The wretchedness of the hangover, the throwing up, or, worse, the inability to throw up, the dread of what might or might not have happened were so alarming and terrible that, blow me, an hour or two later I would start the procedure that guaranteed the whole business began again. What choice did I have? The feelings of disgust were terrifying and only another drink could quieten the demons.

But in the early hours of a new day the task of getting my hands on more alcohol could be a job of Herculean proportions. Who sold vodka at eight in the morning? Was there cash to purchase it? If I had the cash, how could I guarantee that my shaking hands could carry out the transaction without me looking what I was – a shambling, sad, pathetic figure? Who else but a desperate person would be waiting outside Tesco at that hour to buy a miniature? Or, if funds allowed, a quarter-bottle. Who else would have stood at home for the minutes leading up to eight o'clock, holding on to a chair in case she fell down, and practise handing over the money? The hope being that the rehearsal would avoid the embarrassment of my hand shaking and thereby threatening the sale.

I was so sick and so paranoid I actually believed that my mother had, as she said she would, forbidden any off-licence in Liverpool or London to serve me.

Once the purchase had successfully been made and the neat

Smirnoff had quelled the worst emotions, there was the knowledge that having started the day with a drink it would, as surely as day follows night, end in more chaos.

Somewhere in that day too, I would be asked by someone who cared to promise, as I had fruitlessly promised Charlie on that first date, that I was going to pull myself together. An idea so unrealistic that whoever demanded it of me might just as well have suggested I change the booze in the bottle into water before I drank it.

Sometimes, sensing the extent of my downfall or terrified that Charlie or Emma or Penrose or my mother would throw in the towel and disown me, I would move from bender to cold-turkey sober. The process became a familiar one. The first half-day without a drink was bearable. But as soon as my system began to notice the lack of alcohol it had been used to in huge quantities, it would react. I would throw up, shiver, be unable to sit still. In this desperate state my body's need for alcohol was so strong that, if I had been locked up out of harm's way by my mother, I would search for cough mixture, aftershave, anything that I knew contained alcohol, to calm the terror that would come over me both mentally and physically.

These days a wise doctor would bring someone down slowly from an onslaught of drugs or booze, but a quarter of a century ago the awareness of the problem was in its infancy. My ways of coping were amateur. Those around me were no more knowledgeable about what would help. So in their muddling, loving way, they adopted boot-camp tactics. Padlock the patient, deny her the drug, teach her a lesson. None of this was the slightest use.

I was to become the girl with the golden future behind me.

On one of my worst days Charlie met me on a station platform. I weighed under six stone and was shuffling along with a face the colour of parchment, eyes sunken, my hands unable to grip. The tremors in my legs were so violent that mounting stairs, crossing a road, getting into a bath without help were impossible. He reckoned I had, at best, less than a month or two to live.

The promising talent who wanted to write like Brendan Behan had ended up drinking like Brendan Behan and writing like Mrs Behan.

Not all of it was bad. For truly what doesn't kill you gives you strength. But I didn't know that then. Any more than I knew what was to become of me.

My return to the *Sunday Times* after nearly six months' absence was greeted by murmurs of sympathy at what had befallen me. I had few discussions with anyone about anything to do with the case. I simply reclaimed a desk in the newsroom and declared myself ready for work.

The same paper whose editor had never got back to me about the possibility of not working every Saturday now readily agreed to my working only two Saturdays out of four so I could be at home for the weekends I had Emma. The only other good news was that Charlie was returning to London to a job on the *Evening News*.

He was selling up Higher Cliff Farm and buying a house on an estate in Kingston, Surrey. Kingston was where his mother lived. It was also where some old friends and their two children of around Emma's age had bought a house. The couple both worked on the local paper. They were good friends to Charlie and it meant also that Emma could attend the same private day school as their children. Gwyneth was to continue as Emma's nanny. She was now firmly established as part of the household.

The husband had been one of Charlie's witnesses, so there was no question of my previous record not being well known in Kingston circles. Both Gwyneth and Charlie's friends were civil to me whenever I visited, but I felt like the 'bad' mother whom everyone out of the kindness of their hearts tolerated (just).

I dreaded having to visit Kingston. I dreaded picking up Emma from school, as I could do on a Friday on my weekends, if I wished. I imagined I stood out with a label that said 'unfit mother – stay clear'. I was even more acutely aware of my status, or rather lack of status, when I recognised one of the mothers as a girl who had been in the year ahead of me at Farnborough Hill.

Work brought few rewards. In my early days at the *Sunday Times* I had been marked out as a young star. I had covered Northern Ireland. The editor, Harry Evans, had chosen me to launch the paper's Insight consumer unit. Along with Robert Lacey, later to be a distinguished author, I cracked the date codes of Walls, the meat product manufacturers. Unbelievably at that time Walls, along with other major food manufacturers, stamped their perishable foods, such as sausages and pies, with a string of letters and numbers. This meant that only the producers knew how old the goods were. Certainly not the shops and most certainly not the customers. Exposing Walls was to lead to all the manufacturers giving up the practice. When today I watch in supermarkets how slavishly people scan the sell-by dates, I marvel at the progress. We made inroads too into getting a better deal for tourists in the early days of the package-holiday business. Most were then offered holidays at resorts in Spain and Portugal. Then, as now, profit margins were so tiny that no tourist was likely to be well compensated or looked after if things went wrong. But this was yesteryear.

A very different me had returned to the *Sunday Times* newsroom. For a start, the talented young girl who liked a drink was well on her way to being a fully out-of-control drunk. It was in the early weeks back at work, joining a crowd at the Blue Lion, opposite our building in Gray's Inn Road, that I first encountered 'the shakes'. Stretching out for my glass of wine from the bar my fingers started to tremble so badly the glass fell to the floor. Another one was ordered without much notice being taken of what had occurred. But I knew I was heading for real trouble.

My nervous system had been blown. My cover, as yet, had not.

I took matters into my own hands. I never again joined the crowd in the Blue Lion unless I had first, privately, had a miniature or two to settle me. It was the beginning of the end.

In the months after my return I reported on Erin Pizzey's newly opened refuge for battered wives, Chiswick Women's Aid. The first of its kind. Today, you would be hard put to name a city that does not offer a facility of this kind – even if they are still run on a shoe-string. Erin, herself, was eventually to fall foul of feminists by stating her belief that women frequently left one violent relationship for another. Or went back to a violent partner however much he beat her up. I can see only logic in her argument. Familiar behaviour, however damaging it might have been, seems comfortable. We gravitate towards it unless we learn not to. So a daughter unwittingly chooses a boyfriend who mirrors her father or her mother. Even when it means that the boyfriend is mean, cold, unable to be there for her. For sons, ditto.

I, meanwhile, was concentrating on achieving untold success in another family trait. Arriving at work with a bottle clunking in a large handbag became a way of life. If I was sent on stories out of town I would barely be sober long enough to interview anyone. When I got back to London it was impossible to write a coherent account.

On one occasion I was sent to the Old Bailey to report on an IRA bomber. The security was massive. So were my shakes. I dashed out of the court to an off-licence and bought a full bottle of vodka and was about to go back to the court when I realised that my briefcase would be opened at the security checkpoint and the contents exposed. I retreated to a public lavatory, drank as much of the neat Smirnoff as I could manage, left the bottle behind and returned to the courtroom. Not, naturally, in any fit state to follow what was going on.

To avoid typing up my story I would attempt to ring the copytakers from my desk at the *Sunday Times*, as if I were dictating from some far-off place. One day in the newsroom I turned to see another reporter mimicking my drunken speech. In a period when my memory was so frequently wiped out by the effects of my drinking it is interesting how acts of cruelty and acts of kindness stand out vividly. The reporter who mocked my condition would years later ask for an appointment to see me when I was a newspaper executive, in the hope of getting some work. If he had been any good I would have used him. But sadly he was no more talented ten years on than he was when he was enjoying my state that day.

One week I returned from a story in Wales and was called in to the managing editor's office. The people I had interviewed had contacted him to complain about me. I was given a written warning.

Home in Liverpool for the following weekend in November, news came through of the worst IRA atrocity to date – 17 people killed in two Birmingham pubs, 120 injured. It was revenge for a ban on a hero's funeral for an IRA man killed by his own bomb in Coventry.

I rang my news editor, imagining that all hands would be needed on deck in Birmingham. 'No, thank you,' he said coldly, when I offered my services. A few months later there was an Underground train crash at Moorgate when a Tube train rammed into the end of a tunnel. Thirty-five were killed. There were calls for blood donors. Because of Emma's birth, I knew I was O negative. A rare group. I drunkenly rang the sister in charge of the *Sunday Times* health department to make my life-saving offer. 'No, thank you,' she said coldly.

In February of that year, Margaret Thatcher, wife of a wealthy businessman and mother of twins, became the first woman leader of a British political party. She was forty-nine. Women of all parties were elated. Edward Heath, one of her four main rivals, sulked. Anne Robinson had another drink and barely noticed.

That summer was to be the hottest on record for thirty-five

years. In August the temperature soared on one day to 36 degrees Celsius. Anne Robinson drank on. Never outside long enough to care whether it was hot or cold.

The war in Vietnam was finally over. And by the end of the year the Sex Discrimination Act and the Equal Pay Act had come into force. These were hailed as the biggest step forward for women since they won the vote. It was now against the law to discriminate against women in employment, training, education and trade union activities and in the supply of goods, facilities and services to the public. In language that ordinary people could understand it meant that a boss could no longer advertise for a 'pretty secretary'. Something called the Equal Opportunities Commission was set up. I barely noticed.

The Birmingham Six, on trial for the bombing outrage the previous November, appeared at Lancaster Crown Court. Inexplicably, I was sent to cover the trial. My ongoing drunkenness was causing me to spiral ever downwards. I formed a passion for one of the defence barristers, who had no idea he was playing fast and loose with a sad drunk.

About two months later he turned up in London to confess that he was married. I went on yet another bender and ended up being collected by ambulance from a women's lavatory on the newsroom floor of the *Sunday Times*.

With kindness, but with no small amount of concern at what embarrassment my state might cause the newspaper, the managing editor suggested I gave work a rest. He could, he assured me, get me a pay-off. Five thousand pounds was mentioned. I accepted. My career in newspapers was over.

That I hung on to motherhood, however tenuously and spasmodically, during this time was thanks to Emma's father. However cruel I considered him during our marriage, however much I questioned his true motives for fighting for custody of Emma, he now came up trumps. He accepted the days I couldn't function. He made an effort to ensure Emma was there for me when I could. We had warred and disagreed on everything.

Except our joint intention to bring her up without acrimony. To be decent and honourable about each other. He kept the bargain. I, as much as I was able to be in control of anything, did likewise.

As I continued to nose-dive, Penrose was offered the job of Rome correspondent of the *Daily Mirror*. It probably comes as a surprise to a younger generation of newspaper readers that the 'red top' newspapers, as they are now called, used to have foreign bureaux. But in the seventies the *Mirror* had a deserved reputation for quality popular journalism. Despite the crippling costs of running a newspaper leg-ironed by the preposterous demands and practices of the print unions, the journalists lived a good and expensive life.

The Rome bureau had been established in the days when travel to and from the Middle East took much longer. The city was regarded as a jumping-off point. The bureau chief was expected to perform an ambassadorial role, and was also there to entertain visiting *Mirror* hierarchy. The young Penrose, with his Naples-born mother, was assumed, wrongly, to speak Italian. In true journalistic tradition, he never let the office think otherwise. In any case, the assumption was probably justified. He had been listening to the language, or at least the Neapolitan version of it, for so long that in less than six weeks he was interviewing policemen in Florence over the phone competently enough for them only to mistake him for a Sicilian.

It was to just about everyone's horror except mine that Penrose agreed to our making a new life together in Rome. I welcomed it because the alternative was to return to my mother. I was unemployable. I had had to sell my flat because I couldn't keep up the mortgage repayments. Like Charlie before him, Penrose, with far more evidence to the contrary, believed that I could turn over a new leaf. Like Charlie after the day trip to France, Penrose asked me to promise I would stop drinking and come and enjoy life in Italy.

Johnny was my soul mate. He showed me kindness through

my worst benders. I loved his company. He was popular, gentle, ridiculously generous and patient. But he too had no idea of my true state. I persuaded myself that for Emma to come out for the holidays and for me to fly home on a regular basis to see her at weekends would work. A new life. A new me.

Actually, my drinking was entering its most terrifying stage. When I turned up in Rome, in late December, I immediately went on a bender. On Christmas Day Johnny had dinner alone at the Hassler Hotel. I was incapable. In early January Johnny was sent to the Sudan to cover the release of a British family held hostage by Ethiopian guerrillas. By myself in a barely furnished apartment and drinking away, I left the doors unlocked and was unaware that the hi-fi, the answering machine and a stack of other office equipment had been stolen while I was out for the count. When Johnny got back a week later, I was in a sorry heap on the bed. My mother was so worried at not having heard from me she had alerted Interpol. The benders continued.

I was alone again for four weeks in March, while Johnny was in Kenya and Uganda. He came back to find the cleaning lady had called the apartment porter and together they had arranged for an ambulance to take the comatose Englishwoman to hospital. I spent five days there, coming round, coming off a bender, without money, without keys, without being able to speak Italian. It was a miracle I escaped. Nothing persuaded me to stay sober. Not my daughter. Not Johnny. Not the glamorous bits of Johnny's job.

I went home each month to see Emma and for the Easter holidays she came out to Rome. Johnny, a talented artist, had hand-painted her bedroom wall with a British Airways Jumbo flying over St Peter's and half of Rome welcoming her. She loved it. She loved the tortoises we had inherited in the garden. She had become so adept at packing a bag and moving from parent to parent that neither the flight nor the country, or even the climate, gave her the slightest trouble. There were two apartments above us. In one lived a delightful young family with an English mother and a daughter of Emma's age. So Emma had friends. But by week two of her stay I was in the grip of one of my benders. That was how I drank. Either I was sober. Or I was flat-out drunk. I had well passed the stage where I was a daily drinker who functioned badly. If I drank I did not function at all. In common with many women, my capacity and tolerance for alcohol had diminished with lightning speed. From the time when it had taken three weeks for a bender to develop from the moment I first picked up a glass, it was now only a matter of hours.

Johnny took Emma off to the beach each day and even introduced her to *spaghetti alle vongole*. Just like Daddy's fishing bait, she said, but she loved it. She would come in and mop my brow and say how sad she was that 'Mummy isn't well again'. Her sweetness and forgiveness made it worse. Wasn't this a movie I had already starred in? Except last time I was the little girl, listening to her mother's weeping, drunken words. Despite everything, Emma returned to the UK saying she had had a great time.

In those early months in Rome we joined a sports club, played tennis and swam. We entertained friends to lunch on the beach at Fregene. When I was well, life was leisurely and unhurried. It was good.

Emma was next in Rome for the summer holidays. A combination of glorious days at the beach together and periods when I was comatose in the bedroom. Enough was enough for Johnny. With tears in his eyes, once Emma had departed after her holiday, he booked my flight too. As he waved goodbye he begged me to go home and get well.

Experts would say this is the wisest thing a loved one can do. But just as I had regarded his part in the court case as gross disloyalty, I passionately resented the idea that he had got rid of me. Not until I was well again could I appreciate that my husband and my boyfriend were dealing with something of which they had no experience.

I no longer had a home in London. I had no money. I was still meant to send Charlie a cheque on a monthly basis to cover my share of his court costs as ordered by the judge. With my tail between my legs I returned home to my mother. She treated me like a delinquent teenager. She locked up the booze. She alternated between taking me on shopping sprees to cheer me up and denying me the use of the car. Not without good reason. When I hoped she was looking the other way, I would buy booze.

Meanwhile Charlie, unhappy at the *Evening News*, had applied for and got a job in Glasgow as editor of the *Evening Times*. Now it was no longer to be the M6 Knutsford Service Station but the car park of a hotel in Carlisle. And instead of Gwyneth, a much more forbidding woman called Catherine. She seemed to show little warmth towards Emma and made no secret of her total disapproval of her charge's wayward mother.

It was during this, the bleakest of all periods, that I took myself on a train to Glasgow after a spectacular week of drinking and arrived on the platform weighing six stone, shaking and unable to walk.

At some point during the weekend Charlie had booked tickets at a theatre for a children's show. I hadn't had a drink since stepping off the train, where memorably the steward in the buffet car had refused to continue serving me. But the result of cutting off the supply of my drug meant my body was in a dangerous state. As we left the theatre it took the combined efforts of Charlie and our six-year-old daughter to walk me to the car. My legs refused to carry me on their own. I left after the weekend in the same state as when I had arrived: a shivering, trembling wreck.

No sooner was I home than I somehow got my hands on more alcohol. The next I knew I was coming round in a hospital bed. My throat was raw. A tube had been thrust down it to pump me out. The following day I received a routine visit from the hospital psychiatrist. Had I, she enquired, considered going to Alcoholics Anonymous? Certainly not, I replied. I had no need for prayers and cold tea.

But I had every need.

A couple of days later, back home with my mother, I made a call. I made my own way to a church hall in Southport. A man who was a painter and decorator told of how he used to get rotten drunk every weekend and then take Mondays off and how he recognised his drinking was out of control. It didn't seem much of a problem compared to mine, but at least I was with others who were struggling. Better still, no one in the room seemed to think I should pull myself together. But they all had husbands and jobs and children. I no longer had my daughter. I had no job. I had no husband. The one man in my life had sent me packing. All I had was a bossy, interfering mother and a shame so dreadful that the only sensible solution was to have another drink. If life was a fairy tale I would have seen sense that first evening and stopped drinking for ever. But I didn't. It would take me some months and a few more near misses of killing myself with alcohol before I finally gave up.

13

Climbing the Cliff Face

As the months went by I lived for my weekends of access. Those heartbreaking journeys up and down the M6 to Carlisle to bring Emma back to Liverpool. The agony of packing up the car again on a Sunday night to hand her over at the dreaded checkpoint to Catherine, a woman I disliked more with every meeting and one for whom Emma showed no love whatsoever. Although Emma, by now self-trained in a way that would impress any school of diplomacy, never complained. Certainly not about her father, whom she adored. Or about Catherine, unless you spotted the tears she would stoically try to cover up but which welled up in her eyes as we parked the car in Carlisle.

It was as if this little girl, old beyond her years, knew better than to add to the anguish that lay just below the surface of the Pollyanna life we were all pretending she was leading. Sometimes, tired of my mother, I would go up to Glasgow and spend the weekend in Charlie's lavish West End house or the log cabin he had purchased on Loch Fyne.

It was appealing and comforting to play happy families. It was tempting to think we could go over old ground yet again and make it as a family. But I knew in my heart it would be for all the wrong reasons. It wasn't right.

Sure enough, when the weekend was as near to perfect as we could get, with good weather, friends staying near by and Emma thrilled that her parents were seemingly together, I would spoil it all by picking up a drink. Why, why, why? If I could have fathomed why the compulsion to drink was so overwhelming, so important, maybe I could have fought it better and stayed sober. When, yet again, I fell by the wayside (often quite literally), others would talk scathingly of my lack of will-power. My selfishness. When I finally sorted myself out, the same people would talk admiringly of the sheer force of my will-power. On both counts I would respectfully suggest they were talking bollocks.

In my defence, I continued to go to AA meetings, however infrequently. Effectively, if nothing else, AA had ruined any thoughts I had that I could become a controlled drinker. Or that my problem was short term. If I had been on a bender, I would turn up in some church hall, greet people with cheeriness and did not mention what I had done, stupidly imagining that no one would suspect.

The pattern was always much the same. Something, anything, would set me off. For heaven's sake, there were enough reasons to drink – poor me, let's pour another. So I would slope off to buy a bottle and within a matter hours I would be back to my tricks. Three days of blackout, of drinking and sleeping. Each time my mother would be sick with worry, unsure whether to kill me with kindness or try to talk me into sense. She at least would call someone I had met at AA. One friend in particular never counted the cost of her time or lost patience with me. She was at my bedside at home when I came round. She never berated me or questioned what I had done. Instead she suggested I eat (a physical impossibility between throwing-up, retching and shaking). She also urged me to keep in touch. The most important thing I learnt was that 'the first drink does the damage'. If I didn't have the first one I wouldn't want the next one.

Almost anyone else would have imagined the best tack with

me would be to mention Emma and how upset/disap-
pointed/hurt, etc. she would be if she knew my state. Another
former drunk at least knew better.

Weeks would go by without me drinking. But as if out of
nowhere suddenly there would be a more overpowering reason
to drink than not. Even though at AA meetings they urged me to
try to live in the day and let tomorrow take care of itself, I found
it impossible not to dwell on what, if anything, lay ahead.

I met nothing but kindness and love and encouragement. I
realised that all our problems, when it came to the detail, were
different. Others didn't have a young daughter growing up without her mother, who was living in another country. They didn't
have a glittering newspaper career behind them. But we were all
dealing with a loss of sorts, be it family or expectations. We had
all come to grief because we could not control how we drank
and that allowed us to understand each other's struggles.

I felt in so many ways like a child. And one, too, taking her
first steps. I longed for life to be normal. I wanted my daughter,
I wanted a home and I wanted a husband. I wanted more children. I wanted to be out of the clutches of my domineering
mother. I wanted to be able not to drink and to feel free from
thinking about it. Free from my record as a failed journalist.
None of it seemed possible.

I was only slowly learning: to wash and brush my teeth every
day; to be in some way well mannered, instead of barking at
people out of fear; not continually taking a hammer to crack a
nut; that everyone was not out to get me. Fear replaced alcohol
as my biggest enemy. I smoked, I shopped, I dreamt, I despaired
of ever, ever getting out of the black hole drinking had thrown
me into. I couldn't conceive of a time when I would be accepted
again as normal, capable enough to hold down a proper job
back in London.

A step in the right direction was unexpectedly being introduced to a man at Waterloo Rugby Club, the grounds of which
were in the same road as my parents' home in Blundellsands. He

turned out to be an executive at the *Liverpool Post* and *Echo*. A couple of days later, with a shaking hand, I dialled his home number and asked if I might be considered for a job on one of his papers. He asked no questions. He must have known I was desperate. He was the paper's general manager, and a journalist. He arranged for me to see the editor of the *Echo*. Within a couple of weeks I had been offered a job as a feature writer on the paper. It was a toss-up whether to celebrate my chance of returning to my chosen profession or to wallow in the misery of the mess and failure I had become. I did both. But at least I was working.

The *Post* and *Echo* were in a newish building in Old Hall Street, Liverpool, near the entrance to the Mersey Tunnel. They must have known that a *Sunday Times* reporter of yesterday didn't end up back on her local paper without a dark history. But I marched in as Mrs Big Time, sat at my allotted desk and covered up my trepidation with a mixture of arrogance and sharp quips. My first assignment was to report on a threatened dock strike. I took the union leaders for lunch. I don't know who was more shocked. The dockers to find the *Echo* feeding them, or the features editor who found out that I had been splashing out at the local steakhouse. When I wrote up my story I felt as I had done all those years ago on my first shifts at the *Daily Mail*. But I had not entirely forgotten my skills. Enough, within a few weeks, for the editor to suggest that I write a weekly Wednesday column.

I had always dreamt about having a newspaper column. Not, naturally, on a local evening paper – although rereading my early efforts, I can only be thankful that I was able to cut my teeth with a relatively small number of people reading.

The skill of popular column writing is often said to be the talent for saying what others are thinking. This will not do. The knack is to look at the subject matter and take it from another angle. My early efforts show how predictably corny I was. But it taught me the discipline of thinking of ideas. It taught me to live with the panic of not having any ideas. I was crawling back to life.

Like Charlie, Johnny never shut the door on me. He never objected when I returned to Charlie. Likewise, he accepted with enthusiasm my coming back and forth to Rome for holidays and, eventually, to report for the *Liverpool Echo* on the selection of a new pope. Two papal elections, as it turned out.

Again, while I was there, and I was well, we enjoyed idyllic times. As much as I ever could with the loss of Emma permanently in my thoughts. Johnny and I were best friends, comfortable in each other's company, and he was a wonderful, considerate lover. His childlike delight in the good things of life, art, food, fine wine, a beautiful building, was infectious. His love of Emma was unequivocal.

He couldn't comprehend why, when there was so much going for us all, I would so often end up in a drunken heap. He more than anyone would nurse me through the withdrawals. Like the others, he pleaded with me to stop destroying myself. Yet to my consternation, while showing such love and sweetness, he would nevertheless drive me back to the airport at the end of a trip, be it for holiday or work, without seeming to be bothered I was leaving. It didn't appear to worry him to be without me. If I rang half a dozen times a week, he would sound delighted to hear from me. If I didn't ring, he never complained. It was hard to know how he really felt. Naturally I wanted him for keeps, even though I recognised his shortcomings as much as he knew mine.

When Pope Paul VI died and a new pope was to be elected, I persuaded the *Echo* to let me report from Rome, offering to pay my own airfare. As cynical journalists, we called it the Pope of the Month competition, since no sooner had the white smoke emerged to indicate the college of cardinals had made their choice, than his successor was found dead in bed and the whole process had to begin again.

I went on another bender, resulting in Johnny having to write my copy for the *Echo*. Coming out of it, with the all-too-familiar shakes and retching, there was an evening when the Rome apartment was packed with foreign correspondents.

Many of them were old colleagues we had both worked with in the past. As men do (I was the only woman present), they began to discuss in earnest Johnny's career and what plans he had for his future. I realised women, or certainly not those of my generation, never take themselves as seriously as their male counterparts, but I was busily raising my eyes to heaven at the pomposity of the discussion when one of the number turned to me with only a brief glance and asked if he could have some more coffee. I left for the kitchen, raging, tears in my eyes. Was this now my role? How much more proof did I need that I had thrown away my life, when men with half my talent thought I was useful for nothing more than filling their coffee cup?

The visit naturally did nothing to persuade Johnny that I was improving much. I went home knowing that our relationship had just taken another step backwards. I couldn't imagine it getting any better. It was back to Liverpool, with no prospects of a rosier tomorrow.

Charlie, to his credit, would take my phone calls of despair as often as I chose to make them. When my column seemed impossible to write, he would guide me through, suggest ideas and boost my confidence. I have never blamed him for my drinking, nor have I ever allowed anyone else to. It is glib in the extreme to suggest that a bad marriage makes someone a drunk. Daily, all over the place, people cope with rotten, destructive relationships, bereavements, loss of jobs, illness and God knows what else without turning into drunks.

It was as well during my worst times that Emma had the security of Charlie. The judge, by all accounts a heavy gin drinker, had failed to recognise my state. On the other hand, if he had declared me an alcoholic, would I have been prepared to accept it? What makes some drunks call it a day and others go on ruining their lives? I do not know the answer. But my last fight with alcohol to date would take place on 12 December 1978.

As had happened so often before, there was every reason to stay sober. Things were looking up. Johnny had been called back from Rome. The days of reporting the *dolce vita* of the city had gone. The Pope was safely installed. The Red Brigade and urban terrorism had ceased making headlines. Even before he packed up his far from overworked Italian life, he had been coming home regularly to work on the background to the Jeremy Thorpe story.

The Thorpe saga had begun in early 1976, when an unknown man named Norman Scott, in front of the Magistrates' Court in Barnstaple, charged with some minor offence, had announced he couldn't get a job because Jeremy Thorpe, then leader of the Liberal Party, had his National Insurance cards. Scott went on to claim that Thorpe and he had had a homosexual affair and that Thorpe had hired someone to kill him and had had his beloved dog Rinka shot dead.

Johnny had covered the story from the start. It was his earlier than anticipated return to London, plus signs that I was improving and at least taking steps to acknowledge my problem, that prompted our at first tentative house-hunting in London.

It would be fair to say that the sight of a house in need of renovation, one of an architectural style to his liking, was what influenced Johnny incautiously to move forward. In other words, 12 Tavistock Terrace, Upper Holloway, N19, was his goal and I only half – well, only somehow – went with the package.

Off the Holloway Road, towards Archway, most of the terrace was early Victorian and Georgian in style. An old Polish gent, who had been a waiter at the Savoy and also cannily a man of property, owned it. The house, which was in a dilapidated state, had been let as individual rooms and had no inside lavatory, no bath and no kitchen. But it had an enchanting L-shaped garden, bigger than any other in the street, with a splendid palm tree. It was thought to have been the original builder's own home. We settled on £33,000. A fortune. We had to take the most expensive mortgage going because of our lack of deposit and status. It was not yet ours, but we were negotiating and like children would endlessly drive past our potential purchase.

It looked as if I was at least heading back to normal life.

That weekend Emma and I had been staying with Johnny's parents, who were now living in Hackney. On the Sunday night, unknown to the others, I packed Emma into the car, drove to the nearest off-licence and bought a bottle. As I went back to the car, there were tears in her eyes. I drank the contents and the next morning decided enough was enough.

It was the start of the long crawl back.

Within the next couple of years I would end up being at home far more than Charlie, because as a writer and a columnist I would not be chained to an office desk like a newspaper executive has to be. While Charlie, as ambitious as ever, would go on to greater and better managerial jobs, spending more and more time at work. Yet Emma was to remain in his custody, care and control.

That was the piece of the jigsaw that I still can hardly bear to think about without the word *injustice* screaming back at me. Living with that reality was far harder than anything I have ever done.

14

Miss Tickety-boo

By 1979 Johnny and I had known each other for almost thirteen years. A friendship which had begun when a nineteen-year-old boy met an older, more mature girl – a twenty-one-year-old with big thighs, a mini-skirt, bright red hair, a dog, a sports car and a devil-may-care approach – had moved on. The boy had become a man and a highly regarded journalist, while the promising, bright girl had regressed to failed wife and mother. A frightened soul who was gingerly looking over the parapet at the future, inwardly terrified by almost anything that moved.

Throughout, girlfriends observed with some envy that Penrose – as almost everyone called him – came just as soon as I whistled, however badly I had behaved. He says generously that he adored me from the start. In those early days he had joined me the first time I was ever sent to do a piece of political reporting – a meeting in Chelsea – because his shorthand was better than mine. In return I bought him a pasta supper at Dino's in South Kensington. As we got to know each other more he obligingly painted the sitting room of my bachelor-girl flat in Sloane Square.

After I married Charlie, Johnny would occasionally turn up at Alwyne Square. He was always a joy to see. He was self-deprecating and very funny. He could make any story interesting. He had a charm and social ease that people found thoroughly likeable and engaging. That included pub landlords, newspaper editors and even husbands. My mother thought the world of him. He was beautifully mannered, courteous, stylishly dressed and, as she continually emphasised, kind.

On the minus side, he was a dreamer, albeit one whose castles in the sky were invariably Georgian houses packed with priceless furniture and works of art. He had rejected a career as an artist or a designer and opted for journalism. But he had a natural talent when it came to houses, furniture and gardens. His life was an infuriating mixture of order and complete chaos. He always looked as if he had stepped out of a fashion shoot for the sophisticated man, his suits cleaned and pressed, his shirts impeccably ironed. He was a very late riser, up only by the crack of midday, wearing, from as far back as I could remember, Jermyn Street shirts and Levi jeans. But if my drinking had been out of control, so was his way with money. He was permanently in debt, being the guy in the pub most eager to buy a round. By the criteria of Mr Justice Faulks he held his own, nay was top of his field, when it came to 'Fleet Street standards' of drinking.

When I had made the decision to return to Charlie, after we had become lovers, Johnny had accepted my choice without bitterness. He would arrive at Higher Cliff Farm and cheer me up. Astonishingly, even my suspicious, jealous husband regarded him as benign and amusing.

Early one morning at the farm, I received a call from the nearby village. Johnny had driven from London during the night, after I had telephoned him in a state. Heartlessly, I sent him back without seeing him. When the reconciliation with Charlie fell to pieces and the court case was pending, he was still at my side. But I would soon push him too far. It resulted in him ringing up Charlie and offering to give evidence on his behalf. Johnny had had enough. The worm had turned. He was very,

very angry with me. His appearance in court held no sway. But for a long time I found his betrayal unforgivable. I eventually had to accept, once I was truly better, that along the way my behaviour had soured and wounded those who loved me dearly. Johnny was not by nature a man easily moved to anger, but there had been half a dozen times when we had ended up having physical fights. Both of us probably the worse for wear. Neither of us knew what we were dealing with.

After Charlie had won custody of Emma, and I staggered on for a while at the *Sunday Times*, Johnny and I had an on–off relationship. Drunken rows, followed by sensational getting-back-togethers. There was no doubt I was a liability to the prospects and reputation of a rising young Fleet Street chap. His star was in the ascendancy. Mine was all too obviously diving down fast.

I would turn up to greet him or join him at the *Daily Mirror* at the end of a day's work, incapable of speech. At one *Daily Mirror* party, held in the chairman's office, I was so blind drunk that I got locked in the lavatory and had to be rescued. His colleagues regarded me as a frightful nuisance. His bosses likewise. When one of his reporter friends was getting married, the formal invitation arrived very pointedly minus my name.

He would move his things out of my flat at my insistence. Or he'd leave in anger. Once, after I'd thrown him out he was sent immediately on a rush job abroad and the contents of his car, which he'd left at the Terminal Two car park at Heathrow, were stolen. The insurance company asked suspiciously why all his belongings had been parked at Heathrow.

I used to dream of how nice it would be to have an amalgam of Charlie and Johnny. That way I could have Emma, someone 100 per cent hard-working and responsible to look after us, and a kind and understanding husband to boot.

'How many slices of the cake do you want, Anne?' a kindly psychiatrist in Liverpool my mother had sent me to during one of my drinking bouts had asked. 'Because you can't have the whole cake.' The aim of the sessions was 'to sort me out'. I suppose psychiatrists still think they can halt an alcoholic's drinking. They can't. Any more than other quick-fire, expensive methods such as drying-out clinics and rehab centres. They can kick-start a recovery. But it needs ongoing, regular monitoring. That said, the cake question is a handy barometer for those of us who like to have it all.

As I saw it, unless I got my head around the bit about not drinking there wasn't going to be a future beyond Liverpool and my controlling mother. There wasn't going to be any cake to have slices of. But even when my drinking ceased there was a big question mark over whether someone like Johnny could truly settle down or be disciplined enough to recognise that there could be a rainy day, instead of pursuing his usual pattern of blowing every single penny and having credit-card companies chase him. Moving around point zero funds, fruitlessly trying to outwit those to whom he was in debt, took up hours of his time.

While Johnny was still commuting between London and Rome, I got a rare chance to go back on the road. The general election, 1979. 'If it's eight-thirty on Wednesday, we're in Leicester.'

A yellowing cutting from the *Liverpool Echo* dated 20 April 1979 describes a journey in a bright orange Wallace Arnold coach, following another orange Wallace Arnold coach that carried the formidable leader of the Tory Party, Margaret Thatcher. Our convoy had travelled through East Anglia and on to the Midlands. It was my first piece of political reporting since covering the 1972 by-election in Rochdale for the *Sunday Times* in which Cyril Smith, a former mayor of the town, became its Liberal Member of Parliament.

For a while I could forget I was Miss Tiddlysquit-nothing from a local paper. Only meeting other journalists who had known me in a former life and had continued their careers on an even keel spoilt the fantasy.

On the second day of the jamboree at least sixty of us, journalists, security guards, press officers and the leader of the Tory Party, ended up in a field on a farm near Eye in Suffolk. The local lapel badges ordered us to 'Vote for Gummer!' John Gummer was a small, anxious man, eventually to become Agriculture Minister in Thatcher's Cabinet, but then fighting his first election. Many years later he would be remembered principally for posing with his young daughter while she ate a hamburger to illustrate that beef was safe and the population was under no threat from mad cow disease. (A salutary lesson for politicians not to parade their children for a cause unless they are 500 per cent sure their case is strong.)

Mrs Thatcher was handed a calf to cuddle. The farm hand said it was only six hours old. The leader of the Tory Party took great care of her charge. The cameras whirred and clicked. We didn't know at this stage that the soon-to-be Prime Minister disliked furry animals, along with small babies, trains, the unambitious and the feckless nearly as much as she detested socialism and anyone who worked for the Foreign Office.

Calf safely handed back to its mother, we marched over the fields. On the way we met a grumpy Denis Thatcher, who was still negotiating his way to the calf photo-opportunity via the muddy yard outside the cowsheds, while simultaneously complaining about 'the rumpus and the reptiles'. His all-purpose phrase for those following his wife.

Mrs Thatcher didn't notice him and didn't halt until she arrived at her orange bus. Immediately the photographers were clambering for more snaps. 'Here, Mrs T. Here, Maggie'. 'No!' Thatcher suddenly shrieked. 'I'll look like a bus conductor-*ess*.' Pause. 'Not', she added, with slow and overly sweet emphasis, 'that bus conductor-*esses* aren't marvellous people.'

Those were early days. A raw Thatcher. Anxious not to put a foot wrong and sometimes cloying and clumsy with it.

According to the *Daily Mirror* the calf died next morning. No matter, for by then we had moved on to Leicester.

At a sewing factory, Mrs Thatcher got behind a machine and set to. 'What are you doing?' I asked. 'An interlocking edge,' said Mrs Thatcher, astonished by my question. I had not a clue what an interlocking edge was. But I was witnessing a leader of the Tory Party and soon-to-be Prime Minister who knew exactly how to do one.

From the start, that was Mrs Thatcher's knack. And the bit of her that both impressed and alarmed. With or without image-shapers, she knew instinctively how to appeal as Mrs Commonsense, who could do interlocking edges and feel fabric and know whether it was suitable for curtains or upholstery. To the satisfaction of her female followers, she was the sort of woman who looked as if her puddings always came out the right shape.

In a way, a little of her was that woman. There was nothing phoney about her showing off her wardrobe at home, as she would subsequently do in a television interview, and demonstrating how she put tissue in the sleeves of her suits and kept her shoes in a colour-coordinated line-up. 'If you make a habit of something it becomes easier to do. Just like brushing your teeth' was one of her favourite maxims.

The trouble was she reminded me not so much of Disraeli or Winston Churchill or Golda Meir or Mrs Gandhi, but of Mrs Platt, my domestic science teacher at Farnborough Hill, who had despaired of my sloppiness and was always recommending that everything be 'garnished with a little parsley'. Also, like Mrs Platt, Thatcher was rarely parted from her handbag and had an identical, inelegant waddle when she walked.

What did I know? During her first election the stress on domesticity and her unalterable views on what she saw as the way forward were precisely the credentials that carried Margaret Thatcher through. She applied the same housewife's principles when it came to sharing her beliefs on economics with the country. 'You can only spend what you have in your purse,' she would explain, time and again. You couldn't fault her simple logic. She was also convinced that everyone wanted to buy their own home.

I imagined Mrs Thatcher lay in bed at night surprised there were not queues of other women challenging her to become the first female prime minister. Like my mother and me, until my marriage, her path to the top had not been complicated by gender, because she had not allowed it to be. She had wisely ignored all attempts to be sidelined because she was a woman, and carried on regardless. This talent to forge on being an important ingredient both in her success and in her eventual downfall.

She was fearless in voicing her opinions and rarely influenced by those around her urging caution or forecasting disaster. In private, she was known to be kind and considerate and would prove non-judgemental when it came to sexual dalliances by her ministers; her concern being only that a good colleague should not be brought down by an unwise affair of the heart. Motherhood, although her adoring public wouldn't know it for years, was not one of her great skills. It was not even one of her interests.

'My mother was always elsewhere,' daughter Carol, without noticeable rancour, has often said. Ye gods again. In a contest with Denis, Mr Justice Faulks would surely have handed over the Thatcher children to their father.

On the final night of the 1979 election campaign I returned to London and waited for Mrs Thatcher to arrive at Tory Central Office. She looked radiant. The country celebrated its Tory victory. Feminists were sent into a spin. A female prime minister, the first in history. But one batting for the wrong side.

In my column I defined it as the movement's magnificent own goal.

Secretly Anne Robinson, part-time mother, newly sober, thought Mrs Thatcher was completely unnerving. All those brains and determination were ordinary enough in my upbringing. It was her knowing how to do interlocking edges and make puddings turn out the right shape that chimed so oddly. Plus her hairdo, which, as my mother observed, 'had neither shape nor make about it'. It was about the only thing my mother and I agreed on.

My mother was becoming increasingly trying to deal with. Her drinking since Emma's birth, strangely, had virtually stopped, as she frequently boasted, having never previously been prepared to discuss her own abuse of alcohol. I didn't appreciate why or how. Yet far from celebrating my newly employable state she had become inexplicably unreasonable. She would cast doubts on my chances of staying upright. At other times she would annoyingly insist, 'Of course, I got you well.' Fragile and emotional as I was, I didn't have the wit to agree and let it drop. Instead, I would set to and argue with her. No doubt she was fearful. She had suffered all the tragedy and disillusionment and worry of the years since my marriage and now the ungrateful wild child was abandoning her. That meant her seeing far less of Emma too. Her anxieties, unspoken and probably unconscious, were another example of how the damage that my drinking did to other people went much further than my loss of Emma.

To understand my mother's state was well beyond me. In any case, my thoughts were selfishly elsewhere. The move back to London was coming tantalisingly close. At his trial at the Old Bailey, Jeremy Thorpe was charged, along with three others, with conspiracy and incitement to murder. He was acquitted. A hollow victory, because by then his political career and reputation were finished. It was, however, a significant date in the 'Penrob' household. That June afternoon, just before the verdict came through, and reporters had rushed out of the courtroom to call their news desks with the result, Johnny telephoned our solicitor and heard that, after months of delay and hesitation on behalf of various building societies, we had exchanged contracts on Tavistock Terrace.

A month later, on 24 July, Johnny was in Malawi, on his way

to cover the Commonwealth Conference in Zambia, when we completed on the sale. I telexed him in Blantyre from the *Liverpool Daily Post*: the telex, framed and faded, still hangs in his study. 'Have a glass of champagne. Tavistock is ours. Love Robinson.'

Our financial status was poor, the scale of works required daunting, so a bridging loan at a punishing interest rate of 20-odd per cent had to be arranged. Who cared? Before long, Emma and I would be together without the interference of my mother.

To the outside world I looked fine. But it is a falsehood to imagine you can abandon your drug and pick up your life without experiencing the dramatic effects of losing your crutch. My condition showed itself in all sorts of small ways. I was still liable to get an attack of the shakes if I was unexpectedly thrown by a situation. Or rather, the more I worried about shaking the more likely it would be to happen. I was ill at ease with people, particularly around those who liked a drink. I no longer enjoyed standing in a pub, or staying up late at night while others drank themselves stupid. I worried endlessly about how to live a life without alcohol, while learning to enjoy myself. The simple logic that life was never going to be quite the same again completely escaped me. 'Give it two years before you make any major decisions,' I was warned by those wiser. 'What you want now mightn't be what you want when you grow up.' But in my panic and need to shed my immediate past, I naturally disregarded any well-meant guidance. Self-will ran riot as I engaged full throttle in my efforts to make life cosy and back to normal.

We'd started attacking the house and as soon as it had an inside lavatory, I reasoned, I could give up my staff job in Liverpool and settle for the meagre amount the *Echo* agreed to pay for my weekly column and any freelance articles.

Since we had no money, Johnny, true to form, being just about the only foreign correspondent in the history of newspapers to return home without a huge nest egg, I sold my sapphire ring to pay for the roof to be stripped and retiled. Johnny got rid of his beloved yellow Alfa Romeo sports car to square the bills on the other building works that had to be completed as a condition of our mortgage. Once my few possessions were installed in Upper Holloway, I arranged with Charlie that, at my expense, Emma would travel down from Scotland every other Friday. I knew that it was further for Emma to come but I was convinced it was vital for both of us.

Holloway Road, Caledonian Road, King's Cross, Covent Garden, Piccadilly Circus, Hyde Park Corner, Knightsbridge, South Kensington, Barons Court and on to Hammersmith and South Ealing, Osterley, Hounslow East and finally Heathrow. There were more than twenty stops on the Tube to collect Emma. As the train made its slow journey I found it impossible not to think of other mothers. Ordinary mothers, who were at this very minute collecting their children from school and putting their tea on the table, before helping with the homework and playing with them. Mothers who could wake up on Saturday morning knowing it was not all going to end for another fortnight the next day. The journey to and from Heathrow was my bit. Emma was to make the flight from Glasgow and the Tube journey twice a month for nearly three years. I would leave hours early to meet her. Hang around arrivals at Terminal One and eventually be rewarded with the sight of her breaking free from her airline minder and running towards me. Around her neck would be a sign that read 'UM'. Unaccompanied Minor. She would have been put on the plane by Catherine, the nanny, and busied herself during the flight doing her homework. We would then make the journey, another hour and a half, back on the Piccadilly line. It took up most of Friday afternoon and early evening but Emma never once complained. She and I would hold hands all the way home.

To my relief, my daughter was becoming much more her own person. I couldn't spot Catherine-isms, in the same way I had spotted Gwyneth's mannerisms. But it wasn't difficult to sense how little she liked Catherine. Not least when it came to packing up on a Sunday night to make the dreaded journey back to Scotland. Quite often she would complain on a Sunday morning of not feeling well. Of having a sore throat. I knew she wasn't really sick and bent over backwards to be firm. It was important not to act independently of her father and to allow her to remain in London, simply because she and I would miss each other. It was tormenting and heartbreaking and, apart from Johnny, nobody, but nobody, knew about it.

To begin with, Tavistock Terrace was an empty shell. In comparison, Charlie's house in Glasgow was an exotically furnished palace. Nevertheless, Emma, as much as Johnny and I, shared the adventure of home-making. For months, because there was no cooker, we were obliged to live almost exclusively on fish and chips and McDonald's – then a novelty as one of the first branches to open in Britain was only a few hundred yards away. One weekend we hired a pneumatic drill and dug out the basement. (*Unfit mother uses child as slave labour on weekend access.*) We whooped with delight when the bath was plumbed in and we had hot water to wash the crockery in it. The kitchen and the kitchen sink came later. Johnny rented a truck and drove to Liverpool to pick up some units a friend was throwing out. We celebrated the Saturdays when we had gathered enough cash or credit to have another luxury delivered. A luxury in our book being a fridge or a washing machine.

Of course, having Emma every other weekend was never enough. I would spend the best part of the days leading up to her arrival planning, longing. Then as soon as she *was* there I would only be able to focus on the horrible thought of our parting on a Sunday night.

One Sunday evening, back at the airport, the BA official in charge of UMs had rather grumpily taken Emma off and I dutifully waited, as required, for word that the plane had departed, lost in my own world of despondency. A good twenty minutes later the same, now even grumpier BA woman came towards me with Emma in tow. She was furious. She had, she said, been calling my name over the loudspeakers to no avail. Didn't I know the rules? I must wait by the desk in case there was a delay, as there had been. The dressing-down was so unexpected Emma burst into tears. So did I. It was tough enough to have to stand around with the flotsam and jetsam of the departure hall and think about Emma returning to the cold Catherine, without anyone marching up to remind me how useless and inadequate and irresponsible I was. The BA woman had no idea where she had landed her two left feet. Why should she? In fact, she had been calling for a 'Mrs Wilson'. The name hadn't registered when it was announced.

I'd often fall silent and sulk when I had every right to speak up, not just with thoughtless airline clerks, but with Johnny, with workmen, with newspaper colleagues. Alternatively, I'd rant until the person being confronted lost sympathy. In my lighter moments I would refer to myself as the belligerent door-mat. Infinitely more important than the rest of the tribe I was silently at war with was Catherine. She genuinely worried me and I had a right to be concerned about my daughter's welfare. The trouble was Catherine was not wicked or irresponsible. On the contrary, she appeared faultless when it came to carrying out her duties, but her demeanour struck me as chilling. A much more difficult thing to object to. Occasionally I would raise my concern with Charlie that she lacked any cosiness or warmth. But Catherine had witnessed too many of my drunken bouts for me to feel I had any authority to complain about her and it was easy to sense Charlie was perfectly happy with a reliable, trust-worthy carer. I imagined he preferred a less influential nanny for his daughter than Gwyneth. But I am not sure we ever discussed it.

Emma was much more grown up all round. Much more accepting than her mother. She compartmentalised her life. Her bedroom in Tavistock Terrace was *her* bedroom. Her toys came out to play. She picked up the pieces from a fortnight earlier without comment. She showed only affection and smiles: for her mother, for Johnny, for her nanna and grandad and for Johnny's parents, Ray and Anna, who vitally provided a sumptuous family Sunday lunch for us all when Emma was in London. Her life in Glasgow she discussed very little. Instinctively she shied away from passing on any information that might cause trouble.

My mother was now limited to masterminding events via the telephone. 'Has the child got friends to play with?' she would demand. Actually, friends were a problem. We knew very few people with children of Emma's age round about. I had no contact with schools for obvious reasons. We would sometimes try to match Emma up with the children of work colleagues. One Sunday we even invited Lady Lucan over for lunch because her daughter Camilla was the same age as Emma. Johnny had got to know Veronica Lucan during the search for her husband after the family nanny had been murdered – mistaken for Lady Lucan by Lord Lucan, who had never been seen since. Veronica Lucan was a very odd woman indeed. 'Nannies can be a dreadful problem,' she announced at one stage during the afternoon. The words hung in the air without anyone knowing quite how to take them. But be it the children of a missing aristo or anyone else's children, it wasn't satisfactory. In common with just about any child I know, Emma refused to be forced into friendships with playmates chosen by others. My other big preoccupation was covering my tracks to avoid answering questions about where Emma was during the week.

The gap between how I felt and how I appeared was huge. 'Annie, you're back and well!' old friends would exclaim. 'How are you?' A big smile would arrive on my face. 'Terrific, wonderful, couldn't be better,' I would insist.

And so I entered the 1980s. Not just Miss Belligerent Doormat but also Miss Tickety-boo! 'Tickety-boo, Tickety-boo, everything is fine – don't let anyone know your secrets.' Childhood lessons run deep.

I know there are women who lie about their age. My age has

never bothered me. But if it did I couldn't face the prospect of lying about it. I learnt in those years how exhausting it was to have a secret. It requires radar in your head on full-scale permanent alert. 'Where does Emma go to school?' people would innocently ask. Cue for me to rush into discussion about private versus state schools. 'Does Emma see her father?' was another question. 'Does Emma ride/do piano/want to come to a children's party next Monday night?' Almost any demand about Emma's routine or her details gave me the horrors. I often thought it was a good job that on the whole people were not nearly as curious as I am. I could spot a flaw in a story in seconds. Now, socially I wouldn't dream of pulling at scabs in an effort to get to the bottom of something somebody didn't want me to know. Looking back, I realise many must have been just as charitable towards the accounts I gave them of Emma and me. They had the decency to understand how painful prying questions can be.

Just as crucially, I wanted Emma to be spared the knowledge of how different her life was from others'. I didn't ever want her to think I didn't want her. But I avoided explaining what had happened, because I didn't know how to tell her the story. I didn't want to be disloyal and tell the story differently from how Charlie saw it. He, like me, was doing his best to show her that relations between us were good. He viewed it as important that I saw school reports and knew what was going on.

But if she suddenly and innocently mentioned school and Glasgow in the same sentence, when we were with other people, I would wince. Wince, but know I mustn't do anything about it. Why shouldn't she tell people where she went to school? Where she lived? Whom she lived with?

I don't know what a shrink would have made of any of us. We did the best we could. For my part, it was just so, so lonely out there, trying to cover up what I saw as the terrible result of my badness. Oh, how I woke each morning, longing for it to be different. But I also woke knowing I was only going to stay sober if

I faced the truth head-on. My days of wiping out the horrible reality of life were over. I had no options. I was going through a living bereavement – as the partners and children of those with Alzheimer's call it. As millions of fathers do, for goodness' sake.

It would have made sense to ask for some professional help. It didn't occur to me. Why should it, when I was occupied in trying to make sure no one knew the situation? Over and above a dozen friends, I never discussed it. Of course, hundreds more must have known but I never allowed myself even to imagine that.

Let us count the ways Miss Tickety-boo was coping. Get back to London. Tick. Own a home. Tick. Have Emma living in London at least every other weekend. Tick. Next? Get married.

Finsbury Town Hall, 31 March 1980. The wedding was entirely the bride's idea. It took me several weeks of nagging, of promising a rosy outcome, to convince the groom. There was no question that we loved each other deeply. There was every reason to question how long I could stay being a good girl. The new me, unaided by alcohol, was less than eighteen months old. It was sweet of the groom to give in so easily. Whatever doubts he had Johnny kept to himself. It helped that Emma would refer to him as Mummy's boyfriend and I wanted her to be able to talk about having a stepfather. It was a feeble excuse. Unworthy of me. Borne out by the fact that in the twenty years since I've never heard her use the expression. Johnny has always been Johnny.

In any case, the playground dilemma would cease to matter to any family by the end of the century. Even by the end of the decade, when the word 'partner' had slipped into the language. By the mid-nineties, when I did a live broadcast for the BBC from the maternity unit of University College Hospital in London, of the ten mothers we interviewed, two had husbands, six had partners, two were going it alone. But in the 1980s, newspapers and magazines were still worrying themselves about what a live-in lover should be called.

Another reason for my haste in becoming a married woman again was that I was desperate to have more children. The soon-to-be Mrs Penrose wore a grey silk dress and a cute little hat. The best man, the worse for alcohol even before the ceremony, was late and forgot the ring. The bride's daughter, aged nine, had her front teeth missing. The bride's mother was in one of her finest beaver hats and a beige suit. And, given that the groom was not a titled barrister but a penniless, irresponsible, if charming hack, she was thrilled. Even my mother had lowered her sights.

The wedding carriage was a friend's ancient Range Rover with Irish number plates. Its owner took the pictures for free. No former girlfriend rushed from the back to object. No former girlfriend even arrived to weep.

I had wanted a Catholic wedding. It wasn't, as I first thought, out of the question. I learnt I could apply for an annulment. It meant, as far as I could work out, a great deal of paperwork, plus some little influence and, hey presto! my previous Catholic marriage would disappear. It was humbug of the highest order. The more I was assured it was fixable, the more pointless it seemed to enter into such a charade. Despite my marriage to Charlie having failed, it was a nonsense to pretend it hadn't existed – or was in some way phoney.

So Father Oliver McTernan, our friend and then a curate at St John the Evangelist in Islington, suggested that instead he would give us a blessing, and after we had done the legal business at Finsbury Town Hall we moved on to the church. We entertained fifty-odd friends back at home. There was no carpet in the house, and the groom and his father had spent the night before painting the kitchen ceiling. But to me it represented a move to ordinariness for which I had longed for so many years.

I wasn't the only one with marriage in mind. In September of that year there burst on to the scene a new girlfriend for the increasingly solid and dull future king of England. Lady Diana Spencer was a nursery-school teacher, who unwittingly posed for photographers in a see-through skirt. She was tall, on the lumpy side, but beyond reproach. Her pedigree was impeccable. Blue-blooded, grander than Charles, some members of her family would later remark. She looked perfectly sweet and harmless. There was even a poignant side to her life. Her mother, declared the papers, was a 'bolter', who had 'scarpered' from the family home with another man and left her children to be looked after by their father.

Sad enough, but then Diana's father had remarried. A wicked stepmother completed the family background. The daughter of the romantic novelist Barbara Cartland, Raine Spencer was a woman for whom the expression 'last in the queue, first on the bus' might have been invented. She and her mother milked the new royal connection for all it was worth, while the less discreet members of Diana's family let it be known that she and her siblings loathed the interloper and had nicknamed her 'Acid Raine'. If you read the small print the 'bolter' tag attached to Diana's mother was unfair. She was unable to hang on to her children after leaving their father. He had won custody, care and control as, strangely, aristocratic fathers were more likely to do. As closely as I continued to follow our new female prime minister and be fascinated by her development, the same would be true of Lady Diana Spencer. In our different ways the three of us would change dramatically over the next decades.

That year too, Charlie was heading towards matrimony again. Sally O'Sullivan was a magazine journalist. Not one I knew. But when I began to hear about 'Daddy's friend' from Emma I suggested we all meet.

The date set was Charlie's birthday in August. Emma was with us in Islington. Her father and his new girlfriend agreed to visit for drinks. 'Good Lord,' yelled Johnny, as he spotted them arriving, 'another you is walking up the path.'

Charlie had chosen a second redhead. To be fair to Sally – and to Charlie – we do not look alike, apart from the colour of our hair. But it was a standing joke among mutual friends for years. Less funny for me. 'You'd think Sally was Emma's mother!' joked a tactless journalist friend of Sally's shortly after I had first met Emma's prospective stepmother. Ouch! Ow! Silent scream, panic, dread, knot in the stomach, ouch again.

Open wound takes the full blast of stray, unguided, deadly missile, said the headline in my head.

15

The Comeback Kid

There's a bloke I know in what's left of Fleet Street who plans to sink his redundancy money into an establishment to be called the 'This Time I Really Mean It Hotel', specially designed for people who've just walked out on their spouses. You could check in at any hour of the night without luggage – there'd be a razor, toothbrush and change of clothes on every pillow, along with the after-dinner Valium wrapped in tinfoil. And there'd be a twenty-four-hour bar known as the 'Gone Too Far Bar' where you drink yourself silly.

Act II of *Jeffrey Bernard is Unwell*
by Keith Waterhouse, 1989

The Gone Too Far Club, as I preferred to call it, had its origins at the *Daily Mirror*, the paper I was to join and where Waterhouse had been a writer and columnist during the seventies and early eighties.

'This time you've gone too far' was what the weary landlord of the office pub, the White Swan (known to its patrons as the Stab in the Back), would say without any hint of irony to one or several journalists who had been roistering in his bar. The main culprit was generally acknowledged to be the talented, funny, bad-tempered-but-attractive-to-women and much married art editor. But there were plenty of others who qualified for membership. After the hapless landlord wisely threw in the towel, the phrase lived on. 'This time you've gone too far' was also spat out by angry wives when their husbands fell home in the early hours. Drunkenness, adultery, putting the job first, putting the family last was an accepted part of working for a newspaper. Nowhere more so than at the *Mirror*.

I had started freelancing for the paper in the autumn of 1980. Largely thanks to Johnny, who had passed on my cuttings book, showing samples of my work to his friend Richard Stott. The two had been young reporters together and Stott was now features editor. (He would end up as the editor.) Stott completely disapproved of Johnny's drunken girlfriend. But he knew I'd been a decent reporter in my prime, knew I was making a fresh start, was impressed with the cuttings and arranged for me to see Marje Proops, the paper's woman's editor and legendary agony aunt. Without doubt the most famous female journalist in the land. And although she resolutely kept her age a secret, I reckoned she was then already north of seventy.

The new Mrs Penrose, dressed in a pale blue wool suit, a cream silk blouse – both from Jaeger – plus demure high heels and carrying a black briefcase, walked through the *Mirror* newsroom en route to an appointment with Fleet's Street uncontested queen. The suit had been one of three potential wedding outfits. Wearing it now I felt like an idiot, self-conscious and so obviously on my way to a job interview. Marje was in a wheelchair, having had a hip replacement operation. She was polite, kind, charming, and suggested I wrote some pieces for the woman's pages. I couldn't have agreed more wholeheartedly. Gone was the arrogance of years before, when I had so curtly turned down work I deemed to be beneath me.

At my own suggestion, the first thing I did was a three-part series about the scandal of private doctors prescribing slimming pills, particularly to young girls with hardly an ounce of fat on them. It was my old stamping ground of investigative journalism.

I knew the ropes. When it was published it caused a few waves and some good publicity. Several more one-off features followed.

It was pathetically easy to shine. The paper had a handful of stars that were kept busy and a second division of feature writers who wouldn't have known a story from a tub of ice-cream. Why should they? Half of them hadn't been asked to write one for years. So, for the hard-pressed features editor, a freelance readily available, who could produce readable copy and was no trouble, came as a gift.

I was even sent on a 'jolly' to report from Cuba. The island was being opened up to British journalists for the first time since Castro had come to power. The report I sent got a two-page spread in the middle of the paper. For that, and for whatever other work I did, the payments were generous. After a few months I felt I could safely give up my ties with Liverpool. My last *Echo* column appeared in the November of that year.

'All credit to Mrs June Quinn, who this week established a new deal for women,' began one of the items. Mrs Quinn's campaign for a married woman to be able to take out hire purchase without a credit company insisting that her husband act as guarantor had triumphed. A ruling by the Master of the Rolls, Lord Denning, decreed that henceforth a married woman must be given credit on the basis of her own credit worthiness. 'But I shouldn't think for a minute this will stop companies having a sneaky look at the state of a husband's financial affairs before they say yea or nay,' I ended. Both the ruling and my comment were signs of a time soon to vanish.

My own professional status as a married woman looked rosier than it had done for years. By the start of the new year I'd been hired as a staff writer at the *Mirror*. Not only hired, but promised that within a reasonable amount of time I could be expected to be appointed woman's editor. I'd never planned or harboured ambitions to be a newspaper executive. It wasn't on my list. Writing, being famous, getting a job on the telly had been. But those dreams had long been replaced by the more obvious ones of having Emma around; of wiping out my dreadful drunken reputation; of just being 'normal'. Not that anyone looking for normality should have been heading for the *Mirror*'s front door.

As my hiring was being formalised a hint of my mother's training came through. Enough of it to know that if you didn't get your wish list on the table at the start you were unlikely to get the perks you wanted for years. So at my meeting with the editor I asked for an office car. We had bartered slightly about my salary and agreed on a sum. That over, he nodded the car through without any trouble. The editor had had enough of admin for one day and of dealing with a woman he barely knew, other than as a previously out-of-hand girlfriend of one of his reporters.

I only learnt later that the trip to Cuba and the car upset the applecart in the small woman's department next to Proops' office where I had a desk. One of the long-serving female journalists had objected to a non-staff member being selected for an assignment abroad and then to a new staff member having transport when none of the others enjoyed it. She complained about both to the father of the chapel, the National Union of Journalists equivalent of the shop steward. A perfect example of the negative value of seeking union support. Rather than admire someone with the *chutzpah* to demand more, you condemned them. Not the way my mother had taught me to operate – or an indication that sisterhood had reached the *Mirror*. Male power ruled. Or, as I saw it, power – which just happened to be male – went unchallenged.

I had to wrap up the loose ends of my appointment with the managing editor, a crusty former news editor who was seeing out his days checking expense accounts. I asked him for arrangements to be made for me to have a space in the office car park. Why, he demanded, did I need a car in the first place? In my usual confrontational and aggressive manner, I said the car had been approved by the editor and if there was now to be further discussion about whether I was entitled to a car, he could 'stuff the job'. The managing editor, a one-time army major with a good war behind him, looked thoroughly alarmed and backed off. 'There's no need to get shirty,' he said sulkily. My mother was right. Men were highly unsatisfactory and had no courage if they were confronted. Why should the ones at the *Mirror* be any different from the ones she used to deal with at the market?

Thank God for my upbringing. A sense of humour plus a galloping lack of sensitivity towards men was vital if you wanted to enjoy the comic value of how the paper was run.

On a social level it was entirely different from that of the *Sunday Times*. Here was not the unhurried, scholastic atmosphere of an Oxford college, but something akin to the spirit today on a stock exchange trading floor dominated by brash young dealers. The *Mirror* executives were talented, dedicated, uncouth, their language foul, their skill at producing popular journalism of the highest standard unquestionable. Very few had formal qualifications of any sort – apart from the editor and one or two others having been to art college. Those with a university degree were discouraged from regarding themselves as superior. It did not mean Holborn Circus was a house of philistines. Far from it. It was just that the scholarship came heavily disguised. The form was dictated by the editor, Mike Molloy. An accomplished artist and art editor, he had been picked out in the late sixties, while still in his twenties, to edit the *Mirror Magazine*, one of the first colour supplements. He had been appointed editor of the *Daily Mirror* at the age of thirty-four. He was thoughtful and politically astute. But his preferred pursuits included night-clubbing, the company of pop and film stars (Rod Stewart, Billy Connolly and Joan Collins were particular favourites), and long, expensive lunches at fashionable restaurants. He led, his chosen team followed. While other newspapers conscientiously invited politicians to formal lunches to keep abreast of what was going on, at the *Mirror*, when you were summoned at the last minute to make up the numbers in the boardroom, the guest of honour would turn out to be David Niven. The cheeky confidence went with the success the paper enjoyed. Even with that success now in decline, with increased and fierce competition from the *Mirror*'s main rival, Rupert Murdoch's *Sun*, the paper continued to be known as the mink-lined coffin. No one ever got fired.

The general policy was more rather than less. In reality, the club could never go too far. The 'chosen', apart from the top level of executives, were the odd social sophisticates, who naturally included Johnny. As for female influence, it wasn't so much a case of just the occasional woman in a position of power. There was only one: Marje. The readers sweetly saw her as the grande dame who was also their gentle, kindly friend, counsellor in times of need and a pillar of wisdom. Like Mrs Thatcher, it was only half the picture. The whole place was terrified of her.

'What do you think, Marje?' one of the men would say in the morning conference to an idea being floated. Marje would pause long enough for the entire room to fall silent. Her long elegant fingers would fiddle with the gaggle of silver bracelets on her arm or the silver chains around her neck. 'I think', she would say, slowly and grandly, 'it's fucking silly.' Marje's main priority was protecting the good name of Marje and her kingdom. So she was only difficult in matters that directly affected her page or department. In her problem page, which would survive like her until almost the end of the century, she took an old-fashioned view of women. She believed that marriages were better mended than broken, a bit of sexy underwear, or even dressing up in a nurse's uniform, was to be recommended if it enlivened a stale sex life and the worst thing in the world was to be alone and lonely. It caused Marje not the slightest problem that there were no female sub-editors on the paper. In fact, any woman considered of even minor importance she saw as a threat to her position. One that had to be ruthlessly taken out.

So the culture of a male-dominated newsroom, a male-dominated sports department, picture desk, advertising department – everywhere except the fashion and woman's page – went comfortably over her head.

The same culture existed in just about every other national newspaper of the early eighties. What distinguished the *Mirror* from the rest was the stupendous level of entertaining and drinking that went with it. Mr Justice Faulks had rightly determined drinking by 'Fleet Street standards' to be well in excess of normal drinking. But had he known about the *Mirror* he would have been obliged to create a separate category to cover the intake of those down the road at Holborn Circus. The paper had a budget suitable for running a small country, even one rich in oil deposits. As the editor told me dismissively when, as newly appointed woman's editor, I naively asked about my department's spending limits, 'There are no limits here, blossom.'

Within this culture, and Marje aside, the quality and talent of the rest of womankind was straightforwardly assessed in terms of each female's 'tits', 'knockers', 'bazookas', 'bum', 'arse', as well as whether 'you could give her one'. 'Getting a leg over', talking up the prospect of 'getting a leg over' or speculating on the night before and whether anyone had ended up 'getting his leg over' being a major preoccupation of most of the executives. The gossip was uninhibited by the presence of women in the form of secretaries, wives, girlfriends or female journalists.

Yet, despite this, the paper excelled at producing readable, imaginative accounts of popular political issues, alongside show business and glamour. It had staunchly and powerfully supported the Labour Party since 1945. It produced 'shock issues' on housing, unemployment and education that were award-winning. It had editorials that backed the workers in a moderate, right-wing Labour way. None of this moderation, naturally, to be confused with the lifestyle of those actually working for the paper.

For the races, Ascot, Sandown, the Derby, Cheltenham Gold Cup, there were helicopters to take us and to get us home. Boxes with the finest views of the course, bursting with food and drink.

Office drivers on standby back at the heliport to carry their over-tired bosses to their beds, if necessary. The same flash, over-the-top level of corporate entertaining went for any event to which the *Mirror* gave its blessing.

Once or twice a year the editor would call for a 'think-tank' to be organised. They took place at the Bear Hotel at Woodstock, near Oxford. A dozen or so executives attended, usually from Tuesday through to Thursday. These were not management people canoeing and abseiling and learning to bond as a team, but more a collective attempt to drink Oxfordshire dry. The level of alcoholic consumption went way beyond the normal intake of Holborn Circus.

At the annual political conferences of the two main parties the *Mirror* ruled supreme. Its executive suite was the location for one long celebration, even if down the road at the conference hall the country looked to be going to the dogs.

One year at the Grand Hotel in Brighton even I stayed up late, partying. It must have been around four in the morning when, as was traditional, Waterhouse was sufficiently merry to want to demonstrate the famous egg trick. This was an elaborate party piece that involved a raw egg, a glass of water and a tablecloth. (Another bit of popular *Mirror* culture that ended up in *Jeffrey Bernard is Unwell*.) The night waiter at the Grand couldn't be summoned so we called room service at the next-door Metropole. A flunkey appeared with half a dozen uncooked eggs and a tray of sandwiches.

The chairman, Tony Miles, who presided over this swash-buckling, was also one of the most colourful of the lot. He was preposterously fearful, forever seeing the future as a giant cata-strophe. As the editor once astutely observed, 'Tony never lets a thought go unsaid.' Miles was a former editor, and one with a credible journalistic reputation, who could spot a flaw in a piece of copy faster than anyone. But not a man of sophisticated tastes. Unlike most of his younger colleagues, with the advent of his second marriage to his former secretary, he had turned into a standard Thatcherite. He seemed to me to spend most of his time agonising about punctuation, house prices and the outcome of the current US soap opera *Dallas*. Not necessarily in that order. Like just about everyone else on the paper, to say he enjoyed a drink was like saying Monday followed Sunday.

For Johnny, brought up in the culture of the paper, all this was normal and great fun. Following his return from Rome (and denied a posting to New York, which I wasn't aware he had asked for), he was given a free-ranging brief, doing investigations and writing and organising features. There were no set hours. There was no urgent need to deliver. He could enjoy himself – and spend as many hours as he liked up a ladder in Holloway, creating our home.

When God wants to punish you, he gives you what you have prayed for. I had the house, the husband and the job back in Fleet Street. I was sober. I was seeing Emma on a regular basis. Life seemed to be looking up. It was all very different and more optimistic than the struggle it had been in Liverpool. But, as my father might have observed, the pieces of the jigsaw did not fit into neat places 'just like that'. *Au contraire.* Far from being happy, my life was throwing up more problems. They were undoubtedly of a higher quality than being in the gutter, looking at the stars. But every bit as troubling. Because, because, because, it wasn't meant to be like this. This bit wasn't on my list. How come, now I had cleaned up my act, how come, now I had stopped being the drunk forever pressing my nose at the windows of other folk who worked and slept and enjoyed themselves, I still didn't fit in? I still didn't belong?

To the credit of the editor and true to his word, within six months I was given the promised job of woman's editor. My transfer was flawlessly executed. Marje called me into her office and confided that she had gone to the editor and persuaded him that she could 'pass on the keys of her kingdom'. No fool, Marje, she had the good sense to work out what was being placed before her and she moved before she was pushed. In turn she was to be promoted to assistant editor. The elevation was a courtesy. She had her page, plus a department of girls who answered her letters. (A bunch kept well away in another building and never, ever mentioned by Marje.) She signed and approved letters to the readers but didn't have the tiresome job of worrying about their problems.

So here I was, woman's editor. A job I never wanted, but a gigantic acknowledgement that I was on the road to professional recovery. But it wasn't making me happy. In my panic to return to 'normal life' I hadn't considered the consequences of being married to someone who enjoyed a good time. How come I'd been able to make my demands to the editor of the *Mirror* when it came to my salary and my need for an office car at the critical point in our negotiations and yet back home I hadn't any idea how best to behave? I didn't know it, but I hadn't grown up. I'd only been washing on a daily basis for a couple of years, for heaven's sake. No one had ever taught me to ask nicely for anything. My mother's take on matrimonial bliss was to demand and get. Why should I consider doing anything different? The more balanced approach, what self-help books in time would irritatingly call 'stating your needs', never occurred to me.

Equally, Johnny had no warning of or practice for how to deal with a new wife, one who had once been his drinking partner but was now resolutely not drinking and paranoid about her husband doing so. In this uncharted territory he did the very male thing of making it clear he did not wish to be monitored or controlled in his socialising. He was back from abroad, back in the office and could see no reason to alter his pattern of life. He, as he pointed out, was not the one with a drink problem. The diversity in what we wanted daily brought us to grief. When it came to celebrating a birthday or another event, Johnny naturally would suggest going out to dinner, as we had always done in the past. I would dread the evening. We would sit, me with my glass of water, he with his bottle of wine, his demeanour more robust and enthusiastic with each glass. My eyes would glaze. I would become angry, tired and tense. It didn't occur to me to say I wasn't enjoying myself. Or to steer the celebration another way. If I'd said I would have preferred to go to the theatre as my treat, Johnny wouldn't have raised the slightest objection. But I didn't have the self-confidence to look after myself. There were moments I could just about laugh at this. But for the most part I seethed with anger.

Short of guidance, I would alternate between bossiness and pleading with Johnny, never clear in my own head what demands of mine were perfectly reasonable and what were foolish and best left unsaid. As the house came together – Johnny showing a remarkable skill in putting together rooms and choosing colours – I would arrange dinner parties. I had learnt to cook and would do so until I dropped, then sit in silence until the last guest had left in the early hours, puzzled and annoyed that it had all been for nothing. My back would ache, my neck would ache, nobody went home before two in the morning. I had to be up for work. Johnny, after a good evening of drinking, would lie next to me snoring loud enough to wake most of Islington. None of this was in the happy-ever-after script. I was utterly failing to enjoy what was on offer and what I had longed for. And none of it could ease the pain of my beloved daughter in Scotland, being looked after by Catherine. And where, oh where, oh where, was my dilemma covered in Germaine's *Female* Bloody *Eunuch*?

A new puppy was an unexpected bonus. A tiny piece of fluff we named Guinness. Chosen by Emma who, aged nine, had promised if she could have an Old English sheepdog she would never ask for anything else in the whole world. Guinness grew larger, but never grew up. We all adored her. Because of the puppy, and my belief that no dog should be left on its own, we also got an au pair. Christine, from Geneva. It helped that if necessary she could also collect Emma from Heathrow. I would be waiting as Emma arrived home, even though leaving the office early was not considered good form.

That summer, I found she was spending a part of it on holiday with friends of Charlie and their children at Charlie's log cabin on Loch Fyne, while Charlie had just launched a new paper, the *Sunday Standard*. He was busy day and night. I was very upset. Mr Justice Faulks never could have envisaged this reversal of roles. But, as his judgement stood, Charlie was within his rights to do what he liked with Emma in the holidays. From where I was standing it seemed so unfair that she should be without either parent, when I would have insisted on taking the time off work to have her in London. What's more, Charlie hadn't told me he wasn't going to be on holiday with Emma except possibly at weekends. He was cross I was questioning it. He said he had no intention of changing things. I was powerless. And I knew it.

I was not to be the only one looking good to the outside world while quietly dying of despair.

On 29 July 1981 the Prince of Wales married Lady Diana Spencer at St Paul's Cathedral. Only weeks after Marje had 'handed over the keys to her kingdom' she went off, still on crutches from her hip operation, to take up the paper's prized seat in St Paul's Cathedral to report on the union. I was next to a large television set back at the office, monitoring the rest of the royal family that included Auntie Margaret in an outfit and shoes that looked as if they had been borrowed from some northern amateur dramatic society's costume trunk. The pages, I noted, fidgeted. The father of the bride, Earl Spencer, only partially recovered from a stroke, looked on proudly. The Archbishop of Canterbury, Robert Runcie, a highly intelligent cleric and normally a pillar of common sense, was swept up enough in the general euphoria to announce that the marriage was 'the stuff of which fairy tales are made'.

It looked that way. As the bride-to-be emerged from Clarence House, we saw a young girl in a billowing ivory silk dress with puffed sleeves. When she entered St Paul's the Queen looked blissfully happy. Even Prince Philip smiled. The crowds cheered.

The joyful day was transmitted to readers through the pages of the *Daily Mirror*.

On the front page 'The Kiss' was the headline over a photograph of the young couple embracing. It conveyed an image of deep love and togetherness. The inside of the paper contained acres more of syrupy, velvety gush.

The readers would have been alarmed had they eavesdropped on the editor as he reached for his special cashmere cardigan that he kept in a cupboard for the odd days when he personally drew up the paper. 'It will end in tears. She's going to be trouble,' Molloy declared. I thought it an extremely churlish and blokey, unfounded and cynical thing to say. And I told him so.

In the summer of that year our little foursome – Johnny, me, Emma and Guinness the Old English – took off for a canal holiday. We didn't want to put our precious puppy in kennels and Johnny promised us that a narrowboat break would be an adventure we could all enjoy. He was so good at making things sound attractive and exciting. As Emma would say years later: 'I often wondered when I was at school why no one else had a mum and a dad and a Johnny.'

'There will be marinas and restaurants all along the towpaths, with launderettes and bathing facilities,' he insisted. He might even have assured me there would be hairdressers and beauticians and manicurists, since he maintains that's the simplest way to get me to agree to go anywhere. Certainly his description suggested we were about to enjoy a level of luxury that only just stopped short of the Carlton in Cannes. Plus the advantage of not missing the dog.

It rained for most of the fortnight. The marinas, restaurants, launderettes, health spas, etc. turned out to be in Johnny's romantic Neapolitan head. At one point, as we chugged along somewhere in the industrial back and beyond of Stoke-on-Trent, with twelve days of dirty washing on board, Guinness, hearing an InterCity train approaching, leapt from the boat and disappeared. We were convinced she was under the train's wheels or lying electrocuted on the lines. She returned, shaking, about ten minutes later.

Despite all its disappointments and scares, we loved the holiday. There were no tearful nights to cope with. No daughter with a UM notice hanging around her neck. The differences in our careers were forgotten. Johnny made every day fun. When we docked for the last time, he ran ashore and bought a cheap camera. Emma looked sensational in her Osh-Kosh dungarees and her flaming red hair. Guinness posed for less than thirty seconds – the prospect of returning to normal life was too much for her. Johnny had left the door of our car open and she raced on to the back seat. She had to be dragged out the other side.

'Best ever holiday,' said Emma. Nothing I heard could have made me happier.

The *Sunday Mirror*, our sister paper, was edited by the impressive Bob Edwards, who was famous for several reasons. He was a former editor of *Tribune*, the once influential Labour Party newspaper. He had twice edited the *Daily Express*. He was an old-fashioned Labour supporter, with a wealth of stories from the time he had worked for Lord Beaverbrook, the legendary Canadian newspaper proprietor of the Express Group. Edwards also had a deserved reputation for loyalty to his friends. (Notably, when Michael Foot was leader of the Labour Party, he refused to complain in the *Sunday Mirror* about his ineffectiveness, even though Mirror Group Newspapers' policy was quite the opposite.) Like most of his colleagues, socialism and campaigning for the country's working class to have a better deal in life ran alongside a lifestyle that would have made the reader weep.

While Edwards could tell a funny yarn, he actually took himself very seriously. There was a story, no doubt apocryphal, that Bob had once been making his way in his chauffeur-driven Jaguar to lunch at his club, the Reform. In St James's the driver knocked down a pedestrian who had walked out into the road without warning. The elderly pedestrian was badly shocked but conscious as the editor of the *Sunday Mirror* emerged from the back of his car, consulted his watch and cried: 'Why does everything happen to me?'

Bob Edwards rang one day and invited me to lunch. I had no idea why. He took me to the White Tower, an old-established and favoured restaurant off Charlotte Street. We were at the dessert stage and had several Beaverbrook stories under our belt before he came to the reason for the invitation. To my astonishment, he wanted me to move over to his newspaper as deputy editor. I could barely believe it and was wild with delight. To my surprise, Johnny did not greet the news as warmly as I might have expected. I hadn't even begun to think about what days I'd have to work and he pointed out that a Sunday newspaper meant working Saturdays, until the early hours. So what about Emma?

He was right. There seemed no way around the dilemma. How could I give up part of my precious every-other-weekend access? The terrible unfairness and injustice of my life sent me into the glooms. Others, not least Emma's father, were free to pursue their careers and arrange their family life to suit. I was not a compulsive stayer at the office. I was happy to balance my life. If the truth were known, the executive part of my job, as opposed to the writing bits I was still doing, was of questionable enjoyment. But who could possibly turn down the opportunity to be deputy editor of a national newspaper? There were then no female deputy editors. It would be an extraordinary feather in the comeback kid's hat. Also there was something disproportionate about Johnny's anger – it wasn't just that he was reminding me that I'd be working weekends but, as he later confessed, it was also a reaction to my impending elevation.

I booked a week at a health farm. A page from my mother's rule book of 'being good to yourself'. I chose Shrublands in Suffolk, for no better reason than that it was about the only one over the years I'd never tried. On the second night there, Mike Molloy called with an even more astonishing job offer. 'Blossom,' he said, 'would you like to be assistant editor of the *Daily Mirror*, in charge of features?' I could barely believe it. From rotten drunk to the hierarchy of a famous Fleet Street paper in less than two years. Plus no worry now about working at weekends. I accepted! Not only would I be in charge of features, but along with the other two assistant editors and the deputy editor, I was to go on the editing rota. The first woman in Fleet Street regularly to edit a national newspaper.

The *Guardian* came to interview me. The *Guardian*'s 'People' page of Saturday, 13 March 1982: 'Anyone noticed any difference in the *Daily Mirror* recently?' asked the lead item. 'Twice in recent weeks it has been edited by a woman. The paper has now gone further than any other in appointing Anne Robinson as assistant editor, a title that offers the holder the chance to sit at her desk until 2 a.m. at least once a week and some Sundays, steering the sheet on to the street. This redhaired Liverpudlian, 37, is undaunted by her success, which comes after only a year on the paper.' Alongside was my picture. The piece went on to report that I was making history, and that I had changed a story I thought insulting to women in the second edition on my first night in the editor's chair.

I didn't tell the *Guardian* that I knew zero, zilch, nothing about newspaper production. I didn't know one typeface from another. I had absolutely no idea how a newspaper was put together. I hadn't been down on a composing-room floor in ten years, and only then at the *Sunday Times* because the lovely chief printer kept brandy in his cupboard which he would pour into the coffee cups of journalists he assumed to have been in the office all night. (Not a difficult deception for me to pull off.) I didn't tell the woman from the *Guardian* either that the appointment was not playing to rave reviews at home. Johnny looked on in horror. In a few short years the woman he had helped to nurse back to normality was now stepping over him without so much as a by your leave. Actually not so much stepping over him as audaciously leapfrogging him. All at the behest of his so-called office chums.

As for Germaine in Britain and Gloria in the USA, nowhere in their campaign manuals setting out the right of equality was the complex problem of a wife becoming the chief breadwinner.

Johnny's reaction was understandable. But he might as well have been speaking Swahili. I just couldn't see it. I didn't appreciate that to have introduced your spouse (former gifted drunk) to your newspaper (your boys' own club) and then watch as those boys chose to promote her out of all recognition was hard to swallow. This time his club really had gone too far.

My mother's response was strangely muted. She said she hoped 'it wasn't going to upset Emma'. Charlie, to his credit, was thrilled for me. So was Emma. And I was very thrilled for me.

16

Undaunted

The *Guardian* came through the letterbox that Saturday morning at around 7.20 a.m. Johnny was up and waiting. The top of the front page also displayed a picture of me, with the caption: 'She who must be obeyed'. I read the interview inside, then Johnny did. 'Better than I thought it would be,' he said when he'd finished.

The final paragraph pointed out that newspapers had changed – it was now permissible for husband and wife to work on the same team – then asked, astutely, had they changed enough to make it easier to have a higher-ranking job than your husband?

'No, I won't pretend it is easy,' trilled the undaunted Anne Robinson. 'But we've known each other for sixteen years and I expect we'll go on fighting and arguing over stories in much the same way.' Hmm . . . Up to a point, Lord Copper.

Further down, the writer offered an eye-opening statistic on the number of journalists on the *Mirror*. Male: 496. Female: 22. The figures included 123 journalists in the Manchester office, none of whom were women. No comment was attached. None was needed.

Other milestones were recorded on the page: an interview with the youngest ever woman to become Director of the

Women's Royal Army Corps. 'The only real limitations are set by the fact that women are not strong enough physically to do some jobs and – fundamental to army policy – they would not be required to fight on the front line,' was forty-four-year-old Brigadier Helen Meechie's view.

'Personally,' she added, 'I would not want our combat role to change. I believe it must remain a man's army, since we do not live in an Amazon-style society.'

Privately, Anne Robinson, aged thirty-seven and a half, thought that highlighting the promotion of women involved a large degree of hypocrisy. I was a chronic drunk back from the dead. But otherwise there shouldn't have been anything remarkable about someone of my experience and talent becoming assistant editor *Daily Mirror* (features). (Newspapers loved brackets when it came to titles.) For women to take a bow and enjoy the glory for being the 'first' at anything while simultaneously complaining about the lack of equality between men and women is itself perverse.

Richard Stott, Johnny's friend, who had championed the case for hiring me and making me woman's editor, had not played any part in my unexpected promotion. But, as a result of it, he was now assistant editor *Daily Mirror* (news). A new title on the paper. We were about the same age. He was a former award-winning investigative journalist, an inspirational features editor who had improved those pages considerably. No one was writing about him.

The *Guardian* account erred in one small detail. I did not stay at my own desk to edit until 2 a.m. I was obliged to move down to the deputy editor's office, opposite the editor's office, a cross between a railway carriage and a giant ashtray. Bench seats hugged three corners of it. There was a huge desk with a window framing the dome of St Paul's. The room was used for morning conference on a Sunday and during the week for other informal meetings. (It was one of the few *Mirror* offices that could be locked from the inside.) In common with all senior executive offices the deputy editor's had a well-stocked drinks cabinet.

While totally at sea about the technology that got a great newspaper out on the street, I was in charge of the news pages, the features pages, the business news, the sports pages and the 'furniture'. Furniture being the cartoons, the letters page and the rest of the peripheral stuff that journalists shove into each edition and which the readers often consider of more importance than the front page and the editorial.

Of the back-of-the-paper bits and pieces the crossword was *the* most sacred. On my first day as assistant editor (features) the deputy features editor, a brash Liverpudlian, had shown me the 'dummy' – a mock-up of the paper with only the advertisements and furniture pencilled in. I'd airily nodded it through. They were his worry. I had not checked the furniture. Even if I had, I doubt I would have noticed that the crossword was missing. Why was it missing? Ho ho ho! 'Vic went to the pub for most of the day to recover from "a girl" getting promoted to a top job,' said one of his workmates. The switchboard burnt for at least six hours the next day as readers rang to complain.

Johnny, meanwhile, was wrestling with his own career problems. He was suffering the classic foreign correspondent's dilemma. The world had been his unchecked oyster. It was hard to think of any other job offer that was going to be as glamorous and exciting and prestigious as running the *Mirror*'s Rome Bureau. He had been given a roving writer's brief, travelling to the USA and Africa, and had masterminded several investigations. Then he had worked with Keith Waterhouse on an experimental project called *Picture Mirror*. It was fine journalism in the style of the old *Picture Post* but the cost was prohibitive and after fifteen issues it was put to rest. He was briefly appointed associate picture editor and then, with little imagination or thought, was made deputy news editor.

The news editor was a sergeant-major caricature for whom discipline came before talent and who considered an hour-long lunch excessive. Like many a sergeant-major he wielded his limited powers with relish. 'Request refused,' he wrote in a memo to one reporter, who had asked for a day off in six weeks' time to celebrate his silver wedding anniversary. 'He's known this was coming for twenty-five years and he's left it until the last minute to ask for the time off,' he explained.

Johnny was temperamentally unsuited to a desk-bound job and answering to a boss with none of his natural flair. If that wasn't unsettling enough he was obliged, on the Sundays he himself was in charge of the news desk, to read out his proposed list of stories at the morning conference to the editor of the day. This, often, was his wife.

Across the office he could see his old mate Richard Stott enjoying power and glory as one of the chosen. Even worse that a newcomer and a female was doing the same as Stott. But for that newcomer to be his wife was too unequal for him to accept with any grace. For the umpteenth time, for both of us, there was nothing in life's training manual on how to behave in the exceptional circumstances we found ourselves.

On 2 April 1982 Argentina invaded and captured the British-owned Falkland Islands, overwhelming the single company of Royal Marines guarding the island's capital, Port Stanley. The only British warship in the vicinity was HMS *Endurance*, on ice patrol. Three days later the Royal Navy Task Force set sail for the South Atlantic. Mrs Thatcher was in her element. To my mother's relief, the Prime Minister's hair was looking in better shape and she was almost certainly undaunted by war. She was daunted only by the horrifying prospect that the Argentinians had got their hands on something that did not belong to them.

'What you do not own, you cannot have unless you ask nicely or pay for it' was, I imagine, her straightforward logic.

The 'undaunted' Anne Robinson found herself editing the *Daily Mirror* as the war shaped up. She was at the helm the night news came through that the British had landed and recaptured the neighbouring island of South Georgia, invaded by Argentina three weeks earlier.

A week after the recapture of South Georgia things in the South Atlantic were looking much uglier. At the start of May the RAF bombed the airport at Port Stanley. The following day the Argentine cruiser the *General Belgrano* was sunk with the loss of 368 lives. Two days later HMS *Sheffield* went down, the target of an Exocet missile, and twenty lives were lost.

When it did, Anne Robinson, by now very daunted indeed, was editing. The lives being lost were not only those of foreigners in foreign wars but the British as well, with ordinary British names. Men who came from Yorkshire, Lancashire, the Midlands. For a generation with no first-hand knowledge of war this was entirely different from any other reporting. Different from the conflict in Northern Ireland, because it was a battle in a very literal sense and the casualties were in double figures and looked like getting worse. To add to the drama, another sign of the times was the British spokesman Ian McDonald, a Ministry of Defence employee with a face like death, and a voice to go with it, who would appear on television in a badly lit studio that made him appear even more sinister. He would read out the bulletins of lives lost in a scary funereal monotone. We were almost entirely reliant on these selective versions of events.

I was also entirely reliant on the backbench. Without the team drawing up the pages and bringing them in for approval, I would have been helpless. Old union practices usually made it difficult to change the paper radically after the early evening, but special deals were done during the battles in the South Atlantic. 'The printers want coming-to-work money and staying-at-work money and distress money for the sort of stuff they're having to put in the paper,' the night editor would joke, except it was pretty well accurate.

By day the war was discussed with relish. As an assistant editor, I was now not only privy to morning conference at which department heads laid out their goods for approval, but also to the sacred *Daily Mirror* leader conference. It was an eye-opener. Apart from the editor and his deputy and Richard Stott, in overall charge of news, there was the political editor, the industrial editor and the leader writer Joe Haines, a former press secretary to Labour Prime Minister Harold Wilson. Their enthusiasm for what was happening was obvious. Each morning I watched them metaphorically lean on the mantelshelf and bomb Dresden all over again. Even those with no war record would chat with excitement about Exocet missiles and all the other killer devices available.

I appeared to be alone in my feeling that on both sides poor mothers' sons were dying. And what a waste and did it really matter about a windy Godforsaken island that a few years ago we had not wanted to keep? I probably said very little. Not out of fear of the reaction, but because if I became overexcited with a glass of mineral water in my hand I was likely to start shaking. First my hands, then my legs would go. My nervous system was a daily reminder of where I had come from and how much I still needed to recover.

When British troops recaptured South Georgia Mrs Thatcher ordered us all to 'rejoice'. She had personally told the Queen of the triumph. When Argentina surrendered in mid-June the message was unequivocal. We were to celebrate victory! The country dutifully obeyed. In crude political terms the Prime Minister had hit the jackpot, won the lottery in the popularity stakes – but for a shorter time than she would have liked. After a while people who felt like I did about the horror of war began to be less concerned about appearing unpatriotic and more vociferous in demanding why so many young men had died for so little.

There were milestones along the way that precipitated the change in attitude. The thanksgiving service at Westminster Abbey in July conducted by Archbishop Runcie was one. The injured victims of the war were stuck in their wheelchairs, hidden behind pillars away from the cameras. The Archbishop, himself with a distinguished war record, wished to pray for the dead of both sides. 'War has always been detestable,' he said pointedly. Mrs Thatcher was furious.

Back at the *Daily Mirror* the Falklands conflict might have been over, but editing the paper still seemed like a war: long periods of boredom, short, oh too short, bursts of excitement. During the week the job was hardly more than a watching brief. Sunday was better, although generally agreed to be the hardest day to edit. The news editor has very little to offer, unless the unexpected happens. There are no court cases, no parliamentary reports. Often a Monday-morning paper ends up as a rehash of the best stories from the Sunday papers.

Whatever the day of the week there's a debatable difference between the most important story and the most interesting one. BBC News normally will run with the former – if it is significant politically, globally, etc. The broadsheets are unpredictable. The tabloids these days take the 'interesting low ground' every time. In the eighties the *Daily Mirror* prided itself on spanning both churches. But what was interesting or passable as a front page to the backbench was rarely something I found readable. Often it would 'splash' – as the main front-page lead is called – on something so turgid I doubted the reader bothered with it – a third-grade political story or an industrial dispute.

I saw a chance on my Sundays in charge to think about doing things differently. Why not a decent consumer story to lead the front page? I was fascinated by consumer journalism. The sort that named names and showed up a big corporation attempting to pull the wool over the eyes of its customers. It wasn't easy to drum up an alternative to the splash the night editor was suggesting. Only occasionally would I spot one and be determined. One Monday it was washing machines and soap powder – despite the sharp intakes of breath and the shaking of heads entreating me to desist. You were not obliged to phone the editor to check on what might lead the paper. Only the leader writer read out the editorial to him. Otherwise it was all yours.

The backbench – all men, naturally – could have got the editions out with their eyes shut. They often didn't want the hassle of an editor of the day having ideas, certainly not a girl interested in washing machines. They liked the editor of the day to be there to nod stuff through and allow them to gather in the deputy editor's office and raid his booze cupboard. The backbench guys were laddish and dreary. I spent long hours wondering what the hell I was doing in a horrible smoke-filled room watching middle-aged men with big bellies and very little imagination drink and light cigarette after cigarette and talk about the 'missus' and their mortgage. And, as the evening drew to a close, how long it took them to drive home to Northamptonshire, where for some reason several of them lived. But since everyone was telling me what a great achievement it was for me to be there, I hardly felt I could complain.

One night my office was heaving with various laddoes quenching their thirst. I was busy reading page proofs. 'I had her back at the office after a session in the pub,' one of them was boasting. I shrieked because I realised my name was attached to the yarn. The storyteller looked only passingly anxious about the invented anecdote. 'Whoops,' he said mildly. 'Sorry, Annie, didn't notice you there.'

Occasionally Johnny, who had no good reason to go home since his wife was still in the office, would turn up from the pub 'the worse for wear' to check how I was doing.

That summer the Prince and Princess of Wales had a son and heir, William, and the Queen woke up to find an intruder in her bedroom who wanted to chat. More importantly, as far as the stressed-out, exhausted and now daily daunted Anne Robinson was concerned, Granada Television invited her to present *What the Papers Say*, a weekly review of the newspapers. A producer from Manchester came to London and took me to lunch at the Gay Hussar in Soho. 'I've watched your rise', he said, 'and if you were a public company, I'd buy shares.' It was a wonderful compliment. For the programme I wrote my own script and wore a beige suit with an ice-green silk shirt. My teeth were wonky, my mascara lumpy. Old technology required the fifteen minutes to be done in one take. I did it on the fourth. 'Don't worry,' the director assured me. 'Some of the blokes like Max Hastings take twenty-four.' I was elated with the result. This was so much more fun than sitting in the big ashtray until the early hours. Fame, television, I wanted it. What's more, if I did television I could be home for my daughter whenever she needed me. And I would not have an unhappy husband who compared his career prospects to mine and saw only unfairness and a raw deal for him.

To mask our disappointments and the unresolved struggle our professional lives were causing us, we seized on the idea of an away-from-it-all summer holiday. Money was tight. The house was unfinished and I knew precious amounts of my husband's earnings were making their way straight into the till of the pub opposite the *Mirror* – or into the hands of restaurateurs. It was his way of rebelling against the professional hole he found himself in.

Our first holiday abroad as a family since I'd been upright assumed great importance. The cost, I convinced myself, didn't matter. After long deliberations we chose the island of Crete. The Minos Beach was a traditional old hotel with large, beautiful grounds and, apart from the main building, had bungalows by the water's edge. We couldn't have made a better choice.

What delighted me was the number of other children around for Emma to play with. There was water-skiing taught by a wizened old man, bad-tempered but an exceptional teacher. Emma had been around too much robust guidance in her short life to be put off by his severity. She adored her lessons. Like so many dedicated and crusty teachers, underneath was a kind, soft-hearted man, who turned Emma into an exceptionally good water-skier. Emma chummed up with two girls. Their father, Derek Wood, was a barrister and would later become principal of St Hugh's College, Oxford. I remember being permanently anxious lest anyone should suspect our true circumstances. I could hardly say to Emma, 'Please don't mention Glasgow. Please don't mention going to school there.' Instead, I would sit nervously on guard waiting to catch and cover up any casual remark from Emma that would cause people to ask awkward questions. It was exhausting. But the alternative was to come clean and face the unspoken disapproval I was convinced would go with my 'confession'. In any case, how stupid would I look explaining myself before the questions arose? Apart from this the holiday was an outstanding success.

Looking back at the photographs I see that by this stage I had stopped feeling such a victim about Emma's clothes. I simply bought the bulk of them. Charlie, after all, was paying for her education. It was only a sign of how unentitled I believed myself to be that it took me all that time to work out simple solutions.

We had also brought with us the dreaded school holiday project, the task set by teachers to punish parents. That year it was the story of vetch. The combined efforts of journalist mother, father, stepfather and, for all I know, stepmother, must have drained Emma. It certainly wore out Johnny and me. Between us we could have written a ten-part mini-series with the material. I didn't know then that teachers smile knowingly when these efforts are returned to them. The labours of guilty working parents – detailed, mounted, bound, professional jobs – are instantly recognisable. Stay-at-home mothers dedicated to their children on a full-time basis do not feel any need to prove themselves and leave the work to their children.

Away from newspaper life and its stresses it was a wonderful, worthwhile summer. The house was incomplete but coming together thanks to Johnny's skill. The garden was sunny. I could afford to give my daughter a home. My chin, if not held high, was moving up from my chest.

'Ever been to China, blossom?' asked the editor after our summer hols were over. Mrs Thatcher was due there on her first visit as Prime Minister. She had been once before as Leader of the Opposition. The itinerary included stop-offs in Japan, India and Hong Kong. He was suggesting that rather than send a member of the political staff, I should go. I jumped at the idea of absconding from the giant ashtray, editing duties and the brain-teaser of whether you could do Northampton from Holborn Circus in under one hour and ten minutes, at two o'clock in the morning, if there were no police patrols on the M1.

For my thirty-eighth birthday Johnny bought me a Cartier watch we couldn't afford, and we celebrated a day early before I flew off in an RAF transporter from Heathrow. The plane was decked out with a bed for each of the Thatchers at the front and reasonable space for her entourage in the middle. Packed economically in the rear were two dozen journalists, an ITN camera crew and the cabin staff. It was silver service all the way.

The Prime Minister allowed her assistant to double as her wardrobe mistress and hairdresser. First stop Tokyo, where we watched her inspect the troops, plant a tree, visit a nuclear power station and generally confuse the Japanese by always being in charge. Next stop, Beijing. Top of the agenda was the future of Hong Kong. 'A borrowed place living on borrowed time,' wrote the late Dick Hughes, the doyen of foreign correspondents based there. Successive governments had passed the buck on the problem of how a century and a half of British rule could be resolved. While Britain owned Hong Kong island outright, Kowloon peninsula and the New Territories had been leased for ninety-nine years in 1898. By the 1980s it was impossible to go on ignoring the arithmetic. The possibility of sovereignty being handed back to China had to be faced.

The Chinese saw no problems. They wanted what belonged to them returned. Mrs Thatcher genuinely thought that if she wagged her finger they would see it her way and allow things to remain exactly as they were. Diplomatically, the trip was a disaster.

Before she left Britain the Prime Minister had received firm guidance from old Sino-British hands who told her she should take care to listen to what the Chinese had to say. Although large chunks of it would be predicable there might be something that turned out to be a disguised hint or invitation. It's a puzzle why anyone wasted time with this briefing as Mrs Thatcher, naturally, went her own sweet merry way.

Pointedly, the Prime Minister arrived in China with only one under-secretary from the Foreign Office. It was a department she distrusted en masse. Most notably absent was her Foreign Secretary, Francis Pym, whom she didn't even like talking to in London, never mind carting him halfway round the world. Once in Beijing, she was extremely annoyed to find that despite telling people what was best for them they weren't listening. It didn't help that all discussions had to go through interpreters. It didn't help that there were endless banquets and at each several toasts with an evil Chinese liquor, a concoction that instantly removed the power of speech from most of the press. With or without interpreters or strong alcohol, the nuances and spirit of the Chinese were all a tiresome riddle to an impatient and straightforward woman who spoke her mind. Also no one was tickling anyone's tummy. Deng Xiaoping, then Chairman of the Central Military Commission, but the unofficial leader, insisted on having his spittoon in front of him and Mrs Thatcher. Did he, or did he not know his European visitor would find it obnoxious? Either way, it was reported to have been heavily used. And even without the Foreign Office and its knowledge of what a tap on the nose and a wink-wink really meant, the message from the Chinese was clear: Hong Kong is ours and we want it back.

For the less politically inclined of the reporting team there was to be a great deal of contact with Denis. He was immensely loyal, decent, well-meaning, extremely right wing, a breed apart from the modern world, unflinchingly supportive in his own way and oh so dull after a while. His tediousness inflated by his consumption of gin. He would have easily fitted Mr Justice

Faulks' category of a Fleet Street drinker, if not a Holborn Circus one.

On a day when his wife was busy arguing with the Chinese government, Denis and I walked half a mile along the Great Wall together. His refusal to find anything about China interesting was so heartfelt, I was moved to ask him as we strode forth where was his favourite place in the whole world? He thought for a minute before deciding: Dallas.

'If I never see China again, it will be too soon,' he announced as he got on the plane at the end of this most delicate of missions for his wife. China, for those of us who had never been before, had knocked our socks off. It was so unlike anywhere else I'd visited. I felt exhausted. The Great Hall of the People, the thousands cycling to work, the antiquated hotels. There was a visit to Beijing Zoo where my red hair ended up more of an attraction to visitors than the animals, so unused were the Chinese to seeing the colour. The hotel staff were as unbribable as the cockroaches that you could hear in your bedroom.

At a cocktail party at the Governor's house in Hong Kong, our next stop, there was a chance to watch and admire just how the Thatcher marriage worked. Denis, gin in hand, was still in full flood on his weariness of travel and the Chinese. Given the bleak results of his wife's efforts at diplomacy it would have been in order if Mrs Thatcher had turned and hit him with her handbag. Instead, inches away, she smiled benignly. The newly married Mrs Penrose was truly impressed. Why didn't Mrs Thatcher reprimand Denis? Why did he drink to excess and embarrass her? That's what I got wrong. He didn't embarrass her. She accepted him totally. Never, in all the time I covered her as Prime Minister, was I to see Mrs Thatcher looking even vaguely irritated with her spouse. Was it the way her generation dealt with a problem that those of us who came later found so difficult? It was some years before I realised that the Thatchers' endearing and impressive relationship was a good example of how a marriage based on low romantic expectations can be a roaring success. There was a deal. That deal said work came first. One partner was not to get in the way of the other. It didn't involve him being any different from what he had always been. He didn't have to adapt. She never woke up hoping this was the day he was going to change. Or this was the day she'd finally manage to teach him a lesson. His money had allowed her to pursue her political goals. That was enough. 'His professional interest in paint and mine in plastics may seem an unromantic foundation for friendship but it enabled us right away to establish a joint interest in science,' Mrs Thatcher would later reveal in her biography. Even with Julia Roberts and Ben Affleck playing the leads, you'd be hard pushed to turn the tale into a sizzling, passionate box-office blockbuster.

On the long journey home, with a brief refuelling stop in Dubai, Clive James wrote a sketch based on the trip for the press to perform. He suggested I play the PM. I borrowed the stewardess's big handbag and hair lacquer. I hadn't expected to see the Prime Minister in the front row of the stalls. 'You do me very well, dear,' she said afterwards, when she invited me back to her part of the plane for a drink. 'Watch out. She'll be very nice then put you down before you leave,' someone warned. 'Are you going to carry that empty glass to the other end of the plane?' she demanded as I stood there. 'Either fill it up or put it down, dear.' In fact, there was no water to hand, only wine. How was she to know about me and my drinking career?

In contrast to the Thatchers' workable partnership, based on plastics and paint, the new Princess of Wales was finding that her husband's love of duty and her dreams of a romantic married life were producing the very opposite of contentment and mutual tolerance. And the cracks were beginning to show.

Sunday, 14 November 1982. It was the morning after the annual Service of Remembrance at the Albert Hall. I was duty editor. The guests of honour the night before had been, as usual, the Queen and Prince Philip. The Prince of Wales came minus his wife. Then whoosh, like Cinderella, Diana appeared, late and after the Queen as several of the papers in their final editions pointed out. One or two had managed to get in a picture of the Princess as she made her way into the building. The photographs and the story nagged me. Something here was badly wrong. What had happened to cause Diana to turn up late? There had to have been a tiff. Familiar enough in any household in the early years of a marriage. In time, couples learn to adapt and bend around each other in a way that allows outsiders less of an idea of what is really going on. But there was more to it than that. Diana had changed a good deal in the last eighteen months. Her fashion sense, for a start, had soared impressively. Gone was the plumpish fiancée and new bride. The weight loss initially had been an improvement, but now I could see a young girl with her shoulder blades sticking out. She was very, very thin.

I called in the royal correspondent, the redoubtable James Whitaker. He and I had known each other since we were both young reporters at the *Daily Mail*. It is hard to think of a more hard-working, genial, dedicated newspaperman. He took the royal family seriously enough to report with care and accuracy on their progress. But he wasn't their slave. Nor was he a chancer, even though he would put 100 per cent into following up his editor's requests. He was also old-fashioned enough to believe that whoever was in the editor's chair should be treated as the editor. 'I think', I said to James, 'we're looking at anorexia here.' 'Leave it with me,' he said.

He was back within the hour. 'You're right,' he said and told me his source. 'Write it,' I said. He did.

Monday, 15 November. The *Daily Mirror*'s front page asked: 'Is it all getting too much for Diana?' As Whitaker put it: 'No one but no one is ever late for the Queen.' His story went on to report that Prince Charles had already announced that Diana was 'unwell' and wouldn't be attending. It also pointed out

Diana's unpredictable behaviour and her weight loss and evidence of her compulsive tidiness. It quoted a source as saying: 'If her shoes are cleaned she wants them put back precisely in line in her cupboard. She is obsessed that everything around her should be perfect.' Most importantly, the story raised the possibility that the Princess was suffering from anorexia nervosa.

Buckingham Palace denied the condition or that there was any suggestion of concern about the Princess's health with a robustness that had I known its full extent would have convinced me of how right we were. Not only did it condemn the suggestion, it quietly reached out to editors and owners of newspapers to cease such irresponsible coverage. It asked them to 'lay off' the young Princess who was finding the intrusion difficult to deal with. The Establishment at work is a powerful machine. The anorexia tale sank. It would not be confirmed for another nine years. Then we would discover that at the time of the Albert Hall incident the royal family was at its wits' end to know how to cope with an unhappy, sulking, weeping, contrary young woman who, during her pregnancy, had actually attempted to throw herself down some stairs.

Back at Tavistock Terrace, and with no Palace heavies to protect us, we, unlike the Waleses, were fighting our battles publicly with plenty enjoying the joke. Johnny, to his credit, did not attempt to throw himself down the stairs. But in true newspaper style, after a long pre-Christmas lunch, he had a row in a pub with the *Daily Telegraph*'s fine arts correspondent and a barstool, which resulted in a broken leg. As far as I could gather, he was reaching to thump one when the other got in the way. I say thump but he might well have simply been lurching uncertainly in the vague direction of a body to ram home a point. Being Italian, the damage to his suit or his face has always been too much of a priority for him to contemplate using his fist.

Just about everyone except me thought the injuries he sustained were hilarious. I had arranged for us to go skiing after Christmas. We were due to leave on New Year's Day with my old

Liverpool friend Maureen, her husband Derek and their three boys, who were all around Emma's age. I had been skiing once in my youth. For Emma and Johnny it would be the first time. 'Penrose is the only man to break his leg *before* the skiing holiday,' members of the *Mirror* club would say to each other gleefully. 'Penrose has broken his leg in three places – the King and Keys, the White Swan and El Vino.' My husband had been taken to St Bartholomew's, Fleet Street's local hospital. The night nurse's father turned out to have been an old *Sun* news editor. A man as well known for his drinking as most holders of the title. She was more sympathetic to Johnny's plight than Mrs Penrose was. Probably because it was someone else's drunken relative and she wasn't going to have to deal with the aftermath. Her approach made up for my deep, deep anger. We celebrated Christmas and threw a drinks party, with Johnny hobbling around on crutches with his broken leg in a cast.

I left for Austria with Emma and without my husband. He was still not allowed to fly. As was traditional for assistant editors, an office chauffeur took us to the airport. Only when the paper began to tighten its budgetary belt in the years to come did I reflect that the cost in overtime for our journey from Islington to Heathrow for the driver on a New Year's Day was more than the entire cost of our ten-day holiday.

Emma was on the nursery slopes for about two days before she moved to the next class up, as fearless youngsters do. Her mother even began to enjoy the experience of whizzing along. There were no shaking legs or hands. Most evenings we ate supper at six and retired exhausted. Another wonderful holiday. 'One of the best again, Mum, and you even learnt to stop and not fall over.' A happy child. It was over all too soon and she was back to Charlie for the beginning of the spring term.

But things were looking up. Charlie had returned to London. No more UMs. No more Catherine. Yippee! This time Emma wasn't returning to Glasgow.

Emma and I had coped as best we could with our partings on

a Sunday night. Sometimes it was fine and dandy, other times it was sad and distressing. Just once I had taken a deep breath and broached the subject with her. Did she want to be here in London full time? I asked. There was a silence. 'I couldn't do it to Dad,' she said, as she reached out and gripped my hand, 'I couldn't hurt him.' There was nothing more to discuss. I had to accept her decision. I couldn't and didn't press her.

Charlie was to be executive editor of *The Times*. His move was no doubt accelerated by his new bride, who had no opportunity to find a job equal to her experience in Glasgow. Also they now had a baby boy, Luke, whom Emma thought was quite wonderful. The family had bought a beautiful house in Campden Hill Square in Holland Park, also in need of much renovation. Their dog Socky, an exceedingly bright mongrel, was threatened with kennels. We took her in while the builders were at work. Emma was thrilled. Guinness never forgave us.

In the sunshine and snow, I reflected on my lot. 'I hate being a newspaper executive,' I told Maureen. We talked late into one night. A useful exercise. If you keep at it long enough and you have someone willing to listen you can find yourself getting to the nub of the problem.

There was nothing I could do about my husband's discontent but I could change my professional life. What I really want, I had heard myself say out loud, is to have a newspaper column again and to do television. It seemed like a pipe dream. I should have had more faith in the unexpected. Occasionally things happen while you are looking the other way.

17

Wednesday Witch

If Marje Proops was the Queen of Fleet Street, Robin Day was the King of the Small Screen. A trained barrister with an agile mind, he had been destined for the Bar and politics. He once stood as a Liberal candidate but early on in his career he had moved into broadcasting. First at the fledgling ITN and then at *Panorama*, the BBC's flagship current affairs programme. Now he chaired *Question Time*. Sixty minutes, as he put it each week, of topical cut and thrust on issues raised by an invited audience. *Question Time* had begun as a six-week filler but was an immediate hit and had become one of the BBC's most popular political programmes.

Robin was special and different. He wore a bow tie, striped shirts, had a loud voice and acted the part of a slightly deaf and confused elderly uncle. One with an eye for a pretty face. His appearance was deceptive. His skill at conducting probing and groundbreaking political interviews, without ever appearing smug, nasty or rude, was unsurpassed. He adored the company of women and was harmless to be alone with. He only wanted to give you his impression of Maurice Chevalier, or demonstrate his soft-shoe shuffle, or sing his favourite pre-war songs.

We'd been introduced at the Tory Party conference. He was highly amused to learn that I was an assistant editor of the

Mirror. I was flattered he even wanted to talk to me. I didn't know then that deep down he was a gentle, kindly man. And a lonely one. He never forgot my birthday from that year until he died, sending me a card or telephoning with best wishes. He underestimated his appeal. He fretted as to why he earnt less than those in light entertainment. 'I could do it!' he said to me once when we were discussing Michael Parkinson, his chat show and his vast earnings. 'Those pop stars – all you have to say to them is "Hello, and good evening and are you on heroin?"' After our first meeting Robin unwisely insisted to his *Question Time* producer that I would be an excellent guest for his programme. 'Robin's suggestions rarely work when it comes to women,' said the formidable Barbara Maxwell, when I turned up at her invitation along with several other hopefuls for an audition lunch. We had an hour and a half in between mouthfuls to look and sound promising enough to perform live.

I was in two minds about the outcome. Excited that I might pass the audition, while quietly terrified, knowing I was far from ready for a serious discussion programme that required a breadth of knowledge of politics I did not have. I loved the gossip of Westminster. I had no interest, however, in the fine detail of, say, employment law. Even more vital than knowledge, I lacked experience of performing in front of a camera.

Apart from *What the Papers Say*, I'd begun to gain a little know-how on a local London programme. For no other reason than that I was the only female executive in Fleet Street without the tag of woman's page or fashion page after my name, I became a regular guest on Thames Television. A once-a-month simple, cheap, half-hour afternoon slot in which distinguished newspaper people, whom viewers barely knew, would sit around to discuss topics in the news.

Anthony Howard, then deputy editor of the *Observer*, and Peregrine Worsthorne, the *Sunday Telegraph* columnist and later its editor, were the two mainstays. I became the third. Politically, Howard and I should have been on the same side. But it was obvious from the first programme that he was competitive and liked to score points. I was an easy target. Perry, on the other hand, was endearingly kind and if you admired his tie, which was not difficult, he found it impossible to deny you his natural good manners and charm. Being the unashamed crumpet and the amateur between two giants was not something that bothered me.

If the challenge had been to write my opinions down rather than speak without notes, I might have shone more brightly. I had some experience as a columnist, but, sadly, there didn't look to be the remotest chance of getting a column at the *Mirror*. Then the paper didn't have a 'Wednesday Witch', as the Princess of Wales came to refer to the weekly columns in the tabloids written by women. The reason was because the club had got its fingers burnt. A couple of years before, and with great trepidation, it had hired Bel Mooney, a writer and journalist with a considerable and well-earnt reputation. The hiring must have required much late-night soul-searching in the office, in the pub, in Tramp nightclub. The *Mirror* had a reputation for not buying in names but home-growing its talent. Eventually the decision was taken. Sadly, Bel and the *Mirror* never gelled. Bel wisely resigned. Marje heaved a sigh of relief. Her place, top of the bill, was again secure. What I didn't know was that Tony Miles was restless about this Wednesday omission. And again Stott moved in as my campaign manager.

'You've got a columnist here in your midst,' he insisted and offered me up. He alone had seen my efforts from Liverpool. The reaction was muted. Miles started each day pondering the possibility of Joanna Lumley, the actress. Marje's choice, naturally, was no one. Whenever my name was floated she suggested, with a touching look of concern, according to Stott, that the pressure and stress might threaten my health and start my drink problem over again. It didn't wash. The rest knew her intentions were wicked, but a cowardly air of sheer terror prevailed towards dealing with an outraged and upset grande dame. Stott had another go. 'How long', he demanded, 'are we going to sit around and not appoint a woman columnist because another woman on the paper mightn't like it?'

In February 1983 I was called in by the editor and offered the job. I was shell-shocked, stunned and overjoyed. It was probably a combination of Stott's shaming and the thought of an actress they didn't know or understand that sealed my chances. I would be expected to continue as an assistant editor, running the features pages and doing my time on the editing rota.

My first column – it actually appeared on a Thursday in the early weeks – was a five and a half out of ten effort. The main piece looked at the visit of the Princess of Wales to a housing estate in Scotland where she had received a warm welcome from a group of young mothers. Coming from my background I had never quite been able to grasp why people took the royal family seriously. Why, especially, I asked in that first week, did young mothers living in bleak conditions not express more anger and resentment at the very obvious differences in Diana's life as a wife and mother and theirs?

Within a few years we would all be asking awkward questions along these lines. For the moment, I got the only thing required of a new 'voice'. A big postbag. I had hit upon one of the half-dozen subjects from which a columnist can guarantee to get a reaction. Royalty. In the coming weeks I also attempted to share with readers a bit of my home life. It was a deception that would continue for years. The happy picture of a busy wife and mother struggling with the everyday ups and downs of normal life.

Daily Mirror, 17 March 1983. 'I understand Duran Duran are currently on tour. This surprises me since there are times when I could swear they live permanently in my house. Their faces stare down moodily from several walls. They are rarely silent. And whether or not educationalists agree, my twelve-year-old insists that maths homework is vastly improved if done wearing Duran Duran sunglasses, a Duran Duran T-shirt and singing "Save a prayer for me" at the top of your voice.'

I also wrote a scurrilous piece about Joan Collins. 'Sitting in the hairdresser's one day I found myself next to a tall, scrawny-faced, middle-aged lady who had only a small amount of wispy hair. By her side was a large do-it-yourself tool box.' I explained how, during the next hour or so, I watched open-mouthed as she took years off the clock by daubing on her face most of the contents of her mobile intensive-care unit, and added three or four swatches of hair to her head. The actress was furious and sent an angry letter to the editor, which we published below a huge headline, 'The Bitch Bites Back'. 'I do not use "half-a-dozen layers of tarantula-like eyelashes – nor do I use three or four swatches of hair,"' seethed Ms Collins. The *Mirror* columnist was unrepentant: 'Dear Joan,' ran my reply. 'If I had some false eyelashes I'd weep into them. Love Annie.' The editor and his club chuckled away.

I was more satisfied with the chance to have an opinion on the aftermath of the Falklands. The money from the fund set up for the families of those who lost their lives was to be handed out in sums dependent on the rank of a lost husband or son. 'I didn't give my donations to keep a major's widow in a better class of sherry,' I protested. I denounced Victoria Gillick and her campaign to prevent the pill being made available to under-age girls. 'If my under-aged daughter was being prescribed the pill I'd like to know about it. And so would any caring mother.' Again, up to a point, Lord Copper.

My more obvious profile in the paper must have jogged the memory of the scary Barbara Maxwell of *Question Time*, and I was invited to be a guest on the programme. I prayed. I daily read every newspaper ten times over. I tried to remember the names of every member of the Cabinet. I genned up on nurses' pay and the troubles of the Catholic Church, which was then objecting to one of its priests, Monsignor Bruce Kent, leading the Campaign for Nuclear Disarmament.

On the night of the programme, which was to be recorded 'as live' at the Greenwich Theatre, I wore a bright emerald green jumper. The line-up was myself, the Right Honourable Norman Tebbit, then Secretary of State for Employment, Jim Mortimer, General Secretary of the Labour Party and Neil Mackintosh, then head of Shelter, the charity for the homeless. I remember my amusement at seeing the very unsmiling Cabinet minister being powdered with Revlon 'Touch and Glo' just before we went on.

Robin introduced me thus: 'Anne Robinson is further evidence of how women are steadily scaling the heights of power. She is an assistant editor on the *Daily Mirror* and one of the paper's columnists. As assistant editor she is often in complete charge of that paper and is the only woman who actually edits a Fleet Street paper.' He added: 'One of her editorial subordinates on that paper is her husband, who presumably knows on which side his bread is buttered.'

I remember getting a round of applause for demanding an increase in nurses' pay. Otherwise I said nothing useful. Looking at the tape for the first time since then I note that my hair, a much brighter red (quite natural), was almost down to my shoulders and since I was shy and embarrassed I looked down at my pad as I spoke. Add my voice, and all in all it was a passable impression of the Princess of Wales in her early shy Di period. I fled from the studio in shame. When I got home I rang my mother. 'Oh pet, your green jumper looked lovely,' she said. A couple of days later I received the traditional producer's note in which it is customary to praise a particular part of the guest's performance. Mine read: 'Thank you for coming to the Greenwich Theatre for *Question Time*. We all thought your green jumper looked splendid.'

Very few people are television naturals. To perform well on television, as with most other tasks in life, requires confidence. Confidence in how you look. Confidence in your opinions. Confidence allows you to hold the stage whoever is in charge of the discussion or interview. It comes with practice. I didn't have any. And boy, did it show. I slunk into my office at the *Daily*

Mirror the following day. No one said a word. There wasn't even a compliment about my green jumper. It took about a fortnight before I stopped reliving the ghastliness of my major television debut.

One Monday, a little later, I found myself missing from the weekly editing rota. Great, I thought. A reprieve from the giant ashtray and 2 a.m. finish and the having to get back into work eight hours later. The following week my name again wasn't there. I caught the editor at the top of the newsroom. 'Is there any reason I'm not down to edit?' I asked. 'No, blossom,' said Molloy, 'but go off and do more television. That's what you're good at.' This was worryingly vague, to say the least. Before I could ask another question, he had gone. I was stunned and perplexed. How dare he be so patronising? What had I done? I knew I was rubbish when it came to management skills. I didn't know how to ask my staff nicely for anything, but nor did half the other executives. I was a better journalist than most of them. I couldn't think what, apart from my tactlessness, I had done to be dropped from the first team.

I left for home, waiting until I was alone in my car to weep tears of anger. Rejection was very hard. In my sensitive state of desperately wanting to put my past behind me and to succeed it was a body blow. The club had invited me to join and now they were throwing me out without so much as a decent reason, never mind a court of appeal. I didn't have the courage to demand to know more about my sacking.

Once my indignation had subsided, it dawned on me I was being offered a peculiarly wonderful opportunity. If I could do the column and do television, what more could a girl ask? Or, more relevantly, what more could a mother who wanted to be at home with her daughter wish for? But these benefits took time to sink in.

Before they did, we had another disappointment. Ever since Johnny and I had married I had longed to get pregnant. An astute reader might well ask if history was repeating itself. Why was I seeking such a solution when my second marriage had yet to settle down? Was this not as 'feckless' as my first decision to get pregnant? Yes. The unsatisfactory explanation is that clever, grown-up, quick-witted, decent people frequently make decisions that are as irresponsible as those made by half-educated youngsters that at least gives them an excuse not to know better. When the pregnancy happened, however, it was short-lived. It didn't even last long enough for me to tell Emma. Within a few weeks I started spotting. Confined to bed and ordered to rest, I rang girlfriend after girlfriend. One brought round her vast library of mother and baby books. I was astonished how few at the time referred to miscarriage. By the following weekend it was all over. I was whipped into hospital for a D&C. The consultant was irritated by my questions. Was anything wrong? Would I get pregnant again? Why had it happened? I received no useful answers. 'Watch out, she'll say everything was your fault,' one of the club told Johnny helpfully. I soon discovered what he meant. Almost immediately I went into a black depression. It was similar to what I had felt in those early days of my marriage to Charlie after the abortion, although at the time I had never connected the two. Johnny was at his best. Gentle, kind, understanding. But it was impossible to console me.

One Saturday, in desperation, he bundled me into the car and drove me to Gloucestershire, my favourite county, in the hope that a trip out of town might help. The countryside looked so appealing that we came back determined to move, if not out of London, at least somewhere more green and gentle. We put the house on the market and were offered the asking price within a couple of weeks. Our house 'showed well' said the estate agent. That it did was down to Johnny. We raced round looking for a new home and found a Regency dream – in Johnny's terms anyway – at the bottom of Keat's Grove in Hampstead, overlooking the heath. (Astonishingly the Christian name of the owner's daughter was Penrose. She had been named after her mother's university lecturer.) It was semi-detached, the stucco painted white, with a delicate wrought-iron balcony, and was set back behind a deep garden. To me it looked glamorous and elegant and beautiful inside and out. To Johnny's more critical eye it needed everything doing to it. It hadn't been updated in twenty years. It was 'tired'. It only had one bathroom and a very old kitchen, but it was Hampstead, we told each other excitedly. Even though our renovations had increased the value of Tavistock Terrace more than threefold, we still had to take out a colossal £100,000 mortgage. No one we knew had a mortgage of that size. We went ahead.

My daughter was growing up. Charlie had included me in discussions over her new school in London. We went off to be interviewed at the City of London, at Queens Gate and at More House. I was delighted to be part of the process but, as usual, embarrassed that anyone should know our background. We chose More House in Knightsbridge, a small but much recommended Catholic day school for girls. The headmistress was impressive. There were no uniforms, which delighted Emma, although in my book uniforms are a godsend to parents wishing to promote a speedy exit to school every day.

Emma was learning to play the double bass – not an instrument that travels easily or makes wonderful sounds on its own, but it was an appealing example of her eccentricity. At More House she excitedly joined the school orchestra. She was to prove herself exceptionally good at chemistry, maths and physics. She even won a special award for maths. An honour indeed, because she had been required to catch up and take on a new syllabus when she moved from Glasgow. I look back with shame that, in two households full of journalists, her strengths in the sciences were probably received with muted congratulations.

I realised I had on my hands a daughter who was not a great reader. How could this be? I bribed. I promised her one pound for every book she completed. Alas, my child was neither greedy nor bribable. Even now she's a slow reader, although a thorough one. She has also retained her complete lack of interest in money. She is altogether a less impetuous, more considered person than her mother. She is not a spendthrift. She is impressively free of her mother's terrible shopping habits. She has learnt nothing from my bad example in that direction. 'I'm glad', a Manhattan furniture salesman once told me when she dragged me along to his store in Greenwich Village to help her choose a sofa bed, 'I'm not her greengrocer. I can see Emma walking past a cauliflower for a couple of weeks, undecided about buying it.'

I can take no credit for Emma's gift for music. I can perhaps take a tiny bit for her gift for mimicry. Around this time I heard her take off Brian Walden, the Midlands-born presenter of London Weekend TV's political interview programme *Weekend World*, and realised that she only had to hear a voice once to be able to copy it. By the age of twelve there was also no avoiding her quick wit. A survival technique, she now claims, borne from years of having to make herself heard when all about her, at either home, were noisily interrupting whatever she was trying to say.

Once Charlie had been back in London for a time and was heavily office bound, I plucked up my courage and tried again to change the arrangement. I met him for breakfast. I said that I was now at home and sober and well and asked if he would consider letting Emma move over to live with me. It was a reasonable request. I was truly these days a part-time journalist. I had taken seriously the editor's carte blanche instruction 'to do television'. I had pointedly ceased to involve myself in overseeing the features department. I had calculated that I would be left alone and not confronted about only coming into the office to write my column and see my page through. And I was right. For more than half the week I was as free as air. Free to take Emma to school. Free in the evenings for when she came home. Free at holiday time. Charlie didn't need to pause to consider my request. He knew his answer. 'I think things are better left just how they are,' he said. I felt dejected. And furious.

Another general election. June 1983. Four years since the last one. Only four years since I had been a drunk, living with my mother, reporting for the *Liverpool Echo*. Four years since Margaret Thatcher, with her conviction politics, uneven teeth, big bows on her blouses, flat hairdo and high-pitched simpering voice had first triumphed. The Prime Minister had changed too. Her politics were the same. But the teeth were now straight. The big bows had become little bows. The hair had stiffened, but had not yet evolved into the truly magnificent meringue it would eventually become. Her intended look of concern, when she considered an interviewer was being particularly dim, remained. The voice had been lowered, although no amount of elocution lessons could help soften her image. She was rotten at being publicly sincere. And, as Keith Waterhouse famously wrote, she continued to talk to people as if their dog had just died.

'A quite extraordinary thing happened to Mrs Thatcher at 2.37 last Friday afternoon. She met and had a conversation with a Labour voter,' began my account, for the second time, of the leader of the Tory Party's campaign trail. Military precision had replaced the haphazard travelling arrangements of 1979. Mrs Thatcher's purposeful desire to make a good impression on television had also risen a notch or two. 'Here is an election where you might think there were only two votes, those belonging to the ITN and BBC cameramen,' I observed. She was barefaced in her wooing of the media. Michael Brunson, ITN's political editor, had cause to blush. 'Where's Michael?' she would ask time and again. But never noticeably 'Where's Denis?' That worry was left to another half-dozen voices. 'Where's Denis?' was what the security guards, Thatcher aides, public relations men, media managers, hangers-on and daughter Carol would be demanding wearily when yet again the Tory leader's consort went missing. Mostly he was to be found back in the crowd discussing small businesses and how to run one. Carol was there to write her own 'in-depth' analysis of her mother's election for the

Daily Telegraph. Maybe nothing struck her as interesting. I looked over her shoulder late one afternoon outside a bakery in Stockport. Her pristine notebook said only: 'Mummy looked relaxed.' When Denis did catch up he was goodness itself in not letting his boredom show. In factories he would view the objects coming towards him on the conveyor belt and marvel, 'Ah! There's another one the same.'

And my, did we see some conveyor belts. We stalked through bakeries, tweed factories, breweries, electronics works. Their owners were staunch Conservative supporters. The workers almost certainly were not. 'The scarves are seventy per cent cashmere and thirty per cent wool,' one of the women was rehearsing to herself at the mill we were inspecting in Inverness. Her name was Cathy. She told me that she had been laid off and was only back temporarily for a month. But 'Ma'am, it's seventy per cent cashmere, thirty per cent wool' was all she said obediently to Mrs Thatcher as she passed by.

Far more exciting for Anne Robinson than Mrs Thatcher was the sight of Norman Mailer. The *Mail on Sunday* had thrown bundles of money at him to report the campaign. On the trip he bumbled along obediently like the rest of us. My hero! I longed to ask him about his life, his writing, his marriages, his wild days. What he'd learnt, what else he wanted to do? Where was he going? Was he happy? Did he still smoke pot? Instead, I just trailed behind him like an adoring puppy dog. So much so that when we arrived at a Manchester brewery and Mrs Thatcher was being greeted by even more Messrs Robinson (owners of the brewery) than there had been Messrs Warburton at the bakery we had just left, Norm and I were alongside each other.

Together we faced a small, vociferous group of women waving banners and demanding an explanation about local education cuts. One of the women protesters, a *Mirror* reader, recognised me. 'Anne,' she yelled, 'I'm Gaynor. Come here and talk to us.' I went and Norm followed. 'This is Norman Mailer,' I said. 'Well, he can listen too,' said Gaynor, without looking up.

In a field outside Northampton a Tory rally had been arranged. A ticket-only, loyal supporters affair, the worry of how to appeal to the masses could be safely put aside. Here was a different Thatcher. More strident, harsh, raw. 'We believe in freedom, independence and opportunity according to talent and ability,' she announced. The crowd cheered. The 'Dam Busters March' played. 'Oh, Daphne, what we'll do for England,' said a woman to her friend as she looked down at their patent-leather high-heeled shoes squelching in the mud.

On my last day with Mrs Thatcher on the hustings, we ended the afternoon at the Ideal Home Exhibition at the National Exhibition Centre in Birmingham. Most of Mrs T's campaign this time around had been used to stress the need for good management. Unemployment was rising to a worryingly high level. She believed in biting the bullet – that pruning and cutting back and making Britain more efficient were vital. But once inside the vast exhibition building she was back in her old routine. That of Thatcher the homemaker. She had not lost her touch. Playing with an egg whisk she declared with a completely straight face, 'I am here today mostly as a housewife.'

That summer we joined the Wood family and returned to Crete. The school project was Queen Elizabeth I. Emma was growing up. A young lady now with breasts, beautiful red hair and a wicked sense of humour. A temper, but the sweetest of natures. We had booked three bungalows at the hotel. The girls, the two Woods, Jessica and Rebecca, and Emma, were to share one. The parents would be either side. We were taken aback when we arrived to find that we had been granted a mention in the hotel visitors' book the year before. It was not a rave review. A guest reported that he and his family had had an excellent holiday marred only by the 'loud-voiced toffs on the terrace at night giving their opinions and sneering about other people's newspaper reading habits'. Visitors who didn't know their place. We resolved to be better behaved. Or at least to keep our voices down.

Incredibly, despite this being our second holiday together, Derek says now he had no idea of our true circumstances. No idea Emma lived apart from us. No idea I had had a drink problem. No idea of the decision of one of his number, Mr Justice Faulks. It demonstrates to what lengths I must have gone to guard our secret, and how Emma kindly fell in with my unspoken wishes. It shows, too, how unnecessarily preoccupied I was with my position. Or rather my lack of position, as I saw it. How much energy I wasted.

Historical footnote: 30 November 1983: 'The career of a Crown Court judge with a taste for whisky was in ruins last night after he was fined £2,000 for smuggling,' reported the *News of the World*. Judge Keith Bruce Campbell, leading counsel for Charlie in our custody battle, had been arrested with a friend, a used-car dealer, on his cabin cruiser with 125 litres of whisky and 10,000 cigarettes. 'Well, you know our way of life,' he was reported to have told a customs officer. 'We drink perhaps half a dozen bottles over the weekend.' The judge, a former Tory MP and a father of six, was a week later removed from office by the Lord Chancellor for misbehaviour. The only judge in the twentieth century to be so disgraced in this way.

18

Part Monster, Part Magic

Robert Maxwell was a giant of a man who arrived in the middle of a hot summer's night and took over the *Mirror* empire. It was akin to highway robbery. 'Editors are taught by experience to fear no one except policemen in patrol cars late at night,' wrote Bob Edwards in his autobiography, explaining how unprepared those in the building were for the event. (His book, *Goodbye Fleet Street*, is one of the very best accounts of that period.)

Edwards, as editor of the *Sunday Mirror*, along with the other editors in the group, felt the full force of the new proprietor. The year before, it had been announced that the Mirror Group's parent, Reed International, wanted to sell off the newspapers. This casting adrift looked like having ominous consequences. There was the awful spectre of a new owner not understanding the custom and practices of lunch, of expenses, of office drivers on quadruple overtime taking executives to the airport on bank holidays. In retrospect these worries were groundless. The new boss was never against largesse. That was to be the problem.

Robert Maxwell strode into the main entrance off Holborn Circus just past midnight on 13 July 1984. By reputation he was an ogre, a bully, a crook, a liar, an egotist and a charmer. Nothing he did in the following six years disproved this judgement. Which was why it was all the more lamentable that so many people who should have known better chose to trust him and believe what he said. Maxwell had a self-belief and lack of self-doubt that covered up a fear of failure, a fear of appearing a fool and a horror of loneliness.

He was part monster, part magic. The majority of people experienced the former, and I found him neither odd nor scary but, thanks to my mother, almost touchingly familiar. He was a bully first and foremost and bullies always behave better with those who are not frightened of them.

Within days he had sacked the chairman and several of the executives. The editors and the club were still all in place but dealing on a twenty-four-hour basis with a man who made their behaviour look normal. Immediately he made a friend of the chief leader writer, Joe Haines, who had called him a crook in public, but who became one of his closest allies.

A lot of crazy things took place in a short space of time. Since I regarded myself as one of the injured parties of the previous regime's unjustness, I quietly looked on and laughed.

For example, Maxwell immediately ordered the hiring of women executives. Fine by me, as I had no wish to return to the giant ashtray. The snag was where to find female newspaper executives of note. The editors grabbed whom they could. Jo Foley, former editor of *Woman's Own*, and Dee Nolan, former features editor of *Woman* magazine, were not the sort anyone at the *Mirror* would have regarded as suitable. Maxwell ordered one to be given the deputy editorship of the *Mirror*. There was already a deputy editor, so she was appeased with the title of managing editor and a new black Porsche. The other one became features editor. Unfortunately, that had by now become Johnny's job. He was demoted to a side office with an even more worryingly vague explanation than I had received at my demotion from the editing rota.

Few days were dull. One morning, not long afterwards, Maxwell decided – perhaps on the advice of a cleaner or a driver or a secretary – that columns were not what people wanted. Readers wanted news. For a few weeks my column and others were redesigned to disguise the fact that they were the product of a single author. Even this failed to upset me. I hadn't come across such ridiculous, incontestable, unrestrained dictatorship since 13 and 14 Market Street. As time went on, Maxwell became more and more like my mother. It was secretly pleasurable to watch grown men shake in fear at his bellowing and carry out his orders irrespective of how absurd his demands were. I had never been of the 'hate men' school, but the natural order at the newspaper was for the guys to yell and scream, and a lot of women found it tough. So watching the reaction to Maxwell was rewarding confirmation of all that my mother believed. Men were essentially very scared, or 'windy', as she put it.

It helped that just before Maxwell's takeover I had been approached for the second time by the editor of the *Sun* to take my column there. I didn't want to go to the *Sun* but it was useful to know I had a choice. I also suggested to Johnny that we put the house on the market. These were not safe times to be committed to a vast mortgage. Maxwell heard about my *Sun* offer without my telling him. I had actually told Joe Haines, who, along with his many gifts, was, I knew, completely hopeless when it came to keeping secrets. Maxwell called me up to his office. He doubled my salary. Was there anything else I wanted? he asked. 'Yes', I said without blinking, a Mercedes with a telephone. 'You shall have one,' he said. 'With a telephone?' I reiterated. 'With a telephone.' I felt like Cinderella who was going to the ball in a frock and tiara and, what's more, a coach better than anyone else's. I was also my mother's daughter. I insisted he made some calls. I knew, and he didn't, that the idea of a columnist demanding a car of as high a quality as the editor's was not going to be sanctioned further down the ranks. He rang his transport manager: 'Get her a new Mercedes immediately.' The transport manager said meekly that a new Mercedes order could take nine months. 'Tell them it's for me,' said Maxwell. At my request he called in a secretary, dictated a letter detailing the increased salary and car and signed it, there and then.

A week later the phone at home rang. Maxwell was in America making a multi-million-dollar bid for a publishing company. His name was appearing on the front of the business pages on a daily basis. Johnny took the call and passed the receiver to me. 'Bob here,' he said. 'We've found you a grey Mercedes with blue upholstery. Will that do?' Twenty seconds of his time. I thought he was very good news indeed.

I am not sure if the bizarre and unworkable idea of a '*Mirror* train' chug-chugging around the country so that the new publisher could make public appearances and meet the readers was Maxwell's own. If it wasn't, it was tailor-made to suit his conceit. 'Robert Maxwell will lead the crusade, supported by a host of *Mirror* writers,' announced the front page. While it sounded harmless enough, the mechanics of getting the show on the road were a great deal more complicated. The project had every chance of running off the rails and it did. For a start, Marje refused to appear on any platform – train or meeting hall – with her arch rival, the *Sunday Mirror* agony aunt, Claire Rayner. The days of anyone other than pop stars such as Pink Floyd or the Rolling Stones filling a town hall on a wet evening when there is plenty to watch on television were over. We played to an audience of about fifteen one night in Cardiff. Less than thirty in Northampton – or was it Peterborough? A few faithful elderly *Mirror* readers, a few cranks and a few militants. The dullest of dull accounts of the various trips took up acres of space in the papers.

Maxwell enjoyed himself to begin with. When we arrived in Cardiff he toured the city's shopping precinct with a flunkey from the Town Hall. Ordinary people thought he was quite amazing and greeted him as if he were royalty. Only more useful.

'What would you like to see improved?' he would ask as they mobbed him. Better litter bins said one. 'Write that down,' said Maxwell to the flunkey from the Town Hall. It was an early example of how people with good brains will suspend critical judgement when in the presence of a powerful person. In Maxwell's case, the size of his personality was matched by the width of his girth. He exuded authority. The fact that he had absolutely nothing to do with Cardiff's dustbins or the clout to change them not only went over the heads of the people in the precinct, it failed to register with the man from the Town Hall.

Maxwell's confidence was boundless. Naturally, within a couple of days he got bored with the train and moved on, declaring he intended to resolve the miners' strike. We were left to chug away without him.

The miners' strike interfered with but not resolved, he galloped towards a visit to and a fundraising appeal for Ethiopia. Then an appeal to save the Red Devils flying team. It was not unusual to see half a dozen pictures of him scattered through the *Daily Mirror*.

I continued to chuckle quietly. It helped that he genuinely liked women. He came into the category of a brother with older sisters. I never once found him to be unapproachable. He preferred to abuse those who could not answer back. His daily madcap requests included the order for each of us to fill in a form to list our ambitions and our thoughts. Journalists sat at their desks agonising. I hardly bothered. I didn't believe that Maxwell or anyone else would read them. There was a rumour that our phones were being tapped. That turned out to be true.

In the evening Maxwell would sit up in his office on the ninth floor, bored and lonely. As Johnny would eventually discover, the result could be catastrophic for an assistant editor in charge of the paper. He would telephone to interfere, to meddle, to dictate new front pages.

There was the first party political conference where he rode into Blackpool like the new king of England. As they had been in

Cardiff, ordinary people in Blackpool were mesmerised. His knack of being able to speak to them not as if their dog had just died, but as if he and they were pals was genuine. Colleagues would fall under his spell, convinced that they alone had his ear, only to find after a few short weeks that he had tired of them and somebody else had gone to the top of the class and was being allowed to give out the pencils.

Like my mother, he had little sense of the effect of humiliating people in public. So a son, a daughter, an editor would be barked at, ridiculed, ordered around. I worked out there were a few tricks to dealing with him. One was to stay out of his way as much as possible. Second, only to seek him out on matters of supreme urgency. Always, always to get his signature for anything he promised. Without it you were sunk. In my case I only bothered him to arrange a better deal on my salary. To this end, I twice improved my cars. 'With all the extras,' I added each time and made him sign a bit of paper. One day I bumped into Marje in the corridor. By now, she and I rarely saw each other. But if we did she was always pointedly polite. 'Fred is waiting for me,' she said (Fred was her driver). 'He's delighted with our new car, dear.' 'Oh, what's that?' I asked, without much thought. 'A 280E Mercedes with leather upholstery, cruise control and alloy wheels.' Seventy-something years old she might have been then, but she was no slouch when it came to making sure she had a motor as good as the other female columnist's.

Charlie Wilson's career was looking more promising and demanding than ever. Fantastic for his admirers. Dreadful for his ex-wife who could only see her daughter every other weekend and one night during the week in between.

Rupert Murdoch certainly knew a dedicated, talented, hard-working, tough newspaperman when he saw one. On 5 November 1985, to the shock and astonishment, and in certain quarters dismay, of Fleet Street, Charlie Wilson was appointed editor of *The Times*. The previous editor, Charles Douglas-Home, had died after a long illness. In his place, for the first time, a non-university-educated journalist was in charge of *The Thunderer*. It was interesting to watch the reactions and to marvel at how the Establishment worked. Charlie could not move for invitations – be they royal, or political, or to appear on television. He was a most important figure in the land.

What very few people knew was that Murdoch had chosen exactly the right man for a difficult job that needed to be done: a top journalist, also capable of taking his newspapers to a new plant at Wapping fitted out with the latest printing technology. And, in the process, discarding the old printing workers and their restrictive and costly union practices. The move would blow up into a major industrial dispute in which Charlie was threatened with physical harm and Emma, to her delight, was provided with a bullet-proof car to take her to and from school.

The year before his promotion, while still executive editor of *The Times*, Murdoch had tested the skills of his man. He had asked Charlie to take a temporary job at the *Chicago Sun-Times* and sort it out. Charlie was so good Murdoch offered him the job full time at a million dollars a year. Charlie eventually rejected the deal, he says now, primarily because of Emma. He didn't want her to have parents on different continents. Had I known then that it was a possibility, I would not have let Emma go without a legal challenge. Indeed, Charlie would have had to apply to the courts to take Emma out of the country, and I, the mother, now sober and working part time, would have had a very reasonable case.

As it was, the Chicago trip presented a bleak prospect for me. When Charlie told me about it he was uncertain how long he would be away. But I automatically assumed that during that time Emma would be living with me. To my horror, nothing of the sort was planned. 'Sally has broken her collarbone in a car crash. Dad wants me to stay and look after her,' announced Emma. I couldn't believe it. I didn't know how to handle this. For the first time I was truly not prepared to allow what I regarded as an injustice to pass. But how did I go about it without causing a row?

How, when I had promised so faithfully, as had Charlie, to present a united front, could I challenge his decision?

We got nowhere on the phone. Charlie became angry. I thought about it for days. Sally had Luke but also a full-time nanny. If she needed more help, surely she could pay for it? I suppose it would have been healthy to blow up there and then, shout my case and to hell. Instead, I tackled Charlie again. He didn't see the problem. We rowed over the phone several more times. It was like the old days. I wept in despair as I thought about the situation. It came to me that, as unlikely and ridiculous as it was, Emma now saw me as the one without problems. The stoic parent who swallowed the partings and the separation without complaint or emotion. Of course she did. I had spent so long disciplining myself to behave nicely. I was over-conscientious, and it was allowing me less than I deserved.

I could hardly have Emma as the piggy-in-the-middle, pleading with her to let Sally and her injury be looked after by nannies and cleaning ladies or whatever. But I could legitimately lower my mask. In Hampstead one evening I sat her down and told her the story of her father and me. Not in any dramatic or lopsided way, but enough to wipe away any doubt about my vulnerability. I stressed how much I missed her. I reminded her that she had asked me to leave things alone. I knew and respected her wish that we did nothing about her living with Charlie. But I genuinely felt that in his absence she should be with me. She listened quietly and said she understood and she would tell her father. Which she did.

Charlie relented. And Emma came to stay with me for the final stint of his US posting.

During that time I felt truly liberated. I wanted everyone to see Emma with me. I would go out of my way to tell people I had to rush home to pick Emma up from school. Or take her to school. For just a little while I could hold my head high. Emma did not need to take an overnight case to More House on a Friday. She did not have to commute between homes. We carted the double bass back and forth to school. We went swimming. We walked on the heath, although Guinness had never recovered from leaving grimy, traffic-clogged Holloway and disliked Hampstead!

My brother, to Emma's annoyance, arranged to have her portrait painted by an artist friend of his. Emma hated the sittings. She hated the picture. But it was another sign of what I saw as 'normal life'. Not having to make arrangements to fit in with other people for the every-other-weekend routine. Or suffer the horror of explaining to the artist that her sitter was not available most of the time. (If it had had to be done during the precious access visits the portrait would never have been completed.)

Charlie was back from Chicago all too soon and Emma returned to live at Campden Hill Square. It left me feeling even more frustrated about an outdated and irrelevant court decision of a decade before.

One of the dilemmas of my circumstances was that I knew no one else in the same boat. I knew working female journalists. I knew others who were recovering from years of alcohol abuse and were attempting to rebuild their lives. But I didn't know another struggling teetotaller who had leapfrogged her husband at work and who had lost custody of her little daughter, whom she missed more than anything else in the world. Yet was forced to look on helplessly as the father with custody was spending more and more time on his career.

19

Her Last Command

My mother had become much easier to deal with as she saw my life settle down. She would never recover from the trauma of her precious only granddaughter being in the custody, care and control of Charlie. But as time went on her accusing tone had dropped. I sweetly imagined she had come to understand a little better how things were. But one day I heard her talking to my brother on the phone and I realised that she was still bossing him around – or was busy still 'controlling' him, as any kind of bossiness is now fashionably called. It taught me what kind, wise people had been trying to convince me of for a long time. *You* have to change if you want other people to change.

I hadn't realised it but I had grown in confidence. Like bullies the whole world over, my mother did not mess with strength. She messed with weakness. Nowadays, when she rang, she would say kindly, 'Am I interrupting you, pet?' as opposed to the old way, which would be to launch into a conversation with 'Get a pencil and write this down.' Or 'hello' in that dreadful way that sent me back to my childhood when you knew you were in the doghouse but were not sure why.

The good news was that she continued to approve of Johnny. More and more so as time went on. He was unfailingly courteous and considerate to her. She loved his style and stories, his laughter. 'Make sure you look after him' was the order. Not in any way to her a contradiction of what had gone before. In her simple logic you took great care of anything valuable.

It is hard to pinpoint the first stirrings of unease about her condition. But over a period of months I realised she was sounding as if she was battling against depression. Everything seemed to be troublesome and a burden, although she never called it that. She was now past seventy. Not old by today's standards and she looked well and slim. But her thyroid was giving her trouble. She began to see a specialist. At first I considered her moans and frustrations – 'your father doesn't understand; you can't leave anything to him' – no more than normal. She had scaled down her business. She was too old to contemplate expanding when neither of her children was interested in inheriting it. She, like most despots, was hopeless at hiring and keeping staff. She didn't trust them. She imagined they talked behind her back, or were trying to steal from her. Be it cleaning ladies, drivers, block men (who cleaned the poultry), their length of service was short.

The old St John's Market had been pulled down and she had taken a warehouse in Liverpool 7, near the university. A building that I imagined had once housed horses and carts. When that too was marked out for redevelopment she moved her storage to Crosby. She was still buying on the market and supplying hotels and ships, but the competition was fierce and age had slowed her down. More than I knew.

She phoned me one day to announce that she had noted an advertisement in the *Crosby Herald* in which the local authority was offering to fund new businesses. She had made an appointment and taken my father along. To his astonishment she told the woman clerk that she was a trained hairdresser and wanted money to start a salon. It was an indication of my father's lifelong policy of never making waves that he sat through this without apparently telling her she was out of her mind. She thought quite the opposite and was waiting to hear how much money she was going to be offered. She had, she said with her customary air of satisfaction, 'put the woman straight on a number of things, particularly when she asked what experience I had of hairdressing'. I couldn't decide if I felt sorry not to have witnessed this most bizarre of happenings, or marvel at my affable father's ability to let her be herself.

Clearly she was restless and was at times leaving reality behind. She complained she never got to go anywhere and how much she would love to be at the Cup Final. I naturally proceeded to get my hands on Cup Final tickets, only to have her say that 'your father and I couldn't possibly face the journey'. Another time, she started harking back to an osteopath who had treated her at Champneys years before. If only she could find him, she said. Again I searched and searched and came up with his number. She hardly responded. Over several months I realised that just about anything and everything was starting to worry her. Her hairdresser, her manicurist, her accountant, her housekeeper. The criticism of my father got worse. She told me she was convinced he was hiding her jewellery, stealing from her purse. I didn't really worry until she rang to say the checkout girls in the supermarket were talking about her behind her back. She then rang a friend of mine in Crosby to say that I had told her never to visit me in my house again. She called me as many as four or five times in one day, in a state, complaining about her specialist. She began to boast she always took the new *Vogue* away in her handbag from the hairdresser's. Did she think they didn't notice? Obviously not. I rang my father who shrugged off my concerns, saying, 'You know your mother'. He didn't seem bothered. Which was odd because she was now insisting that my father was selling her jewellery. I immediately defended him. Old habits! Why on earth would he be out to distress her? That made her cross. The next time I saw them together I felt guilty that anyone could ever think ill of him. He was his gentle, cheery self. That weekend she turned up in London in a filthy old dress.

Another shock. My mother, of all people, had wardrobes full of clothes. This dress had stains down the front. So did her coat. She didn't seem herself. She forgot the name of the dog. She kept mispronouncing the name of our then dog carer and now my PA, however often I corrected her. It was Karen standing there who convinced me how strangely my mother was behaving.

As well as her thyroid problem she was being treated for diabetes and a few weeks later rang to say that the consultant was demanding money from her and that there were unpaid bills. I rang the consultant and asked what was going on. Of course she didn't owe him any money, he said, it was her age. She was seventy-three. The arteries of her brain were hardening was how he explained her condition. Why didn't he warn me about what was to come?

Five months later she fell and broke her hip. In hospital, she was not herself one little bit. I put it down to the drugs. But couldn't ignore the other evidence. The business was reduced to a part-time book-keeper and driver. She had almost ceased to trade. She had sacked yet another cleaning lady. She had ordered the house painters off-site halfway through the job. The gardener of many years' standing had been dismissed in much the same way. The hospital sent her home as soon as she was able, with the help of my father, to cope. He would carry her up to bed, for she could barely walk. One week she called and said my father was no longer looking after her. I sensed big trouble and left for Liverpool within the hour. What met me was eye-opening and shocking. The house was a complete tip. Worse, my father was clearly sick, and she was making no sense. I tried Social Services and got answering machines. I bundled them into the car and drove them to London. The journey was one of the longest I can remember. My mother moaned and cried and yelled and screamed. She was terrified of what was happening to her. 'Where are you taking me?' she asked over and over again. Whatever I answered failed to reassure her. My father held her hand patiently. I got them up the stairs in Hampstead. With four floors and no lavatory on the same floor as a bedroom, it was an impossible house in which to care for two invalids. Our GP diagnosed my father as having a ruptured hernia and needing immediate surgery. I had scarcely considered him. My mother was a bigger problem in the long term.

She would only allow my father to administer her insulin. How could I nurse her? She was distressed enough when he left her side even for a minute, although when he returned he got the full force of her anger. An ambulance was called and both of them were taken down the road to the Royal Free Hospital. My father was put on the list for surgery but only with reluctance did they admit my mother on to a general ward.

The next morning she looked better and rested. Her calm, I discovered, was because she was unaware she was in hospital and thought she was back at Champneys, her health farm. We were all delighted to keep up the pretence. My brother arrived from France. Her children viewed the illness differently. Peter found it hard to accept he had essentially lost his mother. I took on the fight against the hospital that wanted to discharge her now they had stabilised her condition. Each day Peter would put her in a wheelchair, take her down to the café in the basement and read to her from *The Times*, determined his proper mother would return. I fired letters off to those in charge. To the registrar. To the houseman. My father's surgery was successful but he needed time to recover. Were they suggesting, I demanded, that a seventy-one-year-old man, less than a week after major surgery, could look after his demented wife?

In panic I rang Help the Aged. I also rang the Alzheimer's Society, then known as the Alzheimer's Disease Society. A number in south London. The woman was wonderful and offered to send me a booklet. I recall the calmness of her voice and the fact that she asked for no money. (My gratitude to the society remains. I bat on its behalf whenever possible and I am proud to be one of its vice presidents.) The booklet was a revelation. Apart from my mother never having wandered out of her own front door, every other symptom was familiar. I promptly marched in and told the doctors at the Royal Free what the problem was. The registrar said my mother was no more than a little forgetful, and dismissed my diagnosis.

Annoyingly, at times she could appear so normal. I watched open-mouthed one afternoon as a senior houseman turned up at her bedside and she enquired about his children, their education, his holiday plans. Here was the old Miss Wilson in action on her market stall back in Liverpool, behaving exactly as she did with the surgeon's wife who used to be a nurse.

What was I to do? A sick father, and a lunatic mother now prone to violence if she didn't get her way. Only dogged persistence won the day. I insisted that she was assessed again, and properly, instead of the cursory ten-minute job designed to get the hospital off the hook. After six weeks in the psychiatric unit the same psychiatrists who had pronounced her 'mildly confused' changed their assessment to 'severe dementia'. Full-time care was advised.

How, where, what? Emma was taking her O levels, Johnny was stuck at the office, and we had hit another crisis. This time brought on by his debts. Somewhere in the middle of all this he had come home and announced that his pal, the manager at the bank, had solved his cash crisis. He had agreed to a loan on the joint account, secured against the house. 'Hang on a minute,' I said. 'This means I now owe half of six thousand pounds.' 'Are you going to be difficult?' he asked. What now, Germaine? Revolution or submission? Marriage first, principles second?

It was another sign of the times that a bank official – despite what legislation might be in place about equality – felt no need for a wife to be consulted on a joint account.

I hardly had a moment to consider the full effrontery, being too busy fighting the system on behalf of my mother. I rang dozens of nursing homes, hoping to place her. I considered the idea of hiring full-time nursing staff. But how were we to manage without a single loo on the right floor? How were we to cope with full-time staff and my father living with us? None of the nursing homes we visited was suitable. Matrons with long red fingernails unnerved me. In several we would clearly have had to play down my mother's true condition. Not one looked as if it was meant for a confused, cantankerous old lady who needed love and understanding.

At one point I found a kindly Irish nurse who cared for people in her own home. My mother lasted forty-eight hours before her wailing and crying disturbed the whole house. She had not slept since she got there. We moved her on to another home, where she caught pneumonia and ended up back at the Royal Free Hospital.

Fear, guilt, panic, despair. We put our unsuitable house on the market. I started to investigate renting a ground-floor flat for my parents. But in my heart I knew my mother was no longer able to live a normal life – to live at home. The consultant at the Royal Free suggested Friern Barnet, a forbidding, bleak, Victorian, former lunatic asylum that had become a psychiatric hospital. Thankfully, it is now closed.

It was harrowing. Long dark corridors. A ward with two dozen women in various stages of undress and distress and madness. Moaning, repetitive behaviour, rocking from side to side. Within a couple of days they had kindly taken my mother for a perm and put her in some polyester clothes because it was easier for them to cope with the laundering. What had I done? She was indistinguishable from the other old ladies. The family's most powerful, dominant member, the one who fought all our battles, was now in an institution and reduced to a state of permanent helplessness. How badly I had failed the one person who had never refused to support me, however misguided her help might have been at times.

Her memory would come and go. I was taking my first steps on breakfast television with a ten-minute spot reviewing and previewing television. 'Get to Harvey Nichols,' she said, looking up one day. 'That thing you're wearing has no shape and the hem isn't straight.' It was her last command.

My father would spend each day at Friern Barnet holding her hand. One night, when he returned home, he had with him the smoked-salmon sandwiches he had made for her that morning. She had refused his food. He was weeping openly. 'She's not going to get any better,' he said quietly.

He was right. Increasingly she slept. She caught a bad cold which turned to pneumonia again. A nurse and a young female doctor called my father and me into the office one night to 'discuss treatment'. They were talking in riddles, debating whether to give my mother antibiotics. I couldn't make sense of their dilemma. 'What', I finally asked, 'is the problem with antibiotics if they will clear up the infection?' 'They prolong life,' said the doctor. 'Give them immediately,' I ordered.

But my mother had had enough. She was rushed back to the Royal Free. Emma sat quietly with her for every available minute when she was not at school. She alone was capable of dealing with her nana's condition with kindness and lack of panic. To Emma my mother responded by smiling and clutching her hand. Emma was the last person to receive a glimmer of recognition from her. She died a week later.

We took her home and buried her with full Blundellsands honours. I was moved that one of the many who turned up at her funeral was Terry Field, a one-time Militant MP but before that a fireman, and a part-time van driver for my mother. He was incredibly fond of her. Perhaps she and the Militant Tendency had more in common than either would have thought.

I didn't weep much. I was relieved when someone said that some things were 'too important to cry over'. My father was inconsolable, my brother confused. We had lost my mother months before. I was only relieved that her distress was over. She did not deserve her undignified end; I felt and still feel I should have done better for her. We cleared out and sold up 47 St Michael's Road. So many memories. Wardrobes full of her clothes. Nowhere could we find one of her last purchases, an almost flawless, £50,000 diamond ring. I imagine she hid it and forgot where. It was not insured.

At my suggestion, my father moved to a flat in London near us. He was very lonely and I noticed he kept up with Crosby through the local paper and writing letters. I thought having him live near me would avoid a rerun of a sick parent at the other end of the country. I was wrong again. He wanted to go back. He had corresponded with an old friend who had lost her husband shortly after my mother died. Eventually they got together, in a most Catholic style. Separate bedrooms, Mass on Sundays, but under the same roof in a garden flat we had found him back in Blundellsands. His choice of new partner would have horrified my mother, and I don't think his new partner ever approved of my mother, whom she had known briefly when they were all in their twenties. She certainly openly disapproved of my father's children.

I was mature enough to be thankful he had someone who cared for him dearly and looked after him. He had been a fantastic husband to my mother, in his own way. He had been a greater and more productive influence on me than I gave him credit for in his lifetime. He, like Denis Thatcher, had been totally accepting of his wife's achievements in a way that younger generations find unnerving and difficult. Such unselfishness deserves praise and admiration. He loved to be liked and to be amusing. My mother found this a weakness, although in her own way she loved him. My father lived on happily until his eighty-fourth year. A stroke and a heart-attack in quick succession right at the end were thankfully his only dealings with hospitals and infirm old age.

20

Points of View

Emma got ten O levels. She had worked hard, and she deserved them. The only one that eluded her was French. I think she took it three times. Even before the results, she asked if we might let her go away to sixth form – it was what several of her friends were planning to do. It seemed like a good idea. She was an only child commuting between two parents, and was entitled to have a rest from permanently living with her head and belongings midway between Holland Park and Hampstead. Charlie and I toured several schools. At Charterhouse we were part of a group of parents. 'Don't you edit *Options* magazine, Mrs Wilson? I'm such a fan of *Options*,' said a housemaster's wife. 'No, I don't edit *Options*,' I said. 'That's Emma's stepmother.' I probably stuck my tongue out at her too.

Emma was offered a place at both Charterhouse and Rugby, but she had fallen for Millfield, the progressive co-educational school in Somerset. It was much more free and easy and, best of all, she could take Marcus, the pony Charlie had bought for her when Lily, his new baby daughter, was born. At the moment it was kept at Charlie and Sally's farm in Leicestershire but the idea that she could ride and hunt in term time was too good to miss. Millfield it was.

Emma did economics, history and communication studies

for A level. It is likely that the other schools we looked at would have been stricter about study, but at Millfield she formed friendships that have stayed with her since and it was a useful stepping-stone to being away from home. Or in her case, homes.

My career took a step in the right direction too. It was a dinner one night at Jill and Michael Foot's home in Hampstead that did the trick and launched my television life proper. Michael had been Leader of the Opposition but was now retired from front-bench politics although still an MP. A scholar and a gentleman whose political ambition never came before his sense of honour and his duty to his friends. He had taken the job of leading the Labour Party because he was asked to. Jill hated the backbiting and the criticism he had to endure.

Jill had been Britain's first female film director. She was a great supporter of the women's movement, knew more about the history of the suffragettes than anyone else, but still cooked her husband's breakfast and sacrificed her own career for his. She was a great wit, a great beauty, a great cook and I regarded them both as second parents.

That night, at their big comfortable house in Pilgrims Lane, another guest was Peter Noble, then editor of *Screen International*, the movie industry magazine. 'I want to be on television,' I announced forlornly. 'Who knows you're out there?' he asked. He had a point. I couldn't just sit at dinner parties like a spoilt teenager, moaning. Peter told me the tale of a movie director who was on his uppers but had gone out to Hollywood, put himself about and was now more successful than ever directing *Dallas*.

Next day I dropped a note to my old friend Robin Day. Robin called a week or so later and said that he'd spoken to the editor of the new BBC *Breakfast News* and he was desperate for decent journalists on screen. At the time the programme was fronted by an old hand, Frank Bough, and Selina Scott, a beauty who had been poached from ITN. In addition there was a young girl called Debbie Greenwood, who had been a Miss UK. If she can do it, I remember thinking, I'm definitely sure I can.

Johnny came to my rescue again. Then still features editor at the *Mirror*, he was negotiating a deal with Selina Scott's agent James Kelly of IMG, Mark McCormack's organisation. Over lunch, he suggested to Kelly that if IMG was looking for new talent he should consider me and he sent him a couple of tapes of my TV appearances. Kelly was interested enough to invite me to lunch. With the recommendation of Robin, and the clout of IMG, the next I knew I had been hired to review and preview television for ten minutes, live, once a week. It was a start and a good one. Within the year I was asked to stand in for Barry Took, the host of *Points of View*, a long-established programme in which the BBC allowed itself to be shot in the foot by airing comments from viewers that were invariably complaints.

With *Breakfast Time* a few hundred thousand people, with luck, might catch your performance. I was now to have the chance to perform on prime time! I stood in on *Points of View* for a month. The first week I was in a horrible bright blue suit and big hair. My delivery was slow and stilted. I sounded like some amateur on a programme teaching English to foreigners. But the wind was in the right direction. BBC bosses had had enough of Took, a well-known scriptwriter now in his sixties. His style was jokey. Viewers would pose questions in their letters, read out by a 'voice', and Barry would shrug his shoulders and say cheerfully, without giving any particular answer, something along the lines of 'hey ho, and on to the next letter'. A sharper approach was more in keeping with the times. By November I was offered the job. It meant a weekly programme with as many as nine million viewers.

For nearly thirty years men – Robert Robinson and Kenneth Robinson before Barry Took – had presented *Points of View* and there was no provision for a woman doing the job. No dressing room had been arranged, there was no discussion about wardrobe, no scope for payment for clothes. No credit for writing the show. Considering *Points of View* was screened immediately before and after major programmes into which millions were sunk in lighting, in costume, in fees to artists, it was a poor deal. It took half a day to script it, and another half-day to record it. The pay was around £300 per show. Who cared? I would have paid for the exposure. I was on my way.

Emma wasn't so sure. When we went to Paddington Station the following Easter to put her on the school train to Millfield she said, nicely, would I mind not coming on to the platform because she didn't fancy all the questions about who her mum was? I chose to take it as a compliment.

My father, thankfully, was beside himself with pride. 'I was at the bus stop', he would report, 'and this chap started to talk about *Points of View*.'

Please sit up straight, class, and answer me this: how do a couple deal with their joint finances when the woman earns more than the man, the man has no liking for economy and the woman has had so much chaos in her life she retains a horror of debt? Supplementary question: how does a man whose mother never put him on her knee when he was a baby and said, 'When you grow up you are going to marry a woman who will become more famous than you, earn more than you and will for many years not give a toss about how this affects you' cope when it happens?

Another leap into the unknown that no one has addressed. (I am not certain that anyone has yet addressed the sensible way to deal with joint money.)

Germaine Greer, indeed, questioned the whole concept of marriage, regarding housework, shopping, cooking, even beautifying yourself as a concession to your husband. The tone of the speeches of the day from the women's movement was defiant and adversarial. It was about opposing the system. It was about how men hated women. It was about stating your rights. It was *not* about the Marje Proops school of marriage that said a bit of sexy underwear could liven things up. Or even my lovely friend Jill Foot's idea of marriage, which was that each day in any relationship it was better that at least half a dozen things went unsaid.

Jill claimed to support feminism, but she and I knew that her own values were different. She was a shocking flirt and she loved keeping her husband happy. She boasted that she had no idea how much he earned as a Cabinet minister until she read it in the paper. This might have been heresy but what couldn't be disputed was the enduring love she and Michael had for each other. 'Your marriage won't work, Annie,' she would say gently, 'unless both of you are prepared to put the other one first and never do anything to make each other unhappy.' Except, of course, Jill had happily sacrificed everything career-wise. She wrote the odd article and had been commissioned to write a book on the history of the suffragettes. But her life as an outstanding documentary film-maker had ceased as soon as she married Michael. I found it hard to work out how I could have a marriage as happy as theirs without throwing my hands up on work. But why should I?

In any case, how could I give up work when it was my steadier hand in financial matters that was keeping away the creditors?

So yet again we threw ourselves incautiously into the unknown. Shortly after my mother's death we had managed to sell our house in Hampstead at a good profit. We split the proceeds. I was exhausted from having to try to keep abreast of Johnny's finances. He cleared his debts and invested his share in renovating a flat in Belsize Park. Financially independent lives seemed to be the answer. I imagined that if we kept our money apart it would prevent me from having to play finders-keepers and fret and nag about bills and commitments. It would leave him free to spend his money how he liked. And to face the consequences if he got into debt again.

I bought a house in Kensington and was alone responsible for the mortgage. It was where I had always wanted to live. With my earnings in television it wasn't difficult to manage. It also meant with Charlie around the corner that Emma could come and go without anyone counting. I wondered why I hadn't thought of it earlier.

So Johnny set out to find us a second home, in the country, into which he could sink the profit from the flat he had done up and sold.

The Cotswolds is generally agreed to be one of the most attractive areas in England. William Morris once described the village of Bibury as 'surely the most beautiful in England'. (Having said that he wisely made his home in nearby Kelmscot.) Bibury is popular with tourists. Americans love it, as increasingly do the Japanese. I had always romantically thought of it as about as far removed from the suburban life of Blundellsands as was possible, with its rolling pastureland, dry-stone walls, charming little stone cottages, wonderfully grand houses with tennis courts, all wrapped in the elegance of yesteryear.

Although London born and bred, Johnny had connections with the Cotswolds, where his aunt Nora and uncle George had moved in the early sixties to a magnificent Grade I listed house. He had first visited Bibury in 1976 while investigating the Jeremy Thorpe case. Jimmy Collier, a former West Country farmer and Liberal candidate, had turned Bibury Court, a spectacular Jacobean mansion, into a discreet hotel. Jim had obliged his friend Thorpe when Norman Scott first threatened to expose his relationship with the Liberal leader by taking Scott in one Christmas. Johnny had interviewed Jim and learnt nothing from him. But he did discover Bibury and had fallen in love with the area.

The hunt began. Jim knew of a cottage for sale. Or was it three? Again in need of every sort of renovation. Johnny couldn't have been happier. He was due to take ownership of the curiously named 4 & 8 Arlington Corner in September.

That summer we took off in the car for Elba and a month-long holiday with Emma, her friend Helen and their A-level revision. Johnny had visited friends on the island the year before and said we should rent the villa they had taken. He promised unparalleled levels of luxury and, most appealingly, a private beach. On arrival I discovered the beach was in fact a crop of boulders at the bottom of 120 steps cut into the cliff face. I do not like climbing. I do not dive. Thankfully, we discovered a private tunnel linked the property to a five-star hotel. Sand, sun-loungers and a manicurist! Johnny said the find rescued the holiday. The girls bathed topless. We all got sunburnt.

On the return journey we suggested to the girls that we might extend our trip to do a little cultural sightseeing. Groans could be heard from the back of the car. Two seventeen-year-olds plugged into Sony Walkmans politely looked up for all of ten seconds as we passed the Leaning Tower of Pisa on the autostrada.

Bibury was a major success. Johnny had a stable built in the paddock and Emma brought Marcus there so she could ride him during the school holidays. She loved the young crowd in the village. She had begun to hunt, both with our local hunt, the VWH, and in Leicestershire with Charlie. Millfield, like our houses close by in Kensington, fudged our separations. For the first time things began to feel normal. As if it was just a question of a daughter away at boarding school, instead of one to whom you had restricted access.

Charlie hoped Emma would apply for Oxbridge. I was less eager. We were both wasting our time. Robin Day suggested her having a day in Oxford. 'That always changes their minds,' he advised. But he hadn't met Emma. 'My feet hurt because my shoes were too tight and I never want to go there again,' she announced after Charlie had gone to some trouble to arrange for the father of one of his *Times* journalists, who was head of an Oxford college, to see her over lunch.

As usual Emma was firm. She knew what she wanted. She wanted to study film and television. But she wanted a decent course, she said. Not one taught by English teachers who had little knowledge of the industry. That meant America. Charlie investigated. It was either Los Angeles or New York University and the Tisch Film School. She opted for Manhattan. Charlie and I agreed to split the cost.

As a 'Wednesday Witch', among the most reliable subjects for my scrutiny in the mid-eighties were Mrs Thatcher and her power, the changing status of women and the royal family. The third thanks to Diana. She was a glamorous gift, guaranteed to improve the look of any page.

In the summer of 1986 Sarah Ferguson married Prince Andrew at Westminster Abbey. This time I, not Marje, had the ticket. It was for a view from high in the gods. Female members of the press who'd got carried away and worn big hats were obliged to remove them because of the limited headroom.

'Diana spent most of the time at her brother-in-law's service looking hunched up as if waiting to see the dentist,' I wrote. No wonder. Away from public gaze, the marriage was not heading for the rocks: it had already hit them with a thud so loud it was impossible for the royal reporters to ignore. Fleet Street wasn't prevented from writing what it knew. Rather, it was guilty of refusing to let go of the fantasy. The daily crop of pictures of the Princess, or the pictures of the couple, continued to be matched with words such as 'dazzling Diana' or 'brave Di' or 'a proud Charles'. This was messing with reality on a grand scale.

Dazzling, certainly; brave, hardly. Brave, as the headline writers saw it, was when the Princess went on a visit to comfort sick children – despite having a tummy upset. What I on a Wednesday of the same week would be moved to view as 'Diana hitting another hospice each time she fears her popularity might be waning'.

As for proud husband – that was somewhat far-fetched. One night she gave an impromptu performance at the Royal Opera House in Covent Garden with Wayne Sleep the ballet dancer. Her husband said he was 'absolutely amazed'. A clever choice of words. He was furious. Diana had rehearsed the Billy Joel 'Uptown Girl' routine with Sleep in secret. Charles regarded it as undignified. 'They hardly speak to each other these days,' James Whitaker told me.

Yet the same summer the couple allowed Sir Alastair Burnet of ITN to make a film about their happy family life. Whitaker reported that Charles had vetoed many of the planned scenarios. I reviewed the first of the film's two parts. Sir Alastair, using his special D-Day-landing voice, was not the best choice to interview the couple, who appeared silly and affected, I wrote. I'd often suggested Diana should not just look good in public but should start to make speeches. By the time of the film I conceded she had at least 'rid herself of the Sloane Ranger speech defect whereby every short reply sounds much like a cat meowing'.

In fact, by now the couple had not only ceased to have a sex life: they avoided even being under the same roof, if they could help it. Diana's affair with James Hewitt had started. Charles was back with Camilla.

Historical footnote: The death of Mr Justice Faulks, aged seventy-seven, on 13 October 1985: 'He will be remembered as much for his wit and humanity on the Bench as the mild controversy his remarks occasionally caused,' said his obituary in *The Times*. It reported that the judge had not taken kindly to the liberalisation of the divorce laws and had complained: 'All you have to do is fill your wife with gin, give her a complaisant lodger and file your petition next day.' And 'a husband might just say he found it intolerable to live with his wife because she wears pink knickers or nothing at all'. *The Times* admitted the judge could be 'over hasty', quoting the time he had suggested assaulting your wife was acceptable for a miner but not a gentleman.

My low, burning contempt for the legal profession continued. 4 February 1987: 'Ignorant, clumsy, crass, dense, cruel, insensitive and incompetent,' read the front page of the *Mirror* written by me about a judge who had jailed three members of a gang. He sentenced one man to fourteen years for burglary. The other two got only five and three years, respectively, for rape. It had been a vicious rape of an innocent young woman, who was a virgin and completely unknown to her assailants. 'Her trauma was not so great,' Mr Justice Leonard decided.

'I do not know how you measure the trauma of being raped against the inconvenience of being robbed of your jewellery and video-recording machine,' I opined. 'It is staggering to comprehend how a judge could so senselessly underestimate the extent of the young woman's ordeal. Even worse, how he could reach the conclusion that such an ordeal counts for less than replaceable material possessions.' I asked for two further examples of the insensitivity of men, who were supposed to have the wisdom of Solomon, to be taken into consideration. Judge Brian Gibbens had recently told a thirty-five-year-old builder who had sex with a seven-year-old girl when he was drunk: 'It strikes me, without belittling the offence, as one of the kinds of accident which happens in life to almost anyone.' While Judge Stanley Price had allowed a man to go free a month after he was found guilty of twice raping a six-year-old girl. 'How long must we sit back short-changed and powerless while disgraceful conclusions like these are reached?' I asked.

In another column I quoted a prosecuting counsel in a rape trial in Winchester. 'One cannot imagine circumstances of worse indecency than a man having to watch his wife being raped on his own bed,' he said. 'Well, I bloody can,' said I. 'I can imagine being the man's wife'.

The 1987 general election. Mrs Thatcher's third. The voice had been coached down a full octave by now. In the worst of winds her hair never moved. She had discovered shoulder pads. The bows on the blouse, big and small, had been retired. Other important matters not so visible: she had fallen out with her campaign team; her campaign team had fallen out with those handling her public relations and advertising; she had terrible toothache. We saw less of her pitying smile, much of her ruthlessness. No modern-day spin doctor was telling her to glide like a butterfly or to appear all things to all men. She was at her best stinging like a bee. We spent a day in Devon inspecting guide dogs for the blind. For someone who disliked animals she briefly gave a passable imitation of a dog lover when the news came in that Labour had its hands on an incriminating videotape of Thatcher in opposition. In it she had said that if unemployment ever reached the million and a half it had under Labour 'we would have been drummed out of office'. Unemployment, as we patted yellow Labradors, had well exceeded that figure. When asked about this, mid-pat, Mrs Thatcher said: 'We are looking at guide dogs for the blind.'

In the Midlands Mrs Thatcher addressed a Conservative rally. It was hot and the heat did not become her. 'The audience at Solihull appeared to have been addressed by a particularly animated and bossy beetroot,' I reported.

Like Robert Maxwell and my mother, Mrs Thatcher's natural bullying allowed her to avoid being confronted or challenged, be it by members of her Cabinet or by the press. Both were too frightened, too respectful. Memorably, during the 1983 election she had come unstuck and deepened her distrust of the BBC when during a phone-in on *Nationwide* a Mrs Gould from Cirencester had tackled her about the sinking of the *General Belgrano* during the Falklands War. This election, during a tour of a school in Chatham, I witnessed a young local reporter, with reckless but admirable disregard for her own safety, do it again. Mrs Thatcher had been sailing unimpeded through the classrooms that morning. In particular admiring the craftwork and telling a bemused fifteen-year-old that his fishing trophy would need a design rethink because it was going to be tricky to dust. But at the question-and-answer session that followed Elizabeth Fahey pointed out that the school only had a budget of £250 a year for books and so teachers were forced to buy their own equipment, and the youngsters talked in despair about leaving to face unemployment. Mrs Thatcher tried auto-pilot: a long, irrelevant and intensely boring explanation of education authorities and how they were run. It didn't wash. Ms Fahey persisted. 'Here you are running down the school,' retorted Mrs T. That didn't wash either. The gloves came off. 'This press conference is for the travelling, not the local press,' Thatcher snarled.

A political foul, deserving of a free kick. You didn't have to love her. But you had to admire her. She was duly voted back in.

That spring, not just the country, but the BBC Radio 2 7.30 to 9.30 morning show was daringly put in the charge of a woman. Its usual host, Derek Jameson, a former Fleet Street editor, was on holiday. I remember being scared rigid for weeks beforehand. It was live, unscripted radio. And I was setting a precedent. The station still had an edict in force that two numbers by female artists couldn't be played back to back, for heaven's sake. The edict remained but by the start of the next year I had my own show on Radio 2 on Saturday mornings, replacing Michael Aspel, for whom I had also stood in.

The comeback kid was indeed spoilt for job offers. That spring Robert Maxwell asked me to consider an editorship. A Fleet Street editor's chair was still to be occupied by a woman. Television and radio had fortunately got to me before Maxwell came shopping for a new boss for the *Sunday Mirror*. I concluded that I preferred being *me* to a large audience, than having a rerun of the long nights in the giant ashtray. In any case, I was realistic enough to know that Maxwell might change his mind even before he appointed me. Either way, the fact that I was being asked to become the first woman ever to edit a Fleet Street newspaper wasn't attractive enough for me to give up a more controllable media career outside the power of a mad newspaper proprietor. Plus, I still wouldn't have relished working late Saturday nights when Emma was often with us.

The offer taught me that you should always seek advice from the people least likely to be influenced by fear: either the awful fear of you turning down a fantastic job, or the unwise risk of giving up the security of your current employment. It also helps to bounce it off someone who is not easily impressed. 'What would you want that job for?' asked my friend Maureen. 'You hated it last time.' Then there was my lovely Italian mother-in-law, Anna. She happened to ring me the day the offer was made. 'Whatsa happening?' she asked in her usual cheery, half-English way. I told her I had been offered the editorship of the *Sunday Mirror*. There was a pause before she blurted, 'But when are you gonna be on *Blankety Blank*?'

With our careers no longer on a collision course, the cottage in Gloucestershire giving us more pleasure than we ever imagined, life couldn't have been better for Johnny and me. Emma by now could ignore the straitjacket of access terms as laid down by a court a decade and a half earlier. We had all stopped counting. She had passed her driving test. She was waiting to take up her place at university. I only went in to the *Mirror* to check my page proof, and once the fax machine arrived rarely made an appearance. Ever since my demotion from assistant-editor duties my working week was hardly ever more than three days.

Johnny, however, by now assistant editor (features) – my old job – would have to take his turn editing the paper on a Sunday. With reluctance he would leave early in the morning from Bibury and often drive back in the early hours of the following day. The *Mirror* was not the paper he had joined eighteen years earlier. The one that respected his talent. He began to hate even having to walk through the main door.

In the autumn of 1988, the day after it was learnt that Greek shipping magnate Christina Onassis had died of a drug overdose, his career at the paper came to an abrupt end. He was duty editor. Maxwell, upstairs and in a mood for trouble, began to interfere. He wanted to know what Johnny was doing with the story, who he had covering it, how many pages he was giving it. Maxwell ranted, he claimed he had exclusive information but had not been asked for his help, and then childishly said he was giving his version of events to a rival newspaper because Johnny had not consulted him.

Johnny's relationship with Maxwell had never been good. Maxwell rightly suspected that Johnny despised him. The Onassis drama was one too far. Johnny had had enough of Maxwell. He negotiated a pay-off and was free by the end of the week. It was a welcome relief. We celebrated. More time in the country. No dashing up to London and back. No more 2 a.m. finishes. No more Maxwell madness. And Johnny with money in the bank.

We began making early Christmas plans. Johnny has always been the best at Christmas. Each year he decrees what colour the wrapping paper should be. It hurts his artistic eye if tones clash around the tree. That year he excelled. MNO time! Money No Object was what we call any opportunity to take the eye off economising. Well, that was the problem really. Johnny lived in the permanent worry-free land of MNO. Until trouble was an inch from his face.

That Christmas I had a call from Alistair McAlpine, then treasurer and deputy chairman of the Conservative Party. We'd met at a Tory Party conference at Blackpool one year when he'd introduced himself and told me he always read my *Mirror* column in the bath because the paper was an excellent size for people with short arms. Could we come to his house at West Green the day after Boxing Day? he wanted to know. 'It really will be fun,' he insisted. It was. A small luncheon with a guest list as follows: Margaret and Denis Thatcher, Terence Donovan, her favourite photographer, and his wife Diana (she and I had been at Farnborough Hill together), Willie Shawcross and his soon-to-be wife Olga Forte, Henry and Tessa Keswick. Alistair was at the top of the table, with Mrs Thatcher to his right and me to his left. Johnny got Denis.

The unusually wide and overly decorated table – it groaned with neatly clipped box in terracotta pots and pyramids of fruit in glass vases – prevented Mrs T and me, the hound that had harassed her during three general elections, from having much of a chance to chat during lunch. It was after the shepherd's pie and vintage Krug that we stood in a huddle in the drawing room with three or four of the others, discussing property prices over our coffee cups.

'I always tell young people', the Prime Minister was saying, 'to buy a BIG house at the very beginning. Then they won't have to move when they have a family.' The coterie, hound apart, nodded in unison and whispered, 'Yes, Prime Minister.' My eyes shot round. Was I dreaming? Had I heard right? Had they heard right? 'Actually, Prime Minister,' I found myself saying as a terrifying silence filled the vast room, 'not everyone can afford a big house at the beginning.' There wasn't as much as a pause. 'I bet', said Mrs T, wearing that sickly-sweet smile I had so often seen her use on television, 'that you've made some money out of houses while I've been in office.' We had! We had! It was game, set and match.

What neither Johnny nor I had anticipated was the shock to the system of him being without a full-time job, his colleagues and his identity. I was too busy enjoying my media fame to notice – just as I had been when I'd become Johnny's boss. Change is difficult. Even change for the better. Moving from being part of an organisation, enjoying the everyday life at the top end of that organisation, enjoying having an important role, then it vanishing, was tough. But to have to do it while your partner is basking in her glory is tougher still. I recognised none of this in Johnny's situation. We never talked about it. It didn't help that for some time he too didn't realise quite what was happening to him. When he did, he put on a brave face. Our relationship, which had held together through rough times before because we genuinely loved each other, began seriously to crack up. It moved imperceptibly to separate existences. We no longer chatted. We pursued our own interests.

It didn't help that Johnny spent his pay-off in record time and still had a commitment to pay for his house in the country. Again, like Scott Fitzgerald's definition of going broke, our marriage fell apart slowly and then very quickly.

As always in times of difficulties, we took our positions. I withdrew, Johnny became more gregarious, staying out and enjoying the company of the local landowners and farmers, who, pleasurably for him and without any training, easily fitted into Mr Justice Faulks' 'Fleet Street' drinking standards.

Small differences became bigger ones. Unspoken resentment chilled the air. I remember my husband going to London to a dinner and not minding if he came home that night or stayed out. I remember him telling me he had escorted the female editor of a magazine, a woman we knew slightly, back to her house over the river near Waterloo, in a taxi. I only wondered vaguely if anything had gone on. It was a sure sign things were doomed.

Johnny also found his creditors moving in again and said he might have to sell the house. Neither of us outwardly acknowledged that this was an ever greater indication that we were dividing our spoils. The shall-I-sell-the-house dilemma continued for months. As it did, I became more reluctant to lose our country base. So I offered to buy it in a simple transaction. In exchange, Johnny bought a small flat in London to do up. As with everything he ever put his eye and his talent to, the one-bedroom basement in Vicarage Gate, Kensington, was superb by the time it was completed. He planned to sell it at a good profit, which made sense.

Before he did, there were more and more signs we were heading towards a break-up. With my Radio 2 Saturday-morning show I regularly had tickets for new West End productions, if the lead players were coming on as my guests. For one Pinter play, Johnny failed to turn up. His apologies were half-hearted. My anger was uncontrolled. I felt wiped out. I could see no way forward this time. I was not even inclined to look for one. I felt my husband was hostile.

Next, I defiantly took a holiday in Florida on the island of Sanibel, in the Gulf of Mexico, with an old friend, Julie Hamilton. Johnny met me at the airport when I returned. Strange, because we had a local driver for airport pick-ups. On the way home he told me he had rented a small cottage from one of his farmer friends, in order to start writing a book. He was making plans for his getaway, aware that, should I choose to ask him to leave, he had no local home. It was but a small step to our parting.

Only the memorable events of the demise of Thatcher, which had us both on full-scale alert for every single Westminster television bulletin, and back temporarily to our old routine of discussing the minutiae of a good news story, created the illusion that we might manage to stay together.

An extraordinary chain of events was taking place at Westminster. Mrs Thatcher's departure was only sudden if you hadn't listened to the rumble building up in the jungle. She most decidedly turned a deaf ear to it. The poll tax, or the community charge as it was officially called, but which even her own Cabinet gave up on as a name, was to be her downfall. More broadly the problem was that nobody was on quality control. What we call in our house 'crap control'. I use the phrase mostly to describe what happens when people live alone, without a voice at the other side of the bed asking: 'Do you know what you sounded like this evening at dinner?' Even knowing that a partner is simply watching often curbs the worst excesses. He or she who goes home to a silent mirror has no critic.

The Prime Minister 'forgot herself', as the nuns at my school might have said. She wouldn't listen. She believed only that she was right. The poll tax had a shocking effect on ordinary Tory voters. I had a driver at the time who worked out that with two sons over eighteen at home, his council-tenant household was paying more than the squire in the village with a multi-million-pound mansion, 600 acres and three children at boarding school. Overnight he went from a Thatcher lover to a Thatcher hater. A pity, really, that he wasn't *her* driver.

The upshot was that on the morning of 22 November 1990 Margaret Thatcher resigned. She went before she was booted out. She looked unlikely to have a majority in a second ballot of her MPs, whose votes were ordered after the challenge to her leadership.

I was disgusted by her male colleagues, who had neither the courage to stand up to her nor the brains to replace her. On her final day as Prime Minister she excelled herself. When she left Downing Street for the last time, a tear could be seen running from her eye. People probably didn't know it but even as a junior minister she'd never been against a weep to get her own way. She moved briefly to a house she and Denis had bought in Dulwich and then back to central London. One interior decorator brought in to advise was reported to have spent most of his time listening to her rather than helping her choose soft furnishings. The house in Chester Square, when its interior was completed, looked chic and sophisticated. A couple of months later some Thatcher touches had been added. Antimacassars on the chairs and sofas. Doilies under the vases. Grantham had been restored.

But it took years before Mrs Thatcher, soon to be Baroness Thatcher, was restored. She, like Johnny, and the thousands upon thousands she had been responsible for, learnt first-hand how tough it was having to face being at home instead of at work.

The long-running effect on Johnny and me meant we finally parted.

Why, I kept wondering, is it that famous people marry, divorce, remarry 'just like that', as my father might have said. They didn't appear to be in pain or to suffer.

Johnny had been part of my life for a quarter of a century. He had been a major and influential part of Emma's life from when she was nine months old. His was the artistic temperament she adored. He was the one who was never too desperate to get to the office that he couldn't meet her at the airport, repack her suitcase. Take her to art galleries, discuss architecture and design and listen to her moans; just put her in a good mood. On holiday in Rome when she was tiny, he had once spent a day with her searching until they found exactly the right doll. 'What do you say?' I asked of her when the pair returned triumphant with their purchase. 'I want a pram for my doll,' she announced. Johnny didn't reprimand her or call her spoilt. He roared with laughter. And went out and bought her a pram.

If he was ever cross with her – and it was rare, very rare – she took it seriously. There was no question that her relationship with Johnny would continue. It helped that by the time Johnny moved out she'd gone to New York.

Historical footnote: In the summer of 1990, the Royal Bank of Scotland held a lavish reception to mark the opening of its new flagship office at the Angel in Islington. I was no longer a customer after the débâcle with the joint account. Johnny still was. The same bank manager who had felt no need to consult me about whether I was happy to have a new overdraft rang to ask if Johnny would make sure he brought me to the reception. His bosses, he said, wanted as many 'faces' there as possible.

21

Home Alone

Charlie had travelled to New York to install Emma. I followed for a fortnight's stay. We deliberately spaced our visits to give her ongoing support. It was vastly different from anything she had known before. She was in a university hall of residence in Washington Square, down in Greenwich Village. Her roommates were all gentle out-of-towners. It wasn't at all the den of evil I had imagined. A year later she admitted she had hated the first couple of months.

I didn't know then that her choice would mean we would lose her to America. I didn't know then that I would follow her.

There were still several awkward pieces of the jigsaw to put into place, but Emma and I were enjoying plenty of time together and our relationship was to change.

In another Maxwell negotiation, I had secured an even better deal. I argued that over and above my salary I was turning down a number of lucrative advertisement offers because of my column. This was only partly true because the BBC would not have countenanced me being connected to commercial deals. But Maxwell, who loved nothing better than the incomprehensible side bits to contracts, agreed on a new salary that put me over the £150,000 a year mark. Plus, an annual 'retainer' of another £50,000. At my request, he threw in half a dozen first-class trips to New York per year.

A few weeks later he called me to his office to say he couldn't pay me the money because Joe Haines had complained that I was now earning more than he was. 'Okay,' I said, 'give me a lump sum as a bonus and leave my salary looking less than his.' He did, signing the cheque there and then. I didn't mention the deal to Joe, who was now on the board of Mirror Group Newspapers,. Fortunately, though, he was as hopeless as ever at keeping a secret and one day dropped a bombshell. 'Do you know why they stopped you editing?' he asked me. I never had really understood and remembered my tears of rage. 'Keep this to yourself,' he ordered. 'The Palace got at the Reed International Board when you splashed on that Diana story. The Reed Board didn't want you in charge of the paper after that.' I was astonished. Was he sure? I asked. 'Yes,' he said. I marvelled at the power of the Establishment and still believed, as the whole world soon got to know, that Diana had an eating disorder.

It hardly mattered by this time, except to enjoy the irony. Had we bothered to pay attention, far worse things were happening at the *Mirror*.

Away from work, I celebrated my freedom for a couple of months and then experienced the loneliest two and a half years of my life. Not for the first time, the removal van had arrived and taken half the furniture. Significantly, it was easy to divide. So intent had I been on separating our finances we knew exactly who owned what painting or piece of furniture. Emma, from New York, said only that she hoped each of us would be all right. I had imagined at forty-something, with money, a well-known face, and two homes and plenty of friends, the world would be at my feet. It wasn't. It's very hard to form new relationships in mid-life. Particularly if you are not a party type. It's very hard to live on your own. To work hard and be bothered to organise a social life. A couple don't have to have a social life. They have each other.

'How do I date?' I remember asking Emma in one desperate phone call. She giggled and said, 'Oh, don't worry about it.' But she had grown up and flown the nest. I could not look to her to replace a husband. Nevertheless, it was an important time in our relationship because for much of it I was leaning on her. I needed her strength. Her wisdom. I was relieved that I had the means to visit her often. The BBC even allowed me to broadcast my radio show from New York from time to time.

That year Maxwell too was busy in New York, and by a strange quirk of fate so was Charlie, on Maxwell's behalf. Charlie had left *The Times* and become editorial director of Mirror Group Newspapers, and Maxwell had charged him with the responsibility of buying the *New York Daily News*. Charlie negotiated the difficult deal, including facing down eleven trade unions.

By the time I walked into the *Daily News* in October, the deal was finally tied up and I witnessed the same bank hold-up effect that had gone on at the *Mirror*. The editor of the paper was attempting to stay sane and get his editions on to the streets, while pandering to the demands of the new proprietor. Pictures of Maxwell walking through the streets of New York dominated the pages, not only of his own newly acquired newspaper but others. Television news bulletins, equally, couldn't get enough of him.

I'd arranged to see Maxwell because I fancied a column on the paper. My daughter had embraced the city and I reasoned that once she graduated she would find many more work opportunities in America than in Britain. Why not join her? I even took Emma with me to meet him. 'You must have a green card,' he told her. 'We'll fix it.'

'A bit of Nana in him,' said Emma as we left.

I joined the Maxwell family a couple of nights later at their hotel suite. That autumn Maxwell had been exposed in a BBC

Panorama programme. Some of it was too complicated to understand, even to a seasoned Maxwell-watcher such as me. But it was enough to rock his already unstable financial situation. The bankers were beginning to call in their loans.

Not that you would have known it. He was launching the *European* newspaper in America. A lavish affair to take place the following evening at the United Nations Building. As I waited in the drawing room of his suite, the *Mirror* editorial for the following day was faxed to him. 'Take down these changes,' he ordered to no one in particular. Three of his offspring scrambled for a pen. It would have been impossible to follow the speed of his dictation. But I recall him insisting that a reference to the Pope should be preceded by the word Catholic.

In the middle of all this he announced he was hungry and that someone should order Chinese food. Mrs Maxwell appeared. I hadn't met her often but when I had she had always been courteous to her husband. Now she was being uncommonly short with him. She snapped at his suggestion about where to order their food. He barely noticed. Instead he beckoned me to the lift within the suite. We went up a floor to a bedroom to discuss business. As always, I insisted on writing down our new contract arrangements. The only paper I could lay my hands on was the tiny pad at the bedside. The arrangement was that I should have a weekly column in the *Daily News* for £50,000 a year. 'Make that evergreen,' he added. I wasn't sure what it meant but I wrote it down. He talked about the *Panorama* programme and his fear that it might ruin him. He talked about his son Ian. He talked about his daughter Ghislaine, whom, he hoped, I might take under my wing. 'You have never badmouthed me,' he said. 'People complain that you can twist me round your little finger,' he added. 'But you have talent.'

We returned downstairs and I asked his PA, in the middle of the pandemonium of the Chinese meal being served, to type out what was on at least a dozen tiny sheets of the hotel pad. She did and it was signed. At the United Nations party the guest list was incredible. I left for London the following day.

Three weeks later he fell, or jumped, off his yacht. His body was recovered two days after.

On the day the news came through, I was dining at the Savoy with James Whitaker, whom I intended to co-opt on to the *Daily News* column. We returned to the office to find two reporters at the entrance. 'Can you comment on Robert Maxwell being lost at sea?' one of them asked. I laughed. Maxwell rumours went round all the time. Only when we got to the newsroom and saw the editor's face did we realise it was true. Before long, the parlous state of Maxwell's finances was uncovered. He had robbed the pension funds. Thousands of decent, hard-working people in businesses he had bought up were left with no retirement funds. It was appalling.

Throughout Maxwell's ownership there had been rumours that he was stealing from the pension fund. The whisper would go round the office. But journalists are notoriously bad at looking after their own finances. We dug and threw up dirt on anyone famous, but we failed to monitor what was happening on our doorstep. Nevertheless, I was prepared to go on television, not to *defend* Maxwell's actions, but to point out that cowards had made his behaviour possible. Bankers, accountants, lawyers, who should have known better, who should have learnt on day one of banking, accountancy or law school about the likes of Maxwell, said yes when they should have said no. In the sixties he'd been declared unfit to run a public company by the Board of Trade. The end of the story could disappoint. But surely not surprise.

It was also important to point out that outside his office on any given day was a line of people. Many of them recognisable, distinguished members of the House of Commons or the Lords, waiting to see him. To ask a favour. He was a soft touch. I saw none of these people come forward and admit they had been to him with a begging bowl. In his lifetime they were only too happy to feast on his money. When the scandal was uncovered, they dealt in half-truths by just condemning him. For my part, I always took it for granted that Maxwell's word was only as long as the day. It puzzled me that others chose to believe him when he promised them cars, promotion, trips abroad, holidays, but never safeguarded the promise by getting it in writing. 'Does this mean I won't get my green card?' asked Emma when she heard the news.

One of the few highlights of my miserable years living alone: my daughter was in the movie business. While Emma was a student she spent a summer vacation in Los Angeles. Resourcefully she had headed there to increase her experience and had managed to get a production assistant's job on *The Distinguished Gentleman* – an Eddie Murphy movie. By chance the director, Jonathan Lynn, was British. Although I'd met him once I did not know him – but he was quite wonderful to Emma. I welcomed him to the National Union of Parents, which decrees that all of us give other parents' children the sort of breaks we like to see our own kids benefiting from. That summer we continued our role reversal. Emma had the job. Mum came to visit. Daughter fixed a deal at the best hotel in Brentwood and suffered her mother standing on the side of the set. There is a scene in the movie where Mother can be seen in a walk-on part. (It's the bit in the church.)

When the movie came to Britain I sat in the Odeon in Kensington High Street, furious to see that as the credits rolled the audience filed out and there was hardly anyone left in the auditorium. Emma's name was almost the final one.

The next vacation she was helping on another movie in New York, *The Night We Never Met*, starring Matthew Broderick, written and directed by Warren Leight. Proud Mother was again being tolerated on set, this time in a side-street off Seventh Avenue.

*

I wasn't the only estranged wife. To the shock of some, and the relief of others, in December 1992 the then Prime Minister, John Major, announced in the House of Commons that Prince Charles and his wife were formally to separate. He also said that the separation would not necessarily prevent Diana from becoming Queen.

This turned out to be as fanciful as his statement a couple of weeks earlier after flames had engulfed the state apartments at Windsor Castle. 'The people' would be only too willing to pay for the restoration, said Mr Major. They were not. The Queen had to fork out for repairs herself.

Diana went on publicly to outclass, outstrip and outperform her in-laws. She had two weapons they could not counter. She was fearless and she knew how to play the press. Like a wounded but untreated wild animal, she hit out when it hurt because she was more afraid of being crushed than she was of upsetting the Establishment. Like Thatcher, you didn't have to love her but you had to marvel at her balls. When she died in a fatal car crash in Paris in 1997, the anger felt by ordinary people towards a royal family seen as reluctant to acknowledge Diana's importance nearly brought the House of Windsor tumbling down.

Both events illustrated a change in the attitude of its subjects towards the monarchy. A change neither the government nor the royal family grasped until it was nearly too late.

*

Emma graduated from film school in the summer of 1993. Her parents excitedly lined up outside the building in Greenwich Village where the graduation ceremony was to be held. The actor Bill Cosby, presumably also a parent, was behind us. Emma took the equivalent of a first. She had become a scholar in her second year. She majored in film and television and held a minor in fine arts. She planned to spend the next year making her graduation movie.

Two years before, Charlie and I had pooled resources and bought Emma an apartment in New York. Our efforts couldn't wipe out the sadness, the horrible part of our history. But Emma refused (still does) to complain or condemn either of us. We had survived. Charlie better than me. He had his new family, a beautiful, clever wife. I was fast approaching fifty and living alone, and it did not, for the first couple of years, look as if I had any options.

Once or twice, when Emma was back in the UK, she and I met up with Johnny. He had acquired a young girlfriend, he told us gleefully. I didn't feel particularly jealous. Only puzzled that now we were apart he appeared to be running a competent publishing business, had a good love life and was quite happy. 'What do you think?' I asked Emma one evening, after we had kissed him goodbye on the steps of a restaurant in Knightsbridge where we'd all had supper. 'I think it's very sad,' said Emma slowly, not really explaining herself.

I struggled on emotionally, relying on the support of good friends. Professionally, I couldn't complain. The BBC had approached me to host *Watchdog*, its flagship consumer programme. Oh yes, please! Consumer journalism *and* television, what more could I ask?

That autumn I went on air as the programme's host for the first time. I was passionate we should cover big issues, train our guns on large corporations and cease to be a broadcasting nanny, warning parents that this would kill, that was dangerous. We saw the viewing figures creep up and eventually double.

Newspapers, I noticed smugly, increasingly ran consumer stories on their front pages. A little different from my days editing at the *Mirror* when I was the only one who fought for them.

In the summer Emma and I returned to the island of Crete. We stayed at the Minos Beach, the hotel where we had all stayed when she was a teenager. Where she had learnt to water-ski and where us adults had sat on the terrace in the evening behaving obnoxiously, according to other guests.

It wasn't until we had been there a few days and revisited some of our old haunts that I started thinking. We were in Ayios

Nikólaos one morning when Emma said: 'Mum, remember when Johnny spent half the holiday trying to get his sunglasses repaired?' (Johnny and his holiday missions had always occupied dozens of journeys into whatever town we were staying near.)

Suddenly it seemed as if something very important was missing – not having Johnny there. His sense of fun. His infectious enthusiasm for any task he got involved in. His tireless pursuit of good food. For beautiful buildings. What had I thrown away? How did I go about putting the toothpaste back in the tube?

Not a problem for Germaine to solve. Better to consult a down-to-earth agony aunt. *Dear Marje/Abby: I let my husband go and bade him good riddance and now I want him back. How would you suggest I go about it?*

I came back unsure about quite what to do. A voice somewhere at the back of my head told me to wait patiently.

Several weeks later, a blind date fixed up by well-meaning friends – 'you'll find he's very bright and interesting' – had seen me nearly slide off a chair in boredom at a lunch. The following morning I rose early, wrote my newspaper column and then spent four hours in the dentist's chair. Back home, my face swollen, my head aching, I found a string of urgent messages from the editor who needed me to write a leading article for the front page, this time praising the decision of a judge who had freed a student accused of rape. (Both the accused and his accuser admitted to being blind drunk at the time.)

I was still at my desk late that night trying to complete an overdue book review for the *Sunday Times*. Exhausted, I laid my head on my laptop and wept. A combination of fatigue and defeat. I, who had become so efficient with deadlines, with writing, with life, had lost the plot.

Without even thinking about it I rang Johnny. 'Are you all right?' he said. 'No,' I said. 'Stay there, I'll come round.' He did. We have never been apart since. I had finally been beaten enough to show my weakness and my need for him. With relief and joy we were back together. It was like a new courtship. A new relationship. Relief, coupled with gratitude, plus a determination to make it work. We had been through too much not to be wiser.

When our excitement had subsided we talked and talked. I didn't drink and it was boring and debilitating to be with someone who wanted to do so without restriction. Johnny was hopeless with his own money. I had to accept I was in the best position to be the main breadwinner. But I needed to accept that position without believing I was being 'taken for a ride'. We must celebrate our strengths, work around our weaknesses. We must throw in our lot together. Trust was important. Or as my friend Jill Foot, now no longer around to nod her approval, might have said, 'Make his happiness more important than your own.' Nothing remarkable about that, you might think. It is what *for better or for worse* is all about. It is how the most enduring and successful partnerships work, be it in marriage, in business, in friendship, in families. But it had taken me a lifetime to understand it.

The following spring Emma's graduation movie got its premiere in New York. We all went. Johnny, Charlie and me – the financial backers and occasional victim support system for the girl who had been the movie's writer, director and producer. We had all begun to feel nine months was a very long time in the movie business and were anxious to view our investment.

There were quite a few other pieces of work to view before our daughter's. It caused me to ponder at what stage graduate film students switch on to the commercial reality that will lead them to Los Angeles, the Oscars and a beach house in Malibu. In several of the films everyone appeared to be wearing a black T-shirt and seemed to be very unhappy. The most memorable was called *800 Flowers* and was described in the programme as 'ten guys commit suicide inside a VW bug'.

So did we clap when we saw what we had paid for! Emma's film was in colour, shot in the sunshine, had a pretty heroine, at least half a dozen decent gags and, even more encouraging, a beginning, a middle and an end. I should not have doubted her. She picked up four awards.

I turned into a hooligan, yelling hard with motherly conceit. It was a good job we were in New York. As my friend Ruth said later, Manhattan is awash with Jewish mothers and my behaviour would have been regarded as perfectly normal.

22

Resolution

My all-time favourite movie is *Broadcast News*. I often quote the scene where Jane, the clever young TV producer played by Holly Hunter, is desperately directing the cab driver who knows better than she how to get her across town.

For Holly, read me. For Holly, read a whole generation or two of clever, intelligent, quick, talented younger women. Always in the driving seat, because they're not sure anyone else is truly fit to be in charge of the car. For Holly, read all of the young women who chase after a prince and then find he has turned into a frog. At work the clever, over-conscientious woman is heaven sent. She crosses the 't's and dots the 'i's. In her loyal, giving way she will still be there staring at her VDU at ten o'clock at night desperate to get it right while her male counterpart left hours before, nonchalantly swinging his kit bag over his shoulder and heading for the gym. Who could but admire her commitment?

Unfortunately, when she returns home she is still on full throttle. Orchestrating her partner. Organising him to distraction. We do not trust. We do not let our partners be. Why does a clever, otherwise sane woman believe her man cannot find his way to the bathroom without her guidance? *The Female Eunuch* was of huge importance. It was a vital call to women to wake up, to crawl out from under their stones and acknowledge their true worth. They need not put up with shit. It was a warrior's document. So too is its sequel, *The Whole Woman*.

But feminism was never much good at addressing reality. Or as my mother would say: 'What's any of it got to do with the price of fish?'

I believe we should celebrate our freedom, spend our money how we wish, dye our hair, surgically lift our drooping jaws, lipo-suction our thighs – be we working mothers, be we stay-at-home mothers, whatever suits our needs. But, most importantly, we need to learn how to live in harmony with a partner. We are not anti-men, unsatisfactory though men may be. Most of us would rather have one than not.

It is lonely out there. Ask me. Ask the bereaved. Ask any woman who is making her way in the world, while secretly longing to be at home stirring the rice pudding. Who would far prefer to be doing the very things that Germaine regards as a dreadful indication of our oppression.

And why do capable women time and again pick rotten, inconsequential weak men? 'She kept riding into the sunset with a man who didn't have a horse,' Candice Bergen said of her friend Ali McGraw. She isn't the only one.

Desperate women choose badly. But let us not ignore the possibility of a decent, loyal bloke being reduced to pulp.

Biology, biology – it gets in the way. The urge to feed your man. The urge to mother him. To produce and direct him. And he, whose mother has been a strong influence, obeys and then rails against the loving girl who has become a bossy harridan. Biology again.

My mother had been outstanding in shaping me to be independent and confident. But like other mothers of her generation, her message had been find a man to keep you. This double-edged message thrives today. I look round at younger girlfriends and realise that for all their education and emancipation there is still a romantic idea about the knight in shining armour.

Last Christmas, one of my presents to Emma was a bunch of cushions for her apartment. I had each of them embroidered with a slogan. One was something I'd first blurted out years before, when she was trying to cope with a tricky male colleague at work: 'Every month you'll meet an arsehole. He will probably be your boss. When he comes along, don't get angry, just think, Ah, you're this month's arsehole.' Every young woman needs a cushion that says: 'No one is coming along to rescue you.' No one gives you unconditional love except your mother and then only sometimes. The sassy career girl is free to plan her romantic white wedding with all the enthusiasm of an immature adolescent but woe betide her if she thinks her husband is going to fill every gap in her life. When he turns out to be human she may feel disappointed. She should not be surprised.

In my untidy, rickety life the change in opportunities for women has outstripped all the advancements of previous centuries. Hurrah to that. Except I do not believe women are conditioned to accepting the bread-winning role without the nagging doubt that the deal isn't balanced. And just as we are not good at accepting unconditionally that we are the financial backbone, men are often unprepared psychologically to take second place. I had to go back and unlearn the idea that a man should keep me. I had to go back and unlearn the idea that strength was being in charge. 'Mind your own business,' a wise friend once told me when Emma was in her teenage years. Distinguish between what is wrong and what is merely different. It is astonishing how little is one's business once you decide to keep your nose out of other people's.

I am thankful to be the age I am. I do not know if I could have thrown in my lot for better or for worse if I were much younger. I do not know how, aged twenty-five, I could be a warrior during the day and a gentle, affectionate, unstressed person at night. But nor do I think it satisfactory for women to reach their late thirties without a soul mate. And I am convinced that needy, bossy women do not cut attractive figures. (If I had been Bridget Jones's mother I would have put her on a diet and told her to get a decent haircut and a facial once a month.)

And what of the woman who wants to have babies and flinches at the prospect of staying at home or staying away from her work? Can the hand that rocks the cradle cook her husband breakfast, take a board meeting and return to behave like a hooker in the bedroom?

The *Daily Telegraph* runs a glorious column charting the life and times of Kate Reddy, the corporate banker with the tiny children, the well-meaning if incompetent husband and a working schedule only suitable for a young thing with no commitments and double the normal energy. The reason you laugh is because there are Kate Reddys all over the place. Just as there are Bridget Joneses. And if Kate Reddy's diary is a sign that we did not march in vain, I'm glad I never got round to marching. Guilt, exhaustion, the longing for the hurly-burly of the chaise-longue. A wife and mother pulled so many ways she no longer knows who she is.

How do mothers rid themselves of the guilt? I could cry biology again. Except my mother was never guilty. Her rules were her own. She never failed to cook my father's breakfast and supper. In exactly the way that Mrs Thatcher made Denis bacon and eggs every single morning she was at home at Number 10. In both cases, however, they chose husbands who were confident enough in themselves to accept the status quo. They were lucky because, generally, the idea of her at work and him at home is not nearly so neat and workable as it should be. Those of us who have had careers and now have grown-up daughters must conclude that our daughters will have to resort to paid childcare if they want what we wanted.

I don't know how we resolve the child versus job predicament. But I'm convinced now that letting go and letting a partner do things his way without correction, carping and being permanently on quality control help to make for better accord at home.

I'm glad too that biology decrees we will never entirely rid ourselves of being women. Recently, a male television producer whom I have known for years was telling me about the new young team he had put together for a show we were doing. One name on the list I hadn't heard of. I asked what Nina was bringing to the party. 'She has huge and wonderful breasts,' he said. I laughed, then went home and felt guilty. What if a producer talked like that about a daughter of mine?

A couple of weeks later, as we walked off the set of the show, my producer courteously accompanied me to my dressing room. Suddenly in our midst was a young woman. I noticed her pretty face only after I had noticed her magnificent breasts peeping, bursting, through the tiny piece of fabric that passed for her blouse, a couple of buttons doing a heroic job holding the lot together. 'Mikey, Mikey,' she gushed. I had never heard my producer called Mikey, only Michael. 'Mikey, Mikey . . .' 'Not now, Nina,' he said brusquely. 'But Mikey, Mikey,' she persisted, only just avoiding brushing her body against his, 'I just wondered if I could have a day off tomorrow?' He took a split second to agree. Whose way is right? Whose method is most effective? Germaine's or Nina's? Is there room for both?

As for motherhood, I must thank Shirley MacLaine for a valuable lesson. I interviewed her for the BBC when she was promoting her book *Dance While You Can*. I remember her for a number of things. She put her feet on the desk of the radio studio. She complained that we didn't have any water 'without bubbles' and that the traffic outside her hotel room had caused her several sleepless nights. Her lack of inner calm was the opposite of the message of her book – which was her account of coming to terms with herself. Of making peace with herself. She said she had been driven to fulfil her mother's unfulfilled dreams. What remains valuable from that interview was the fact that she was just about the only person I have met who, like me, had been separated from her daughter. She and her then husband agreed that their daughter was better off with her father, growing up in Tokyo rather than in Hollywood. Shirley and her daughter had long vacations together, but the rest of the time Sachi was with her father and a governess.

Shirley MacLaine felt the mother and daughter relationship was still unexplored by the time Sachi had grown up. Only then did they sit down and talk. When I told her I too had a daughter, Shirley melted. 'Let her see you weak. Dump on her,' she advised. 'It worries our kids if we leave the bad stuff unspoken.'

Not being the strong one is hard. Letting go of the past, letting go of being in charge, takes nerve. Letting go is accepting that as parents we do the best we can and it almost certainly falls short.

From the ashes of our lives all of the main characters in this autobiography, Charlie, Johnny, Emma and myself, have healed in a way that we all deserve to be proud of. Emma remains a Manhattan girl. She is a broadcaster of quality these days. Talented and good at what she does. She writes with great wit. She is also a mixture of precision and anarchy. She disapproves of any move I might make to encourage her to conform. Or, as she sees it, to do it my way.

I bought her a sensible suitcase with wheels. She pointedly left it behind when she returned to New York. She feels it is time-wasting to get to an airport to catch a plane before the last possible minute and, like Johnny, she has an irritating habit of never missing one. I become the screaming banshee when she leaves. Drained and exhausted from the tension of entreating her to hurry up.

Why do I so often sound like an old 78 record of my mother as I ask her whether she's got enough pairs of clean knickers? Why are Emma and I so alike in some ways and so different in others?

About three years ago we had a very heavy falling-out. In haste, I had written a piece about wanting to be a grandmother and charged my daughter with regarding Bridget Jones as her bible. She was furious. On the contrary, she said, she had no time for *Bridget Jones's Diary*. Yet when the *Bridget Jones* movie came out she urged me to see it. She thought it was glorious (so did I).

This year, on a job out of New York, she sheepishly leapt at the offer of a spare small suitcase on wheels I was about to throw out. Things change. We must all learn to adapt more easily.

In those two and a half rotten years I was on my own, I learnt to lean on her. She became my rock. She once told a newspaper that, proud as she was of us both, she suffered from having two 'over-achieving' parents. I know at times she sees me as a mirror image of Edina in *Absolutely Fabulous*, the crazy mother with the sensible daughter.

She and I can fall out. We can laugh. We can swear and tell each other the truth in a way that I would never have dared with my mother. But I imagine there are things I do that Emma is promising herself she will never inflict on any children she has. Two years ago, sadly, Charlie's second marriage ended. He looked like he needed a jolly Christmas, and Emma suggested he join us at our home in Gloucestershire and she would make it home from New York. Why not? We laughed when Emma's work commitments caused her to miss that Christmas. Charlie came anyway!

And what of Charlie now? He recently married for the third time. His new wife Rachel is in her thirties – only a few years older than Emma. Another redhead. We hope she will push all our wheelchairs when we are old. He is sixty-six and his editing days may be over, but he is nevertheless as industrious as ever. He's a member of the Jockey Club and on the board of a couple of government quangos, the Countryside Alliance, the World Wildlife Fund and several other charities. Emma and I joke that we should pickle him because he remains wonderfully detached from all the changes towards womankind of the last three decades. He has, he says sweetly, never stopped loving me. When he met me he said he couldn't believe he had found someone so like him, 'bright, vibrant, intelligent, etc.' Yet by our wedding day his doubts were as real as mine. He was genuinely unsure that morning whether to go to the church in Farm Street or Lingfield Races. He reminds me that in the early part of the honeymoon I found him sitting on the bed weeping about the terrible mistake we had made. I, he said, comforted him and told him it would be all right! He says he was horrified to discover there was another side to me. He tells me that the reason he had consulted a solicitor so early in our marriage was because I bit him. I might well have done. It's what girls do to defend themselves against bigger, stronger opponents.

Our standards were different. I did not conform to what he considered to be correct behaviour. The difference showed itself time and again.

As for the custody fight, he says he saw a self-indulgent, wanton, selfish young woman who wouldn't act responsibly and wouldn't have been capable of looking after Emma at that time. And not until three-quarters of the way through the case, at lunch with his solicitor, did he learn differently. The idea of my being an alcoholic, Charlie said, was stunning and it was the first time he became aware that it was not a question of 'wouldn't' stop drinking but 'couldn't'. I was sad not bad.

He recalls that awful Friday evening in Glasgow when he and Emma met me off the train. They were standing on the platform and everyone had left and they decided I wasn't coming. Only taking a second look at the shuffling figure still making her way to the ticket barrier did it dawn on him that it was me. He says that he wrote me a letter afterwards, in which he threatened to stop me seeing Emma unless I got help with my drink problem. I have no memory of it.

It took him at least three years to recover from the experience in Court Four, he says. 'After the first week of the case, I went home to Higher Cliff Farm, lay on the bed and seriously thought of shooting myself.'

For my part, I tell him I found it hard to recover, not so much from the court's decision, but from the fact that it seemed like a lifetime's sentence. That despite my sober years when I was at home and free as air and Charlie was editor of a national newspaper, and like most editors was putting in a twelve-to-sixteen-hour day, plus the socialising it required, he had Emma. I didn't.

But I owe Charlie for playing an essential part in my survival. I will be forever grateful that he did everything he could, with decency and honour, to support my relationship with my daughter when I was sick and in a very fragile state.

He never gave up on me. If he had, I doubt I would be around to tell this tale. He has gone on thinking good of me and being there for me. He has delighted in my professional success. I blame him for nothing.

And what of my brother, the prince of the family? He is nearing his sixties. He is as tall as I am short. His hair has gone from red to pepper-and-salt. He is not a multi-million-dollar businessman as my mother possibly imagined he might be – and which for some time he probably attempted to be. His love of books and his hunger for literature won through. He is one of the finest teachers I know. He too, like Emma, is a natural broadcaster. He edits a literary magazine in California and runs the San Francisco Literary Society, and has his own radio show. Ironically, it turned out he benefited most from the gifts of his father. Yet he is also just about the best person to go shopping with. He doesn't get annoyed or bored. He dresses beautifully. He learnt that part from his mother. He also learnt from his mother to enjoy the company of women. It would be fair to say women adore him. He lives in Mill Valley in Marin County. His partner, Carol, is a lawyer. She is smart and clever and she mothers him.

And Johnny? We never had children. Why? We never found out, although he says he spent enough time in Harley Street successfully filling jam jars with specimens to know that it was nothing to do with him.

We have built ourselves a Cotswold stone house in one of the most beautiful little villages in Gloucestershire, not far from where we first lived. I say we, but actually it is Johnny who designed it, Johnny who supervised every stone being laid, every door frame, every door handle. The garden continues to be his ongoing passion, that and his art collection and his love of anything Georgian, which is why our twenty-first-century rooms are crammed with eighteenth-century furniture.

We have two soppy English setters. We think of ourselves as being like Henry Fonda and Katharine Hepburn in the movie *On Golden Pond*. I work in front of a camera and write for a living. He does the rest. He is my strength and support. But in a different way than I imagined. He runs our business life. 'Do you notice', he says, reading the manuscript of this book, 'that you are always able to remember what you were wearing?' He's right. My clothes, my habit of using earning power as a barometer of my worth, are legacies from my mother. 'I was brought up to despise money,' says a girlfriend. 'You, Annie, were brought up to glory in it.' She considers both faults about equal. I don't. Forgive me if I think that earning power is freedom. It is the abuse of that freedom that sends us in the direction of stormy waters.

Thank goodness, indeed, that, albeit painfully, I had learnt how best to manage *my* earning power. Even though I had no idea that it was about to skyrocket.

23

The Weakest Link

'Never let anyone have the deeds to your plantation.' Another of my mother's maxims. Be independent. Alas, the drawback of jealously guarding your deeds is that you rarely have a chance to enjoy your plantation.

January 2000. I have four jobs. My BBC television consumer show, *Watchdog*, has been successful enough to spawn a second weekend version. Both are live. I am also hosting an antiques show. I have a weekly newspaper column in *The Times*. I have been commissioned to write my autobiography.

So who needs a call from a producer in the BBC entertainment department with news of a game show for which they think Anne Robinson would be the perfect host? Johnny, then my agent and manager, hardly reacts. We get these requests all the time. 'Send us a fax,' he says.

Attention: John Penrose
From: Ruth Davis, Series Producer
28th January 2000
Re: Anne Robinson/BBC Quiz Show Pilot.

The concept:
To give you a brief idea of the format: at the beginning of

the week we start off with 11 contestants who are all total strangers. They have to work as a team over the course of 10 rounds to win a holiday by the end of the week. Every round they successfully complete represents a day's holiday, so in theory they can win up to 10 days abroad. However, only one of them will actually go on the holiday because after every round the contestants have to vote off the person they consider to be the weakest link until it's finally whittled down to one.

And later:

We very much want this show to explore the psychology of the quiz show, so as well as the mechanics of the quiz itself we are also planning on filming the contestants before and after to get their reactions to events, if they feel confident about winning, how they feel about being voted off, etc.

    Anne Robinson would be our ideal host as we are looking for someone who is not afraid to push the boundaries of existing quiz shows, someone who can be firm enough to handle the voting off of the Weakest Links, yet sympathetic enough to soften the blow where necessary.

Mmm . . .

One of *my* maxims: *always* take the meeting. You never know. I'm wearing my favourite pair of tight, black leather Caroline Charles trousers. Just as well. The team that greets me is remarkably young. I doubt anyone is more than thirty years old. They are blessed with that precious gift of youth – boundless optimism and enthusiasm. They have taken a one-and-a-half-page idea for a quiz with 'links' and developed it into a game show. Before I leave, and without realising it, I have committed to attending a 'run-through'. A week later we're in a BBC basement rehearsal room and I'm watching the proposed game in action. It seems a bit too complicated. But there is something irresistible about the energy of the team.

'This show's got legs,' I say to Johnny when I get home. 'Tightened up, there might be something there. Something new and different.' The run-throughs in dingy, under-heated rehearsal rooms continue. The impossibly beautiful producer, Ruth, is relentless in her insistence that we 'practise, practise, practise'. Another of my mother's maxims: 'If you need something doing, ask a busy person to do it.' Despite my diary, I make time.

Every fairy tale requires a prince. Ours arrived a month later. Admittedly, at first glance, Ray did not look like a prince or even a knight in shining armour. He was a bespectacled librarian in his forties, who bounced into our lives wearing an orange shirt, sandals and socks. The whiff he exuded was more body sweat than Eau Sauvage. But he was willing to be practised upon and used as a would-be contestant. He was a veteran with at least half a dozen prime-time television contestant appearances under his belt. He took no prisoners. As we played the game the female would-be contestant next to him failed to answer 'Tinky Winky' to a question about the Teletubbies. 'Nobody', declared Ray – heaving a campish sigh – 'comes on a quiz show without knowing the names of the Teletubbies!'

It clicked. Quiz contestants are not humble wallflowers. They are arrogant, well prepared and my, how competitive. They play along to the cheesy, saccharine handling they receive on the majority of television game shows. But they are worth more than that. They dislike being beaten. They loathe anyone who is beset by nerves or who dithers. They are tough.

Thus for me the final piece of the jigsaw was there. I did not need to ease their disappointment by 'softening the blow'. On the contrary, I could compound their distress. Point out their shortcomings. Ridicule their mistakes. During another rehearsal a few days later I heard myself saying, 'You are the weakest link,' as instructed, then adding, 'Goodbye'. I hadn't planned the pay-off. But somewhere surely must have been a memory of Aunt Liz. She who only very occasionally left her bed and who announced 'thank you' or 'goodbye' when she had had enough of a visitor.

The executive producer punched the air. We had a catch-phrase! Now we needed our one piece of pure luck.

Up at the top of the BBC tree, senior executives were not in the least convinced by the proposal to invite viewers into a studio and insult them. Studio bosses are not paid to take chances. One declared the whole concept unwise. He hated *The Weakest Link*, the chosen name for the show. Before we pro-ceeded, he wanted the idea tested on a focus group.

Time, usually an enemy, was on our side. Quite simply, because there wasn't any. If the boss of BBC Daytime – a woman – was to commission it, she needed to do so immedi-ately to have enough shows ready to fill a gap in her summer schedule. Thus she ignored the cynics and ordered up sixty-eight.

So, in the end, we were blessed not just with Ray and luck but with having someone around who was prepared to use that most old-fashioned of working tools: instinct.

The Weakest Link, by now tightened with fewer players and a cash prize, was launched in August 2000. The summer season is a desert for ratings. Viewers are on holiday or outside in the garden. The disturbing publicity ploy was to allow it to air with-out any advance notice and let the audience build organically.

My appearance? Ruth had been so taken by the leather trousers I had worn to the first meeting she suggested I wear black – with perhaps a hint of colour. The colour didn't work. We went with just black. How was I to know that within months the leather look would have me hailed as a dominatrix? With sad men in their fifties confessing they dreamt of me with a whip in my hand.

The viewing figures for the first show hit the 2 million mark.

Six weeks later, to the astonishment of television executives, it had edged nearer 5 million. By the autumn it was the BBC's Exocet missile, simultaneously running on daytime and prime-time TV.

And by then, when I was out shopping, no one was begging me to fix their rotten holiday, shout at an airline or write on their behalf to complain about their washing machine. In a few short months my identity as a newspaper journalist and television current affairs and consumer show presenter had vanished. I was the mean woman in black. The Rudest Woman on British Television.

To the delight of the bosses, it was also beginning to sell abroad. By Christmas that year Japan, Italy, France, Finland and Australia had bought the show, each station sending its executives to my studio with their would-be hosts. Then tailoring the host, most of them in the afternoon of their years, in black, with spectacles and hair cut short and dyed red.

In America, *Who Wants to Be a Millionaire?* had proved a sure-fire hit. Hosted by Regis Philbin, it had swept the ratings. Upwards of 14 million viewers per show. No one could come anywhere near ABC's triumphant purchase of a British game show. Other stations were in the doldrums about how to challenge its success. None more so than NBC. It had a new head of entertainment, Jeff Zucker. An unlikely choice. A man unaccustomed to the roar of the greasepaint, the smell of the crowd, but a Harvard graduate honed on current affairs. The rising star of the station, fresh from his job as the highly rated executive producer of the *Today* show, was new to Tinseltown. He viewed tapes of *The Weakest Link* and thought it had a future in America. But who to host it? There was perhaps Roseanne Barr. Maybe Judge Judy. Or Richard Hatch, million-dollar winner of CBS's hit reality show *Survivor*. In the meantime, the NBC people came to England to see the British host in action.

Another of *my* maxims. 'Listen to your sane voice,' no matter what others might say. Intuition isn't a fantasy. It's a science.

'You will host the show in America,' said my sane voice. 'Sadly, Annie, the Americans are very parochial,' everyone else said. 'They wouldn't dream of giving the job to a Brit.'

Even my lovely, clever girlfriend Denise O'Donoghue, who owns the highly successful independent television company Hat Trick, creator of many hit shows, including *Whose Line Is It Anyway?*, advised: 'The US will want their own.' But *The Weakest Link* was never going to run along conventional lines. In Britain it had marked a point between old and new: shows of the twenty-first century and shows that came before.

In January we shot a pilot for NBC in London, using expatriate Americans living in the UK. How I loved those contestants. They were feisty, good humoured and smart. Maybe *The Weakest Link* Stateside could be an improvement on the original?

The pilot was a success. 'It has to be Anne Robinson,' Jeff Zucker was charmingly heard to say. 'She *is* the show.' NBC's choice of a British host for *The Weakest Link* was another example of history in the making.

Two dozen or more interviews with the American media followed the announcement. Picture, dear reader, the reporter from the *Washington Post*. The *Post*'s New York-based media correspondent had made the journey to England to interview me. But, apparently, she thought she shouldn't have had to. 'I don't normally interview quiz-show hosts,' she announced as she sat down. 'I am used to dealing with current affairs journalists . . .' And, a little later, 'Why would you want to do this show?' Our correspondent was not disguising her disgust. She knew Jeff Zucker, she said. She thought he had made a huge mistake. The American public wouldn't wear it. Other American journalists who made the trip said the same, even if they put it more tactfully. Most of them, interestingly, added that they themselves *loved* the show but warned that the American public would be appalled by its rudeness. I ignored their fears.

Time and again I had taught, nay pleaded with young

broadcasters to avoid one grave mistake. Which is to imagine there is 'us' who work in television. And out there 'them', the public, whose taste is different, whose appetite is for less challenging material. Take the viewer with you, I have so often urged producers under my care. If you love a show, it's the best guide in the world.

March 2001. The NBC publicity machine sets out to introduce an unknown Anne Robinson to America. We (me, my husband, my agent and my hairdresser) make a flying thirty-six-hour visit to LA to do a round of radio, TV and press interviews, tape a promotional video, pose for publicity shots, generally talk up the show. American TV crews can't get enough of me. A British documentary team follows me everywhere.

By the time we return, a little over three weeks later, America knows a lot more about *The Weakest Link*, and about Anne Robinson. There's my 40-foot-tall image in Times Square. An even bigger billboard on the NBC studios in Los Angeles. My face is on the sides of buses. The phrase 'You are the Weakest Link, Goodbye!' has been spray-painted on sidewalks, flown on banners behind planes over Daytona beach, broadcast constantly on prime-time TV. Already people are using the phrase. It is truly a marketing and promotional triumph.

April 2001. We are in Studio One in NBC's Burbank home. A shrine to Johnny Carson. His pictures are everywhere. We have replicated every aspect of our set-up in Britain. In one corner of the set is the 'village' – an area draped in black where we work out the statistics. My favourite British chocolates are on the desk. My wardrobe is hanging in the dressing room. My pointy boots. My forty pairs of different coloured spectacles.

The studio is icy cold. But the place is buzzing. John, the stage manager, has shoulder-length hair. We have a full audience. The contestants file on to the set. Am I nervous? No. It doesn't occur to me that we might fail. Why should we?

'Let's do it,' I hear myself say. We do it, and do it.

*

A week later the first show airs on American prime-time network TV. I fly to New York – and a week to end all weeks.

The morning after the show's premiere, I am slowly coming to at the Rihga Royal Hotel on West 54th Street when the phone rings. 'Pick me up at my apartment,' Emma pleads. 'We can mooch around the Village, then go back uptown to Elizabeth Arden's.'

This is a mother and daughter ritual. Once or twice a year we shop till we drop. Then throw ourselves into a cab, head for our favourite beauty parlour and raise a manicured hand to my late mother, Emma's nana, who long ago decreed that no situation was so perfect that a facial couldn't make it better.

Her adored grandchild is now a Manhattan girl through and through. She's been here a decade or more, ever since her days at New York University. This is very much *her* city.

I am the bit-part player. I am the mom who looked on anxiously when Emma got a place at NYU's Tisch Film School and crossed the Atlantic to live in a noisy residence hall on Washington Square, and has been proudly following her career ever since.

If she is patient, after shopping in the Village (boutiques with every size from two to six) Mom is rewarded with a visit to Bergdorf Goodman, her spiritual home. 'On a good day,' her daughter will say admiringly, 'my mother can empty Bergdorf's as fast as any of the natives.'

This is not so much a good day, as a rather extraordinary one. Early morning, as the cab makes its wobbly way down Fifth Avenue to Emma's apartment, I catch sight of a placard of the front page of the *New York Post*. 'Host from Hell!' the headline cries. The rest of the page is taken up with a picture of me. Underneath another plaudit: 'The Queen of Mean.'

Emma and I buy a copy of the paper. The *Post* critic hated the show and said so. The front page is merely a message about how horrid I am. Giggling, we make our way to Betsey Johnson. Emma is trying on a pink coat with sequins and I am yelling, 'Get the shoes and bag to match,' when my cellphone rings. It's the West Coast head of NBC calling from Los Angeles with the ratings. We got 15 million viewers. The best numbers in the Monday 8 to 9 p.m. hour for the network in five years.

Two hours later we are heading for the front door of Arden's on Fifth. As we pass Gucci a small crowd begins to follow us chanting 'Goodbye'. My catchphrase.

Emma and I exchange more giggles as a policeman gets off his horse, shakes my hand and says, 'Welcome to America, Miss Robinson.'

'Is this happening?' asks Emma. 'In my town?'

In the courtroom that exists in every mother's head – the one that constantly tries us on the charge of being unworthy – I plead guilty to cruelty. No grown-up child deserves to see her mother on a gigantic billboard high over Times Square. Or splashed across the front of the *New York Post*. No child, quietly minding her own business, in her own space, in her own town, deserves to be so grotesquely embarrassed by a fifty-six-year-old parent, who should be planning her retirement.

That night we go to Michael's for dinner to celebrate. Representatives from the William Morris Agency – who have brokered the BBC-NBC *Weakest Link* deal and are also pitching to represent me in the US – surround us. 'Do they come ready packaged out of a box labelled "William Morris Agents"?' asks Johnny. Each of them has a sharp haircut and an even sharper suit. Suddenly I look at my watch. *The Weakest Link* is about to air. Panic sets in because Michael's, that most chic of show business restaurants, turns out to have no television set. We abandon our dinner and race to an Irish bar further down the street. An ice-hockey game is playing on the big screen. Customers have paid generously to watch it. 'Show me how you operate,' I dare the William Morris guys. Quietly, $100 bills are scattered. The customers, happily clutching them, agree to view their game in another part of the bar. We take their places. Halfway through the show, two waiters from Michael's stroll in with our desserts.

By the end of Wednesday night, when *The Weakest Link* has aired three times, 52 million people have seen the show. Nielsen Media Research reckons that one in five Americans has at some point tuned in.

Fast-forward a month. The catchphrase has entered the language. The ratings are soaring.

At the Lakers play-off game in Los Angeles, the Staples Center is packed. Jim Gray, the NBC sportscaster, guides me on to the court for a half-time interview.

Ahead I spot a familiar face. His gold teeth are visible, his grin infectious. 'You're one mean woman,' Mike Tyson whispers in my ear. Alongside him, sprawled on his chair, another familiar face gives me a lazy wink. I must be dreaming. It's Jack Nicholson. 'Did you call my woman mean?' demands my husband of Tyson. (The champ had nothing to fear. At fifty-four, Johnny is not only supremely unfit but also so Italian he would rather trade his woman than dirty his suit.) But, I've no time to linger or worry about how the threat is received. We are on air. The interview is to promote *The Weakest Link* basketball special to be played during the finals. The crowd acknowledges me. The roar is deafening.

These first four weeks in America have been an incredible ride. In the Ivy restaurant in LA a woman comes to our table, apologises for disturbing me but says she wants to tell me how much she loves my show. And how she tapes every episode. Penny Marshall, no less. In my book, the very finest female movie director.

In Elaine's, in New York, fellow diners rise to their feet and applaud as I leave.

At the Radio City Music Hall for the Up Fronts, where TV networks show the advertisers their wares, I host, live, a brief version of the game in front of five thousand people. The station's head of entertainment announces that the British game import, *The Weakest Link*, has changed the face of US TV.

For the finale of the event, the 'talent' gathers backstage and prepares to take a final bow. Martin Sheen and the rest of the cast of *West Wing* come over to congratulate me. Kelsey Grammar from *Frasier*; the *Today* show team, Katie Couric and Matt Lauer, do the same. Back at my hotel, there's a request for me to open a concert in LA with Britney Spears. (Might Emma just think that's cool?) Or will she be more impressed that I chatted with Shaquille O'Neal on *Tonight* with Jay Leno? And that *NSYNC passed my dressing room, hoping to meet me? Or even that at lunch at the Four Seasons restaurant Henry Kissinger waved?

Six months later and *The Weakest Link* is still up there, defying its critics. The top-rated television show in America among eighteen- to forty-nine-year-olds, the market that advertisers covet.

Finally, one of my favourite maxims: always dream your dreams.

It's the best way to make them come true.

My mother, incidentally, would have adored *The Weakest Link*. She would have been thrilled by its success. It would make up for her dismay at peeping inside my wardrobe and finding that these days my favourite colour is purple.

Epilogue

On Mother's Day 2001, I was surprised there was no card or package from Emma. Then I opened one of our weekend newspaper supplements to find she had penned me an open letter.

Happy Mother's Day, I miss you. Our Saturday calls do not replace a cuddle or your complaints that my breath smells of garlic and my shoes need to be thrown out, or your muttered 'Jesus, Mary and Joseph' when you remember my lack of health insurance. Was there BUPA in Bethlehem?

What's new? My kitchen light is still broken. I still don't have health insurance and, much to your dismay, I'm still not dating a titled barrister. But my hair is pink. So you can be disappointed but not surprised.

The latest man in my life is 'celluloid only'. I have difficulty pronouncing his name but he gives great close-ups. Do you think Emma Del Toro has a romantic ring to it? I am returning your Caroline Charles leather skirt. We both know it is too small for me. Oh, to be a size eight. When I grow up, I want to be just like you. (Cue roll of eyes.) It's my rite of passage to take your mistakes and make them my own: men, work and fashion *faux pas*.

Why are you so concerned? My education at the Anne Robinson School of Life has been comprehensive and colourful. You read me *Charlie and the Chocolate Factory*. You taught me that boys with sisters are emotionally advanced. You made me appreciate the lyrics to 'Harper Valley PTA', 'Rose Garden' and other country classics. You held me, loved me, even when I had mumps. And you agreed to a puppy, even though you knew you would be the one left holding a large elderly Old English sheepdog with hip trouble.

When I was at university in America other mums sent their Allysons and Tammys potpourri and floral bed sheets. You gave me your laptop. And in the middle of the night you defied time zones to solve its printing problems.

You came to my graduation movie with husbands old and new. With love and loyalty. And while Allyson and Tammy were being dragged round the Guggenheim and Ellis Island we stormed the gates of Bergdorf Goodman, Barneys and Saks.

You taught me not to take men too seriously. You humour me through all my relationship mishaps. When I'm inconsolable you hand me half a dozen self-help books and announce 'there's plenty of food in the fridge'.

You've encouraged me to believe in myself and insist I can do anything I want. And yet the world knows you want a grandchild. But you've set a standard. You've triumphed in both career and motherhood. And I smile with pride when an interviewer asks you why you've done something extravagant, and you answer: 'Because I can.'

Would I bring up my children differently from the way you raised me? Hell no. I fear motherhood and the

thought of you not being there as co-pilot starts a panic.
Will I be as ready to give the Agnès B shirt off my back?
To love so unconditionally?

So, Rawhide Robinson, when you are ready to hang up
your leather, assuming my ovaries haven't shrivelled up,
shove a box under the stairs. You never know, I might
pop out some pups.

Love as always,
Emma.